What Heroes Are Saying About
How Heroes Hero

How Heroes Hero is the book we so desperately need
to read and apply to our world today.
Marcos Wittig, Founder & President, COSDECOL, Medellín, Colombia

How Heroes Hero opens our hearts
through kindness, compassion, and the courage to shape our world.
Ezra Teshome, *Time* **Global Health Hero, Rotary District Governor**

How Heroes Hero is a tremendously inspiring read.
As a pediatrician, the book gives me insights into how to empower
young families with wisdom to excel in a world which desperately needs heroes.
Dr. René Bravo, Bravo Pediatrics

This book is incredible!
How Heroes Hero proves that heroism is not an illusion.
Anyone can become a hero. Jens Omli has revealed the magic formula.
Jon Dorenbos, NFL All-Pro, *America's Got Talent* **Finalist, Author of** *Life is Magic*

Jens Omli hit it out of the park. The world needs
this book because the world needs more people who are ready to lead!
Guy East, U.S. Olympic Cyclist, Founder of Hope Sports

Inspiring, powerful, and hopeful.
This is a must-read book for every teacher, every parent, every person.
Fiona Lloyd-Moffett, Teacher of the Year, San Luis Obispo County

A generation without heroes suffers the consequences.
Heroes are needed on every continent, in every country, and in every community. This book is our call to action!
Stone Kyambadde, Wolves Football Program, Kampala, Uganda

I wish I had this book as I was starting my professional life and advancing through the leadership ranks. *How Heroes Hero* is full of examples that are perfect for aspiring managers, irrespective of field or profession.
Tibor Nagy, Jr, 19th Assistant Secretary of State for African Affairs, Former U.S Ambassador to Ethiopia and Guinea

Refreshing, thought-provoking, and inspiring. A must-read!
Marceil Whitney, Founder, Tennis Outreach Programs, USTA Hall of Fame Inductee

How Heroes Hero is a timeless book, which is especially important for our time. *How Heroes Hero* inspired me to reflect on the small decisions I make daily that could lead to a more heroic life in service of others.
Derek Nesland, Founder and President, Courts For Kids

Read this life-changing book—at least twice—and get ready to become a more impactful person.
Lisa Berg, Sport Envoy, U.S. Department of State

HOW HEROES HERO

HOW HEROES HERO

A Description and
A Prescription

Jens Omli, PhD

HOW HEROES HERO
Jens Omli, PhD

© 2024 Jens Omli

All rights reserved. No part of this publication may be reproduced, stored in a retrieval system or transmitted in any form or by any means, electronic, mechanical, photocopying, recording or otherwise without the prior permission of the copyright owner or in accordance with provisions of the Copyright, Designs and Patents Act 1988 or under the terms of any license permitting limited copying issued by the Copyright Licensing Agency.

Published by:
Jengo Publishing
San Luis Obispo, CA, USA

ISBN-13: 979-8-8825-5110-9 [Hardcover]
ISBN-13: 979-8-3290-4776-9 [Paperback]

Printed in USA

Dedicated To
My Parents
Arne & Desa Omli

Contents

Introduction: The Big Five   *i*

HEROISM

Answering the Call	1
Protecting the Vulnerable	11
Projecting Calm	23
Remaining Vigilant	37
Finding Solitude	51
Preparing for Battle	63
Disarming Opponents	77
Defeating Villains	95
Uniting the Village	119
Disregarding Speed Limits	135
Defending Values	153

TRANSFORMATION

Noah's Character Arc	173
Fool's Gold	185
The Great Escape	199
The World's A Stage	217

Afterword: Nathaniel	*231*
Bibliography	*235*
Notes	*241*
About the Author	*265*

HOW HEROES HERO

Introduction

The Big Five

The world is going to be a little bit better after you read this book.

Why?

Because the world needs more heroes.

And I am going to teach you how to be a hero.

We will learn from some of our greatest heroes—people like Abraham Lincoln, Mohandas Gandhi, Martin Luther King, Jr., Mother Teresa, and Nelson Mandela.

I will call these individuals the Big Five.

Admiration for the Big Five is hard to argue. But if you still aren't convinced, consider the following:

> National holidays celebrate their lives.
> Currency bears their faces.
> Buildings, streets, schools, and stadiums are named in their honor.
> Three received Nobel Peace Prizes.
> And one (Mother Teresa) is literally a saint.

We will learn from the Big Five. Not just by reading *about* them, but by learning *from* them—in their own words, whenever possible. A description of *their* heroism is a prescription for *our* heroism.

If we follow their example—and identify, elect, and support leaders who follow their example—you and I will be the solution to many of the problems that we face.

The Big 5 will show us How Heroes Hero. Their stories will help us understand the nature of heroism.

Their heroism started small but became global. Your heroism might remain more local. But heroes are needed everywhere. In big cities and small towns. In small businesses and multinational corporations. Up on stage and behind the scenes. In families, schools, churches, neighborhoods, and soccer fields. The world needs heroes.

The world needs you to be a hero.

So, what does it mean to be a hero?

The word "hero" has multiple meanings. Sometimes "hero" is used to describe people who inspire us with their exceptional achievements (think sports heroes).

But the original meaning of the Greek word "hero" is "protector" or "defender."

Heroism really isn't that complicated. Heroes protect us. Heroes inspire us. And heroes set a standard for us to aspire to.

In literature and film, the protagonist is often a hero. But there are other types of characters in fictional stories, just as there are other types of characters in real life. Each of us, deep down, views ourselves as a character type—or combination of character types.

I have studied self-perceptions by asking people to answer the following question: if you were a fictional character, what type of character would you be?

Hero (puts others above self, does what is right, calm under pressure)
Villain (selfish, evil, disregards wellbeing of others)
Anti-Hero (pursues a noble goal but willing to cheat or hurt others to win)
Villager (stays in the background, waits for others to act)
Damsel in Distress (weak, passive, victim, needs saving)
Clown (mostly interested in entertaining or being liked)
Sage (provides wisdom and guidance from behind the scenes)
Ruler (expects obedience, relies on power and authority over others)
Sidekick (always willing to help, but doesn't take the lead)
Scoundrel (gossips, stirs up conflict, creates drama)
Alarmist (pessimistic, chronically stressed, makes hasty decisions)

Most people do not view themselves as heroes. But those who view themselves as heroes also describe themselves as healthier, happier, and more eager to help others. Being a hero is good for your health. Being a hero is good for your happiness. And being a hero is good for others.

I have also surveyed people to identify the character types that best describe their favorite and least favorite teachers, coaches, and bosses. The results reveal two things. First, the favorite leaders are almost always viewed as heroes. Second, the least favorite leaders are NEVER viewed as heroes.

When I asked people what type of person they would most like to have as their leader or colleague, the results are equally clear: In each type of relationship, most people prefer heroes. So, to be clear...

> If you are a parent, your children want you to be a hero.
> If you are a teacher, your students want you to be a hero.
> If you are a coach, your athletes want you to be a hero.
> If you are a health care provider, your patients want you to be a hero.
> If you are a politician, your constituents want you to be a hero.
> If you are a business leader, your employees want you to be a hero.
> If you are an employee, your boss and coworkers want you to be a hero.
> If you are in a romantic relationship, your significant other wants you to be a hero.
> If you are in the market for a romantic relationship, that person is looking for someone who embodies the characteristics of a hero.

The people in your life don't want you to be a victim, a villager, a clown, or a scoundrel. They don't want an alarmist. They don't want a sidekick. They don't want a ruler. And they certainly don't want you to be a villain. The people around you want you to be a hero.

Deep down, *you* want to be a hero.

One last survey result: When people are asked what type of character they aspire to be, the most common answer won't surprise you. That's right, almost everyone wants to be a hero. But they aren't sure how.

Using examples from the Big 5 and other famous heroes, I will show you how to be a hero.

The way Heroes Hero can be summarized in 11 principles, which I will describe in the next 11 chapters.

The remaining four chapters will dispel a few myths about heroism and will reinforce some of the central ideas of the book:

1. Heroes are heroes by choice, not by birth.
2. There is a fundamental difference between heroes and anti-heroes.
3. Even former villains can become heroes—if we let them.
4. Anyone, anywhere, can choose to live, love, and lead like a hero.

As you read this book, you may see ways in which you are already a hero. And you may see other areas in which you can become more heroic.

I hope you enjoy learning from The Big Five and other heroes as much as I have. And I hope their lessons reach your head, touch your heart, and are manifest in the works of your hands. Heroism is about helping others. Someone, somewhere, will be thankful when you put what you have learned into action.

Let's get started.

Chapter 1

Answering the Call

*There are those who see the need and respond.
I consider those people my heroes.*
-Fred "Mr. Rogers"

Every hero has an origin story.

Superheroes have origin stories. Literary heroes have origin stories. And real-life heroes like Lincoln, Gandhi, Martin Luther King, Jr., Mother Teresa, and Nelson Mandela have origin stories. The origin stories of heroes are surprisingly similar.

Let's look at a couple examples.

The first story goes like this:

In a small city called Skopje, in what is now Northern Macedonia, a visiting priest was welcomed by a small audience, which included an Albanian teenager named Agnes. Agnes listened carefully as the priest talked about serving the poor in India. She had hoped to become a musician or a poet, but as Agnes heard the priest describe the plight of the suffering poor in India, she changed her mind.

Agnes moved to Dublin, Ireland to join the Loreto Sisters as a novice. Her wish to move to India was fulfilled three years later. Agnes spent seventeen years teaching geography and history within the high walls of a stately school, isolated from the indescribable poverty in other parts of Calcutta.

And then it happened.

While on a rickety train *en route* to Darjeeling on September 10, 1946, Agnes experienced what she later described as a "call within a call." While contemplating the suffering that she had seen on her dusty journey to the train station in Calcutta, she was overwhelmed by a feeling of God's love for her and was transfixed on two simple words recorded in the book of John 19:28: "I thirst."

Agnes spent the next ten days in Darjeeling pondering her inspiration, then returned to Calcutta, confident of her new calling: She was to quench the thirst of Jesus by serving those who shared in His suffering. She was to devote herself not just to the poor, but the poorest of the poor. And not just serve them, but to live among them—to live as they lived. To possess nothing and to trust entirely in God's providence. To be but a pencil in God's hand.

Agnes left the Loreto Sisters but she kept her vows.

With the blessing of her superior in the Catholic Church, Father Van Exem, Agnes began her new life in the slums of Calcutta. The "call within a call" transformed Agnes Gonxha Bojaxhiu from Albania into Mother Teresa of Calcutta, founder of the Missionaries of Charity.

The expressed aim of the Missionaries of Charity was to "quench the thirst of Jesus Christ on the Cross for love of souls" by providing "wholehearted free service to the poorest of the poor." Mother Teresa saw the suffering poor lining the streets of Calcutta and accepted the responsibility to care for them.

But Mother Teresa's was not the only life-changing call-to-action experienced on a train.

The second story goes like this:

Sitting in a first-class seat on a train from Durban to Pretoria, where he was scheduled to try a case, a young lawyer of Indian descent saw a white passenger enter his car at the station in Maritzburg, South Africa. The embarking passenger went away and returned with two railway officials. Shortly thereafter, a third official entered the car, saying, "come along, you must go to the van compartment."

"But I have a first-class ticket," the lawyer objected.

As the argument continued, the official threatened to call the police constable.

"Yes, you may," the lawyer said firmly, "I refuse to get out voluntarily."

So, the constable came, took Mohandas Gandhi by the hand, and pushed him out of the compartment, leaving he and his luggage on the platform in the winter cold, as the train steamed away from the station. Sitting in a dark room, without his overcoat, Gandhi considered his options:

> *Should I fight for my rights or go back to India, or should I go on to Pretoria without minding the insults, and return to India after finishing the case? It would be cowardice to run back to India without fulfilling my obligation. The hardship to which I was subjected was superficial—only a symptom of the deep disease of color prejudice. I should try, if possible, to root out the disease and suffer hardships in the process. Redress for wrongs I should seek only to the extent that would be necessary for the removal of the color prejudice. So I decided to take the next available train to Pretoria.*

As he waited for the next train, Gandhi spoke with merchants in Martizburg who "tried to comfort [him] by narrating their own hardships and explaining that what had happened to [him] was nothing unusual." Gandhi spent hours "listening to these tales of woe," recounted by fellow Indians who explained to Gandhi that, "Indians traveling first or second class had to expect trouble from railway officials and white passengers."

When Gandhi finally reached his destination, his troubles continued.

Failing to connect with a friend sent to greet him, Gandhi entered Grand National Hotel to rent a room. But after the manager looked him up-and-down, he said, "I am very sorry, we are full up." So, Gandhi continued to a shop owned by a second friend, who found great humor in his attempt to find lodging, asking with a laugh, "how ever did you expect to be admitted to a hotel?"

The friend went on to explain, "You will come to know after you have stayed here a few days. Only we can live in a land like this, because, for making money, we do not mind pocketing insults, and here we are…you will have to go to Pretoria tomorrow. You will have to travel third class. Conditions in the Transvaal are worse than in Natal. First and second-class tickets are never issued to Indians."

And "with this," Gandhi recalled, "Abdul Gani Sheth narrated to me the story of the hardships of Indians in South Africa."

Gandhi found it much easier to "pocket insults" directed at him than to accept injustice inflicted on others. After experiencing the indignities of daily life for Indians in South Africa, he decided to stay and fight on their behalf. Gandhi vowed to never use force against another person or to yield to force used against him.

What links the origin stories of Mother Teresa and Mahatma Gandhi is not just their mode of transportation, but the fact that they each saw a problem and they each accepted the responsibility to fix it.

See the Need

The origin story of each hero includes a "call to action." But heroes can come from any background. Some heroes are called from the countryside. Others are called from the palace.

Nelson Mandela experienced a privileged upbringing, surrounded by the luxuries of an African monarch. His father was an advisor to the tribal chief, and with the educational opportunities made available to him, Nelson was groomed to follow a similar path. In his early life, Nelson was protected from many of the indignities experienced by blacks under the system of apartheid in South Africa. But as he arrived in Johannesburg to continue his studies, Mandela began to see—and experience—the different treatment of blacks and whites. After he finished his legal training and began defending clients, Mandela's eyes were opened further as he saw white defendants acquitted because they were white and black defendants convicted because they were black. On such occasions, Mandela would simply say, "this isn't right."

Nelson Mandela despised injustice. He hated oppression. He considered apartheid immoral and repugnant. Mandela saw a problem and sought a solution. With his sense of justice violated time and time again, this ambitious young man abandoned his life of privilege to fight on behalf of black South Africans as a leader of the African National Congress political party.

Abraham Lincoln's youth was spent in more humble circumstances than that of Mandela, but like Mandela, his call to action was motivated by a similar combination of ambition and conviction. From an early age, Lincoln maintained a firm belief that "no man is good enough to govern another man, without the other's consent" and that "if slavery is not wrong, nothing is wrong."

From the onset of his political career, Lincoln personally detested slavery. Lincoln was adamant that the practice of slavery must not be expanded as the nation extended its borders westward. When the Kansas-Nebraska act was passed by the U.S. Congress on May 30, 1854, allowing the citizens to decide for themselves if slavery would be allowed within their territories, Lincoln had had enough. Lincoln vowed to devote his political career to halting the spread of slavery.

Start Local

Mother Teresa, Gandhi, Mandela, and Lincoln had eyes to see the suffering of those around them and had the heart to do something about it. They were aware and they chose to care. They saw an opportunity, accepted responsibility, and opened new possibilities for the vulnerable and the suffering around them.

Big things usually start small. And heroes usually begin where they are. Gandhi chose to stay and serve in South Africa (where he had moved to begin what he expected to be an ordinary law career) after finishing his studies in London. Mother Teresa spent almost two decades in India before she was overcome by compassion for—and the conviction to serve—the very poorest of the poor, who lived not far from the Jesuit school where she taught.

Toward the end of his doctoral work in Boston, Martin (and his wife Coretta) King contemplated their next move. As a bright young preacher, he had options, including a job opportunity in Detroit, which would allow them "a chance to escape the long night of segregation." But the South was their home. And both Martin and Coretta wanted to do something about the problems they had seen first-hand as children. They concluded that they could make a bigger difference in their native South. And they felt "something of a moral obligation to return—at least for a few years."

On September 1, 1954, Dr. King preached his first sermon at Dexter Baptist Church in Montgomery, Alabama. The church was just 80 miles from Coretta's childhood home in Marion. As the Kings settled into their new church and community, Dr. King began his tenure by bolstering the education, political action, and social services programs at the church to better serve the sick and needy. His next step was to make countless home visits to become better acquainted with each individual member of his congregation. Then, Dr. King attended meetings held by various committees in the church and organizations in the Montgomery community.

Dr. King became discouraged by his realization that the black community in Montgomery was "the victim of a threefold malady—factionalism among the leaders, indifference in the educated group, and passivity in the uneducated." Though he understood change would be difficult, Dr. King did not lose hope.

Accept Responsibility

Dr. King began his career as a preacher. But Dr. King's call within a call, so to speak, occurred less than a year into his pastorate.

On March 2, 1955, a fifteen-year-old high school student, Claudette Colvin, was removed from a city bus, handcuffed, and jailed for refusing to relinquish her seat to a white passenger. Dr. King was asked to serve on a committee formed to address the issue with the City Commission and the bus company. The committee had limited success defending Claudette or promoting change in the city's bus seating policies. But they were ready to spring into action when on December 1, 1955, Rosa Parks sat down on a bus in downtown Montgomery and refused to get up.

As news of her arrest spread across town, a meeting was organized for the next evening, which was attended by members of the community and local church leaders. The Rev. L. Roy Bennett presided over the meeting and brought forth a proposal for a bus boycott. Three days later, the boycott began. On that morning, Coretta shouted from the living room to Dr. King, who was drinking his coffee in the kitchen, "Martin, Martin, come quickly!" As he entered the living room, she pointed to a bus driving by their home, "Darling, it's empty!"

Later that day, Ralph Abernathy and other church leaders organized a meeting to form an organization to guide the boycott. After Rev. Bennett called for nominations for president, Rufus Lewis stood up and said, "Mr. Chairman, I would like to nominate Reverend M. L. King for president." The motion was immediately seconded and carried and, on the day

Rosa Parks was tried for disobeying the city segregation ordinance, the young preacher was installed as leader of the newly formed Montgomery Improvement Association.

Dr. King later recalled, "I neither started the protest nor suggested it. I simply responded to the call of the people for a spokesman."

Dr. King's willingness to lead the MIA set in motion a series of events that would hoist him to the forefront of the civil rights movement. As he received and responded to countless pleas to assist in cities throughout the United States, from Selma to Chicago, his territory increased.

Dr. King embodied Jonas Salk's observation that, "the reward for work well done is the opportunity to do more." But additional opportunities sometimes come with additional costs.

Martin and Coretta King gave up career opportunities—with promises of better pay and safer surroundings—to answer the call. Their decision came at a significant personal cost. Like Mandela and Gandhi, Dr. King was incarcerated. Toward the beginning the civil rights movement, he was arrested at a sit-in in Atlanta in 1960, arrested again at a prayer vigil in Albany in 1962, and a third time in Birmingham in 1963. Dr. King was always willing to do more, even when the stakes were high.

Dr. King was not deterred by danger. In fact, he developed a habit of rushing to the sound of sirens. "I am in Birmingham because injustice is here," he explained on one occasion and on other, announced, "I am here because there are twenty million Negroes in the United States and I love every one of them. I am concerned about every one of them. What happens to any one of them concerns all individuals." Dr. King wanted to be on the ground, in the thick of it, all the time. He felt uncomfortable when he was away from the action.

Such was the case when he traveled to Oslo to receive the Nobel Peace Prize. Expressing his urgency to return to the South, Dr. King said, "For the past several days I have been on the mountaintop. But my brothers and sisters down in Mississippi and Alabama can't register to vote. I've got to go back. There are those who need hope...I wish I could stay on the mountain, but I must go back to the valley."

Dr. King made the transition from local preacher to civil rights icon not by responding to a single call, but by faithfully answering the continued pleas of those who called upon him to assist in their struggle to be free. "This is not the life I expected to lead," he explained, "but gradually you take some responsibility, then a little more."

Heroes see opportunities. Heroes accept responsibility. Heroes answer the call.

Chapter 2

Protecting the Vulnerable

*Life's most persistent and urgent question is,
what are you doing for others?*
-Martin Luther King, Jr.

Riding horseback to a courthouse in rural Illinois, a young Abraham Lincoln heard the squeal of a pig that had fallen into a hole. Wearing his fancy new suit, he found a railroad tie and positioned it in such a way that the pig could escape. A slightly disheveled Lincoln returned to his horse and proceeded to the courthouse. It was in Lincoln's nature to help wherever he saw a need.

On another occasion, an aggrieved man entered a law office in Springfield, IL to retain Lincoln's services in the hope of evicting the family of a widow whose late husband had owed him money. After listening to details of the dispute, Lincoln answered, "I know I can win your case for you. But at what price? I can distress a widowed mother and her six fatherless children, and thereby gain for you six hundred dollars. I shall not take your case, but I will give you a little advice for nothing. You seem an industrious and enterprising man. I would advise you to try your hand at making six hundred dollars in some other way."

Lincoln defended those who were ill-equipped to defend themselves, even when he could have personally benefited from their mistreatment.

One day in December, 1948, Mother Teresa was swarmed by a group of children as she walked through the Motijhil slum in Calcutta. These first pupils returned the next day to greet her as she stepped across the railway bridge leading to Motijhil. By the end of the month, she received permission to open a "school," which began with twenty-one children gathered in an open space between the huts, learning the Bengali alphabet by tracing characters with sticks in the mud. Enrollment doubled the next day.

Mother Teresa spent the balance of her days visiting families, feeding the hungry, caring for the sick, and discovering the many needs within the community. Her evening hours were spent in prayer and writing.

In her journal, Mother Teresa recalled seeing a dying woman on the street outside Campbell Hospital:

I picked her up and took her to the hospital but she was refused admission because she was poor. She died on the street. I knew then that I must make a home for the dying, a resting place for people going to heaven.

Shortly thereafter, Mother Teresa was able to rent two huts for a total of ten rupees. One served as the first school building. The other became the first home for the sick and the dying.

Thus began the work for which Mother Teresa became known, serving the poorest of the poor in Calcutta, India.

Suffering

As word spread of the little nun clad in a white sari with blue borders, more and more people came to offer money or assistance. Consequently, the need arose to find a residence for those who would join her. Reflecting upon her search, Mother Teresa wrote:

Today I learned a good lesson. The poverty of the poor must be so hard for them. While looking for a home (for a center) I walked and walked till my arms and legs ached. I thought how much they must ache in body and soul, looking for a home, food and health.

When a home was found, Mother Teresa began receiving volunteers. The first ten were Mother Teresa's former students from the Loreto convent school. The new recruits spent their time begging door-to-door and using the money to teach the children, feed the starving, care for the sick, and provide a dignified end to those who were dying.

Though motivated by the lofty ideals of her faith, Mother Teresa remained pragmatic. Mother Teresa believed that "in order to understand and help those who have nothing, we must live like them...The only difference is that these people are poor by birth, and we are poor by choice."

By living like the poorest of the poor, and building relationships with each person they served, Mother Teresa and her Sisters were able to better identify the unique needs of each of the individuals that they served.

Once restored to health, children were returned to their parents or placed in adoptive homes. Each child received an education that would prepare them for adulthood. Men and women were given job training in trades like typing, sewing, or construction, in the hope that with these new skills they would be better equipped to support themselves and their families.

As the Missionaries of Charity established homes in new cities throughout the world, Mother Teresa never presumed to understand the unique needs of the people in the community. When the Missionaries of Charity were to enter her native Albania, Mother Teresa declared, "We have come to give tender love and care, as we do throughout the world," then explained, "We will begin slowly and see what is the greatest need."

The suffering of those around them shaped the development of the Missionaries of Charity. When new challenges arose, the Missionaries of

Charity responded with tuberculosis clinics, ante-natal services, villages for lepers, and hospice care for those dying of AIDS.

One reason why Mother Teresa was so admired is that she served people who were suffering in extreme poverty. Gandhi, Dr. King, and Nelson Mandela were admired because they devoted their lives to those who had suffered the indignity of segregation and subjugation. Gandhi was moved by compassion for the suffering of fellow Indians; Dr. King was moved by compassion for fellow African Americans who suffered under Jim crow laws; Mandela was moved by compassion for those who suffered under apartheid.

See a pattern?

Each of these heroes listened for—and responded to—the sounds of suffering. They were able to recognize the pain and sorrow around them. Instead of lamenting their own suffering, they worked to relieve the suffering of others.

Psychologists use the term "directed altruism" to describe behavior that is aimed at assisting others who are in need, in pain, or experiencing distress. Directed altruism is reactive. Directed altruism is a response to pleas for help or signals of distress.

Some respond to suffering with indifference. But heroes figure out a way to make a difference. When they saw signs of suffering, Gandhi, Dr. King, and Mandela responded with empathy rather than pity. They chose compassion rather than resignation. The suffering of others was their call to action.

Living among the people allowed them to understand the sources of suffering. With this knowledge, they took it upon themselves to comfort those who were suffering *and* address the source of the suffering.

Mother Teresa was especially good at recognizing the many forms of suffering around her. As the Missionaries of Charity expanded their scope, Mother Teresa worked tirelessly to protect the poorest of the poor from the physical consequences of extreme poverty—like hunger, homelessness, illness, and pain—as well as the deeper emotional suffering of loneliness and rejection. As Mother Teresa would often say, "There is more hunger in the world for love and appreciation than for bread."

Mother Teresa focused on addressing the specific needs of each of the specific people she served. "I never look at the masses as my responsibility," she explained, "I look at the individual. I can love only one person at a time. I can feed only one person at a time. Just one, one, one." On another occasion, Mother Teresa said,

I feel called to help individuals, to love each human being. I never think in terms of crowds in general but in terms of persons. Were I to think about crowds, I would never begin anything. It is the person that matters. I believe in person-to-person encounters.

Similarly, Arun Gandhi observed that his famous grandfather "cared about political justice not from some grand theoretical perspective but because he was moved by the plight of each individual."

Bureaucrats see groups. Heroes see individuals.

Individuals and Groups

Why does it matter if we view people as individuals or as members of groups?

Because the way we think and feel and reason about individuals is totally different than the way that we think and feel and reason about groups.

In the 1890s, a Kantian philosopher named Wilhelm Windelband used the terms "idiographic" and "nomothetic" to make a distinction between two approaches to knowledge. The latter, refers to making generalizations about—and deriving principles from—groups. The former, focuses on seeing the unique characteristics of the individual.

The difference between an idiographic and nomothetic approach to knowledge was illustrated when I conducted a study on how children want their parents to behave at youth sport events. Before conducting the study, I asked parents for permission to interview their children. Each parent gave permission to conduct the interview. Then, something unexpected happened: Most of the parents followed up by requesting that I send them a summary of my result, saying something like, "this is such an interesting study! I would love to know how Kailee wants me to act while she is on the field. Can I give you my email address?"

Think about that for a moment.

Rather than asking their particular child to share his or her particular preferences, parents were content to wait for months as I transcribed interviews, analyzed the data, and summarized my findings, so they could learn how children in general want their parents to behave. Then, they planned to use my findings to better understand how their particular son or daughter might want them to behave.

Can you think of a way these parents could satisfy their curiosity more quickly? Or a way that they could receive answers that would be most relevant to their child?

We have become so accustomed to searching for evidence in the form of group-level differences in quantitative studies that, at times, it appears that we have forgotten that it is ok—and sometimes preferable—to simply ask individuals what *they* want, what *they* like, or what *they* believe, as opposed to asking what people in general want, like, or believe.

For parents who are interested in understanding how they can best support *their* son or daughter at youth sport events, an idiographic approach would be quicker, easier, and much more relevant. Over a bowl of ice cream, the parent could simply explain to the child, "I love you and want to support you while you are on the soccer field. How would you like me to act while you are playing?"

Nomothetic thinking can have profound—even global—consequences.

Large populations depersonalize individuals within groups, as famously illustrated by a quote attributed to Joseph Stalin: "If only one man dies of hunger, that is a tragedy. If millions die, that's only statistics."

Tyrants rationalize their evil with statistics. And ordinary people may be tempted to view people as faceless group members. But heroes find a way to maintain idiographic thinking, even when they are responsible for dozens, or thousands, or even millions of individuals.

This may be why superhero stories always include side characters. We don't care as much about Superman saving Metropolis in general as we care about the Man of Steel saving Lois Lane in particular. In Superman's debut in *Action comics #1*, his first three acts were to save a wrongly convicted man from his scheduled electrocution, protect a woman from spousal abuse, and rescue Lois Lane from her kidnappers. Side characters are an essential part of hero stories, not just because they allow the hero to demonstrate his care and concern for vulnerable others, but because they allow the hero to tap into the psychology of the individual.

Heroes don't just see individuals. They protect and guide individuals.

The Shepherd and the Servant

The word "pastor" comes from the same root word as "pasture" and it's meaning is based on a shepherd metaphor. Just as shepherds guide and protect each of their individual sheep, a pastor guides and protects each of his congregants.

Dr. King rose to international fame as an inspiring speaker and civil rights leader. But he was, at heart, a pastor—in the literal sense. Speaking to his congregation in 1966, Dr. King proclaimed, "Some people are suffering, some people are hungry this morning. Some people are still living with segregation and discrimination this morning. I'm going to fight for them." His natural inclination was to guide and protect each member of his congregation, which he continued to do for as long as he was able.

Eventually, Dr. King resigned the pastorate in Montgomery to join his father as an assistant pastor of Ebenezer Baptist Church in Atlanta, where he could focus more of his efforts on the civil rights movement. He knew that a new shepherd was needed to tend to his former flock at Dexter Avenue Baptist Church in Montgomery.

Dr. King focused on serving those in greatest need during each phase of his career. He frequently quoted Matthew 23:11, "He who is the greatest among you shall be your servant," and added, "I want to be your servant." Dr. King remained grounded in service to his congregation, his community, and his country.

Dr. King's commitment to service was inspired by another civil rights leader who devoted his life to serving humanity.

Gandhi's first notable acts of public service were performed in his role as a lawyer—and as a newspaper publisher—defending Indian immigrants from injustice in South Africa. He then volunteered not once, but twice, to serve injured soldiers as a nurse during the Boer War and the Zulu Uprising. Because the ground was so rough near the battlefields, vehicles were often unable to reach the troops. Gandhi and his colleagues carried wounded soldiers—from both sides of each conflict—on stretchers for several miles under the unrelenting South African sun. Then, after serving his fellow Indians in South Africa for two decades, Gandhi returned to his native country to fight for freedom from British colonization on behalf of the Indian people.

For Gandhi, service had profound significance—at least when performed sincerely. Gandhi viewed serving others as an opportunity rather than an obligation. Service was a way to give *and* receive. "The best way to find yourself is to lose yourself in the service of others," he explained, "all other pleasures and possessions pale into nothingness before service which is rendered in a spirit of joy."

Gandhi demonstrated that "power comes from sincere service." But Gandhi warned that service performed "for show or for fear of public opinion stunts the man and crushes his spirit." Gandhi considered insincere service, which is motivated by "selfishness and egotism," to be counterproductive. Unless the servant is focused on the welfare of the people he serves, he is merely serving himself—deriving unjustified satisfaction from *the idea* of serving others. "Service can have no meaning," Gandhi explained, "unless one takes pleasure in it."

Mother Teresa expressed similar sentiments. When her Sisters established a home in Armenia, she asked rhetorically, "why did we come here?" before answering her own question: "We came to proclaim Christ in the poorest of the poor by giving humble love and service and do that with a smile!"

In serving others, Mother Teresa tried to direct the focus away from herself. "No one thinks of the pen while reading a letter," she explained, "they only want to know the mind of the person who wrote the letter. That's exactly what I am in God's hands – a little pencil. God is writing his love letter to the world in this way, through works of love."

Like Gandhi, Mother Teresa was adamant that service be performed for the right reasons. While observing Mother Teresa care for a dying man with an unpleasant odor, a disgusted reporter said that he would never do what she was doing for a million dollars. Mother Teresa replied, "Yes, for a million dollars I wouldn't do it either."

Public Service

Politicians sometimes refer to themselves as "public servants." But not all politicians serve the public. Some only serve themselves. Some politicians view their election victory as a finish line—the conclusion of their quest for power and position.

The term "public servant" is accurate only when politicians see their election as a starting line—a point at which they can begin their tireless journey on behalf of the constituents they were elected to serve. Over time, true public servants eventually earn the respect of those they serve, even when their constituents might disagree on specific decisions or policies.

When Abraham Lincoln was elected president of the United States, he was not universally popular—far from it. Though he is America's most beloved president in *our* time, Lincoln was the most hated president of *his* time—and arguably the most divisive of all time. Remember: in the wake of Lincoln's election as President of the United States, eleven states seceded from the Union and formed the Confederate States of America. No other president has *literally* divided the nation.

But Lincoln gradually earned loyalty and admiration—even from former rivals and critics—through faithful service to his soldiers and citizens during some of the most difficult times our nation has faced. In a letter written to James Conkling in 1863, Lincoln stated, "I freely acknowledge myself the servant of the people, according to the bond of service—the United States Constitution; and that, as such, I am responsible to them." Lincoln's sense of accountability to his constituents and the Constitution kept him focused on serving the needs of the people he was elected to serve and the interests of the Union he was sworn to defend.

As a true public servant, Lincoln acted on behalf of his soldiers and citizens, not his own behalf. He made decisions for their benefit, not his—even when he had to pay a price personally.

Lincoln identified and met the needs of his constituents. He spent time listening to his soldiers. He understood the importance of timely correspondence with friends and families to their morale. Lincoln took action to increase the speed and efficiency of the postal service. The nation noticed. President Lincoln won a second term over his Democratic rival, George McClellan, with the resounding electoral vote of 212-22.

Nelson Mandela, on the other hand, only served one term. Despite his overwhelming popularity, Mandela chose to forgo a second term as president. He believed he could better serve the people of South Africa by relinquishing power—thereby demonstrating that it is possible for an

African leader to do so—than by remaining in office. Mandela realized that by stepping down from his position—and ensuring a peaceful transfer of power—he would have even greater power to serve his people.

There is nothing inherently noble about being a servant—when placed in that position by others. But when a person voluntarily descends from a vaunted position to live among the people and to serve the most vulnerable among them, self-appointed servants earn the admiration, loyalty, and trust of those they serve.

After obtaining the consent of the people, the hero is ready to lead them through trying times.

Chapter 3

Projecting Calm

Fearlessness presupposes calmness and peace of mind
-Gandhi

Sitting in a neatly pressed suit and tie on the sidelines of the basketball court at Pauley Pavilion, Coach John Wooden looked on as his UCLA bruins dominated another opponent. After a questionable call, the camera panned to the bench, and the commentator deadpanned, "Coach Wooden just raised an eyebrow. He must be very upset about something."

Under the pressure of unprecedented winning streaks, mounting expectations, and national broadcasts, Wooden's UCLA Bruins continued to bring national championship trophies back to Westwood. Through it all, Wooden's players seemed almost impervious to pressure as Wooden remained stoic on the bench.

Athletes take on the emotional tone of their coaches. If the coach argues with the referee, the players feel entitled to argue with the referee. If the coach rides an emotional rollercoaster, the players get on board. If the coach loses *his* cool, the players are more likely to lose *their* cool. When players lose their cool, they are more likely to make mistakes that could cost their team the game. That is why Coach Wooden remained calm on the bench and often reminded his players, "emotion is your enemy."

Basketball is a simple sport, which Wooden called "a game of 3's." When a player receives the ball, they have only 3 options: dribble, pass, or shoot. The fundamentals of basketball are essentially the same at every level. Excellence in basketball means doing the fundamental things with greater precision and speed—and making fewer mistakes—than opponents. While practicing and competing, Wooden taught his players to "be quick but don't hurry" and reinforced the importance of precision with a rhetorical question: "if you don't have time to do it right, when will you have time to do it over?"

In basketball, there is a physical game and a mental game. The physical game is against the opponent. The mental game is against oneself—against the thoughts, doubts, worries, and vanities that can distract focus from the task at hand. The players that win their mental game usually outscore their opponent on the court.

Through his words and through his example, Wooden taught his players *about* basketball and *through* basketball. The man known as "Coach" thought of himself, first and foremost, as a teacher. His lesson about basketball concealed larger life lessons. His lessons about emotional control were applicable in any situation. Wooden taught the young men on the UCLA basketball team that when people lose control of their emotions, they are more likely to make costly mistakes, on and off the court.

As head coach of UCLA, Coach Wooden applied principles that he had learned from other exceptional leaders.

When asked to identify the person that he admired the most, Coach Wooden named Mother Teresa.

Calm, Cool, and Collected

Before Mother Teresa became an international figure, she sometimes met resistance from local community leaders in Calcutta. Having acquired a new home for the dying, which had previously served as a Hindu temple, less moderate Hindu leaders assumed the Missionaries of Charity would use the building to proselytize. One day, a prominent Hindu leader from Delhi gathered local youth and led a mob—brandishing stones and clubs—toward Mother Teresa's home for the dying, which she called Nirmal Hriday ("house of the pure heart"). Learning of their approach, Mother Teresa,

> *Stood in front of the door and then walked toward the mob. She greeted the leader without any sign of fear and invited him to come in and see what they were doing. He went in with her by himself. After a while he came out again. The youths crowded around and asked him whether they could now begin to drive out the Sisters. He replied, 'Yes, you can, but only when your sisters and your mothers do what those Sisters are doing in there.'*

Remaining calm, cool, and collected amidst danger and uncertainty is a defining feature of fictional heroes like James Bond, Indiana Jones, and Atticus Finch—and real-life heroes like John Wooden, Mother Teresa, and Nelson Mandela.

On a flight to the Natal region of South Africa in 1994, Nelson Mandela looked out the window and noticed that one of the propellers on the small twin engine plane was not working. Mandela turned to his bodyguard, Mike, and asked that he inform the pilots. Mike saw Mandela quietly reading his newspaper and took solace in Mandela's calm demeanor. Upon landing, Mandela shook hands and posed for photographs with a group of Japanese tourists in the airport lounge, who were unaware of the mechanical failure. After getting into a bulletproof BMW sent to retrieve him, Mandela's eyes widened as he said, "Man, I was terrified up there!"

In his autobiography, *Long Walk to Freedom*, Mandela admitted that, on many occasions, he had been afraid. He was afraid when he was a fugitive from justice, he was afraid as a defendant in the Rivonia Trial, and he was afraid as a prisoner on Robben Island. When he began negotiations with the government, he was afraid once more. But Mandela learned to overcome fear and conceal his fear while he was in the company of other people.

"Calm," Mandela observed, "is what people look for in tense situations, whether political or personal. They want to see that you are not rattled, that you are weighing all the factors, and that your response is measured."

Don't Get Panicky

For most of his public life, Dr. King and his wife Coretta lived under constant threat. Day after day, the Kings received letters from people who threatened to blow up their home. Night after night, Dr. King answered a series of menacing phone calls warning he and his family to leave Montgomery. Despite the ever-present danger, Dr. King remained calm, even during the most stressful times.

While attending a mass meeting at the First Baptist Church in Montgomery, Dr. King was informed that his home had been bombed. He calmly interrupted the meeting and asked those in attendance for their undivided attention. After explaining to the audience why he needed to leave, Dr. King urged each member of his congregation to "not get panicky," and to hold fast to their philosophy of nonviolence.

Dr. King arrived home to find that his wife and daughter were safe. He spoke with the mayor, police commissioner, and members of the media, who were visibly concerned by the prospect of navigating through the angry crowd assembling outside his home. Sensing the volatility of the situation, Dr. King walked out and stood on what was left of his front porch and called the crowd to order.

"Now let's not become panicky," he urged those assembled, "if you have weapons, take them home; if you do not have them, please do not seek to get them. We cannot solve this problem through retaliatory violence. We must meet violence with nonviolence. Remember the words of Jesus: 'He who lives by the sword will perish by the sword.' He continued,

> *We must love our white brothers, no matter what they do to us. We must make them know that we love them. Jesus still cries out in the words that echo across the centuries: 'Love your enemies; bless them that curse you; pray for them that despitefully use you.' This is what we must live by. We must meet hate with love. Remember, if I am stopped, this movement will not stop, because God is with the movement. Go home with this glowing faith and this radiant assurance.*

When his home was targeted a second time, he stood on his porch where twelve sticks of dynamite had smoldered to no effect and addressed the crowd: "We must not return violence under any condition. I know this is difficult advice to follow, especially since we have been the victims of no less than ten bombings. But this is the way of Christ; it is the way of the cross. We must somehow believe that unearned suffering is redemptive." Concluding his extemporaneous remarks on that Sunday morning, he then asked his neighbors to go home and get ready for church.

Years later, while marching in St. Augustine, FL, Dr. King was hit in the head with a brick thrown by an anti-protester. Rather than retaliate or flee, Dr. King stood up and said to his friend, "I'm not going to run, Hosea." One of Dr. King's young white staffers described the incident: "I was scared they were going to jump us, but King was so calm. His eyes—I don't know how to describe eyes like that. You could just look at them and think, well, if he can do it, somehow nothing will happen to me."

Always trying to be the calm, steady hero that the people needed, Dr. King continued marching. As he later explained, "we need leadership that is calm and yet positive. There is no place for misguided emotionalism."

Dr. King was a preacher who practiced what he preached. Time and time again, he guided his followers into danger. Before one march, Dr.

King addressed those gathered, saying, "I want to make a point that I think everyone here should consider very carefully and decide if he wants to be with this campaign. I have to tell you that in my judgment, some of the people sitting here today will not come back alive from this campaign. And I want you to think about it."

On the eve of the march from Montgomery to Selma, Dr. King said, "I can't promise you that it won't get you killed. But we must stand up for what is right." Dr. King not only stood up for what was right, but walked at the front of the crowd, fully exposed to the dangers that he and his fellow marchers faced.

In heroic stories, when the villagers begin to panic, the hero projects calm as he protects them. In fact, calming the crowd is one of the ways in which heroes protect the villagers. Even when his own home was bombed, Dr. King modeled the same level of restraint and self-control that he asked of his followers. Seeing the example set by their calm, cool, and collected leader, fellow marchers who might have felt tempted to retaliate or retreat when harassed or attacked, kept marching forward.

Amidst growing threats to his life, Dr. King traveled around the country with minimal security, clearly demonstrating to both his followers and his adversaries that he was not afraid. "I have a job to do," he explained, "If I were constantly worried about death, I couldn't function. I must face the fact, as all others in positions of leadership must do, that something could well happen to me at any time." Dr. King dealt with the looming danger by focusing on the bigger picture, reassuring himself with the thought that, "my cause is so right, so moral, that if I should lose my life, in some way it would aid the cause."

Unsent Letters

Before the end of the Civil War, Abraham Lincoln and his War Secretary, Edwin Stanton, traveled the streets of DC in an open carriage. Friends and cabinet members pleaded with him to be more careful. Lincoln refused additional precautionary measures because, as he explained, it was essential "the people know I come among them without fear."

Lincoln refused to live in fear. He once remarked, he would "rather be dead than to live in continued dread." Lincoln explained his reasoning: "If I am killed, I can die but once; but to live in constant dread of it, is to die over and over again."

During his frequent visits to the troops, Lincoln sometimes found himself within range of enemy fire—an unusual position for a sitting president. But, while walking among his soldiers and officers, "The President evinced a remarkable coolness and disregard for danger."

Lincoln responded similarly when hazards were more political in nature. Early in his administration, members of his cabinet tried to sabotage his work, make decisions behind his back, and position themselves as challengers for the presidency. But Lincoln's uncanny ability to regulate his emotions and resist the impulse to retaliate in the wake of such attacks served him well during his time in office.

One of the ways Lincoln managed his anger involved writing letters that he had no intention of sending. Lincoln also encouraged those around him to do the same, as illustrated by an episode described by former presidential speech writer, James Humes:

> *One morning Edwin Stanton, Lincoln's secretary of war, stormed into the president's office. Stanton was angry at a letter a major general had written him. Lincoln told him to write him back a letter. At the President's desk Stanton sat down to write. "Stick it to him, "egged on Lincoln, and Stanton penned on furiously. "Scorch the General, "urged the President, and the war secretary continued to vent his rage on paper. "Really scold him," Lincoln pressed. When Stanton finally finished, Lincoln took the letter and tore it up. "Why did you do that?" questioned a perplexed Stanton. "You don't want to send that letter,*

Stanton. Put it in the stove." Lincoln continued, "That's what I do when I've written a letter when I'm angry. It's a humdinger of a letter and you've had a hell of a good time writing it. Now burn it and write another letter."

Lincoln was a master of self-restraint. He taught Stanton one of his tried-and-true techniques. The 16th President kept a collection of envelopes with notes to the effect of: "To Gen. Meade, never sent, or signed." By releasing his frustrations in private, Lincoln prevented his anger from surfacing in public.

The Upside of Anger

Gandhi lost his temper many times as a child but, as an adult, he too became a master of restraint. When the offense was merely personal, Gandhi usually chose to "pocket the insult." But when the issue was a matter of principle, Gandhi stood firm. Even though he was a frequent target of racism and discrimination, Gandhi refused to retaliate.

One day, Gandhi's grandson Arun came to him with tears in his eyes after he was bullied on the soccer field. Arun wanted his famous grandfather to help him get rid of the anger. But Gandhi taught his grandson that anger isn't necessarily bad. Gandhi, who devoted his life to promoting nonviolence, considered anger to be a gift rather than a vice—if used properly. "I am glad to see you can be moved to anger," Gandhi explained, "Anger is good...Anger to people is like gas to the automobile—it fuels you to move forward and get to a better place. Without it, we would not be motivated to rise to a challenge. It is an energy that compels us to define what is just and unjust."

When Gandhi was kicked off the train in South Africa, he was understandably angry. In the aftermath of the unkindness and injustice (and his study of similar indignities experienced by fellow Indians in South Africa), Gandhi was compelled to do something. But Gandhi did not retaliate or lose his temper. Instead, he took time to understand the problem and develop a plan to address the problem. The time that Gandhi spent reflecting on the best course of action was pivotal in his life—and pivotal in the course of history—because the way an aggrieved party responds is what determines whether anger will be helpful or harmful.

Anger, like other forms of energy, is powerful but volatile. And anger, like any other form of energy, can be used to help or to harm; dynamite has the power to create a tunnel or destroy a bridge.

To illustrate this point further, Gandhi used yet another energy analogy: "When we channel electricity intelligently, we can use it to improve our life, but if we abuse it, we could die. So as with electricity, we must learn to use anger wisely for the good of humanity."

Getting angry is easy but controlling anger is difficult. When gasoline or electricity escape from their proper channels, they become dangerous. But just as wires, pipes, valves, and fittings must be robust enough to keep the gasoline or electricity inside the system, a person must be strong enough to experience anger privately while not allowing the anger to escape in public.

Internal anger that prompts public action is helpful. But anger expressed publicly pushes people further away and creates enemies out of the very people you wish to convert. Nobody wants to be splashed with gasoline or shocked by electricity. You aren't going to win anyone to your side by shouting in their face.

It is not the expression of anger, but the suppression of anger, that reveals strength. Countless times, Gandhi demonstrated his strength through restraint. He used the many injustices that he suffered as fuel to motivate his continued struggle against injustice. He transduced one form of energy (anger) into another form of energy (nonviolent action).

Stay Focused

In addition to destroying relationships, uncontrolled anger is problematic because, when people lose their temper or act out of passion, they tend to make poor decisions—usually erring on the side of being overly aggressive. This idea is expressed in the "fixer-upper" song in Disney's animated movie *Frozen*. One of the troll characters sings: "people make bad choices when they're mad or scared or stressed."

This line, sung by fictional characters in an animated musical, contains an important truth. Research on human performance has revealed that anger, fear, and distress cause people to narrow their attention, fixate on only one aspect of a situation, and make reckless decisions. For example, after golfers hit a series of bad shots, they often make an overly aggressive club selection in an attempt to make up for past mistakes. But impatient decisions usually leave the golfer in an even worse predicament.

When we are already in it up to our ears, hasty decisions usually cause us to dig our holes deeper. Hasty decisions rarely help us get out of the hole we dug for ourselves.

There is a psychology to vicious circles: When our minds focus on regrets related to past mistakes and concern over future outcomes, our attention shifts. When a golfer is not intentional about directing her attention, she may fixate on what she is trying *not* to do rather than what she is trying to do. The golfer will pick a target but tell herself, "Don't hit it into the water hazard, don't hit it into the water hazard." Then, kerplunk. The ball splashes into the water hazard. Our actions usually follow our attention rather than our intention.

Long before performance psychologists dubbed this phenomenon "ironic processing," Lincoln understood the relationship between fear and focus. "You cannot fail in any laudable object," Lincoln wrote to his friend William Herndon, "unless you allow your mind to be improperly directed."

Lincoln appreciated passion—in its proper place. He once remarked that, "When I hear a man preach, I like to see him act as if he were fighting bees." But he warned against allowing unregulated emotion to influence important decisions: "We must not be led by excitement and passion to do that which our sober judgments would not approve in our cooler moments." Lincoln "was disinclined to hasty action" and stated that, "In grave emergencies, moderation is generally safer than radicalism."

During his first inaugural address, as the nation was anxious to see what would unfold, Lincoln called for patience, saying, "Nothing valuable can be lost by taking time. If there be an object to hurry any of you in hot haste to a step which you would never take deliberately, that object will be frustrated by taking time; but no good object can be frustrated by it."

The word "patience" literally means "long-suffering." When people are angry, fearful, or distressed, they are motivated to escape from suffering as quickly as possible. This is why, in stressful situations, impatient leaders can appear so decisive—the first option that comes to mind becomes their getaway car. But when people begin to drive without considering the direction they are headed, they often end up in the wrong place.

Lincoln displayed the patience needed to calm down and carefully consider his options before reaching a conclusion. In many cases, Lincoln postponed important decisions until he was able to gather the information needed to make a more fully informed choice.

When leaders of the Wig party proposed a new plan to select candidates for Congress (which would give an unfair advantage to incumbents), Lincoln did not respond hastily. Instead, he carefully articulated his reasons for rejecting the proposal in a letter to General John J. Hardin, which included population data from the most recent census along with the number of delegates proportioned under the old system and those proposed under the new system. During this inter-party squabble, Lincoln focused on facts and reassured General Hardin, "I promise to 'keep cool' under all circumstances."

When startled or scared, humans engage in what social psychologists call "social referencing." When a toddler trips and falls, they look up to see how their parent responds before deciding to cry or brush themselves off and keep going. Through social referencing, toddlers seek clues for how *they* should respond by looking at the responses of their parents. Adults also engage in social referencing—especially during frightening events. But instead of looking to parents, they look to heroes.

Why? Because in stressful situations, people are prone to panic. But heroes project calm. Heroes mask their own fear and put the safety of others ahead of their own wellbeing. Heroes display courage amidst chaos, which helps others feel comforted and protected. And heroes keep a cool head in times of turmoil, which allows them to gather information and make prudent decisions on behalf of others.

Chapter 4

Remaining Vigilant

No decision is difficult to make if you will get all the facts
-Gen. George Patton

During World War II, General George Patton led his 3rd Army through North Africa and Southern Europe at a torrid pace. "Old Blood and Guts" was relentless in his pursuit of Nazi Armies and was unwilling to accept delay on his path to Germany.

Patton was tasked with making decisions on behalf of his soldiers, which would affect their lives—and the outcome of the war. While some generals watched from the safety of mobile war rooms, Patton wasn't afraid to get his boots dirty on the front lines. Patton was tenacious in collecting the most thorough and reliable intel possible. In many instances, he insisted on assessing situations first-hand. For Patton, seeing with his own eyes and hearing with his own ears was an indispensable part of his job as a military leader. He wanted to acquire the best information so that he could make the best decisions.

A leader's effectiveness comes down to their ability to build relationships and make wise decisions. The Big 5—Lincoln, Gandhi, Mother Teresa, Dr. King, and Nelson Mandela—were experts in these essential skills. They were intentional in building trusting relationships with those they served and diligent in gathering the information necessary to make prudent decisions on their behalf.

Heroes insist on developing a thorough understanding of a problem before trying to fix it. This important habit requires a rare combination of humility, patience, and perseverance. Humility to realize their ignorance, patience to delay decisions until they become better-informed, and perseverance to do the hard work necessary to gather relevant information through experiences, observations, and conversations.

Live

Heroes usually live among the people.

Mother Teresa lived at the "Mother Home" in Calcutta, which was situated near the poorest of the poor. By living among the suffering poor, Mother Teresa was able to demonstrate care, establish trust, and develop a firsthand understanding of their suffering. In addition to identifying the unique needs of each of the individuals that she served, Mother Teresa was able to better ascertain the experiences of those not yet known to her, who lived in similar conditions.

Gandhi shared Mother Teresa's belief that understanding should come before intervention. Gandhi believed that to truly help, "We must step down from our pedestals and live with them not as outsiders, but as one of them in every way, sharing their burdens and sorrows."

Prior to his arrival in DC, Lincoln lived a rugged life "out West." He had no problem relating to the struggles of families on the frontier. Countless miles traveled around the Illinois legal circuit provided first-hand knowledge of the insufficient roads and railways used by farmers and merchants who wished to bring their goods to market. Though he was often mocked as a back-woods rail-splitter, Lincoln's humble background equipped him with an endless supply of relatable stories and folksy anecdotes, which were often drawn from the considerable challenges that he faced early in his life.

Due to his difficult upbringing, early experiences of trauma, as well as the death of his son, Lincoln was painfully aware of the suffering experienced by those—in the North and South—who had lost loved ones during the war. Lincoln learned from his experiences and expected others to do the same, confessing, "I do not think much of a man who is not wiser today than he was yesterday."

While the 16th President of the United States did not share Mother Teresa and Gandhi's inclination to live in poverty, Lincoln's White House was no ivory tower. Astonishingly, Lincoln maintained an open-door policy during most of his presidency. When he was in the capitol, Lincoln spent about 75% of each workday meeting with people. On a typical day, a line of visitors would form in the hallway leading to his office. Most came with requests. Some were seeking a job for themselves or a family member. Some lobbied the President for a pardon on behalf of a son or nephew who had deserted his military post. Others requested some appropriation or legislation that would benefit their hometown.

When his secretaries tried to turn visitors away with regrets that the President was unable to receive them, Lincoln would sometimes emerge through the door and welcome them in. In response to cabinet members who questioned the wisdom of his accessibility, Lincoln explained, "They don't want much, they get but little, and I must see them."

By meeting with tens of thousands of constituents—many of whom had traveled from afar—Lincoln was able to understand the cares and concerns of each of his visitors. Each citizen reminded Lincoln of the importance of the task before him. He called these meetings "public opinion baths" and explained that he had "but little time to read the papers and gather public opinion that way; and though they may not be pleasant in all their particulars, the effect, as a whole, is renovating and invigorating to my perceptions of responsibility and duty."

Due to his habit of seeing visitors on a first-come, first-served basis, his conversations were not restricted to members of elite society. Lincoln interacted with a representative sample of citizens, which allowed him to gather accurate information about the beliefs and values of the American people. As Lincoln explained to a visitor, these meetings "serve to renew in me a clearer and more vivid image of that great popular assemblage out of which I sprung."

More than any president before or after, Lincoln knew the American people. He spent countless hours listening to them, learning from them, and laughing with them—often laughing at his own jokes. While residing in the White House, Lincoln still managed to live among the people.

Look

Mother Teresa, Gandhi, and Dr. King spent most of their time where they were needed most.

Throughout the civil rights movement, Dr. King traveled to where the action was. In each town or city he entered, Dr. King spoke not just with the local leaders, but with ordinary people. He made a habit of visiting night clubs and pool halls to speak with young adults.

Pool hall meetings provided an opportunity to understand the hopes and fears of young people and to educate them and recruit them to the cause. "We are in the midst of a great movement and we are soliciting the support of all the citizens of Albany," he explained to those around him, "In order that we can continue on a Christian basis with love and nonviolence, I wanted to talk to you all and urge you to be nonviolent, not to throw bottles. I know if you do this, we are destined to win."

After focusing on the struggles faced by black residents in the Deep South, Dr. King turned his attention North. But he did not assume that his experiences in Southern cities like Montgomery and Selma had prepared him to fully understand the experiences of those living in the urban slums of Chicago—or that his Nobel Peace Prize would provide him with credibility among the residents. Dr. King moved into the Lawndale ghetto in Chicago, explaining to a group of reporters, "You can't really get close to the poor without living and being here with them." His two-bedroom apartment—which mirrored the living conditions of those he came to serve—became his base of operations.

Domestic travel allowed Dr. King to share his vision. International travel helped shape his vision.

In 1957, Dr. King traveled to Ghana, which he called "the land of my father's fathers," to study the conditions in which his ancestors had lived. Two years later, he traveled to India, remarking that "To other countries I may go as a tourist, but to India I come as a pilgrim." Dr. King was eager to learn from those who had followed Gandhi and to become better acquainted with the philosophies that guided Gandhi's quest to free India from Colonization. Domestic and international travel allowed him to discover similarities in the experiences of poor and disaffected people throughout the world.

Dr. King's travels paralleled those of the "little brown saint" that he so admired. Having vowed to stay in South Africa to fight on behalf of Indian immigrants, Gandhi set out on a deliberate fact-finding mission. Gandhi made "a deep study of the social, economic, and political conditions of the Indians in the Transvaal and the Orange Free State." He later recalled, "I had no idea that this study was to be of invaluable service to me in the future." When providing a legal defense for his clients, Gandhi was always equipped with a detailed understanding of the challenges they faced.

When Gandhi returned to India, he maintained his habit of gathering first-hand information to understand problems before attempting to solve them. As he became increasingly famous, Gandhi was frequently called upon to share his thoughts and opinions on a variety of matters. But Gandhi remained firm in his restraint, saying "I can give no opinion without seeing the conditions with my own eyes." At the advice of his mentor Gokhale,

Gandhi spent an entire year traveling around India—learning from Indians—before offering an opinion on matters of any importance.

In the early 20th century, the most convenient way to travel throughout India was by rail. Three types of tickets were available. First class tickets were meant for British passengers, second class for upper class Indians, and third class for poorer Indians.

To better understand the conditions in which ordinary Indians lived, Gandhi set off on "a tour through India traveling third class, and of acquainting myself with the hardships of third-class passengers." When asked why he traveled third class, he said "because there is no fourth." While traveling among the people, Gandhi observed that, "Third class passengers are treated like sheep and their comforts are sheep's comforts." He concluded that:

> *The indifference of the railway authorities to the comforts of the third-class passengers, combined with the dirty and inconsiderate habits of the passengers themselves, makes third class travelling a trial for a passenger of cleanly ways. These unpleasant habits commonly include throwing of rubbish on the floor of the compartment, smoking at all hours and in all places, betel and tobacco chewing, converting of the whole carriage into a spittoon, shouting and yelling, and using foul language regardless of the convenience or comfort of fellow passengers.*

While touring his native country, Gandhi was particularly concerned by the living conditions of those born into the lowest caste—the so-called "untouchables." Much to the dismay of local leaders, as well as the untouchables themselves, Gandhi insisted on inspecting the most mundane details of daily life, including their toilets. Upon inquiring, Gandhi learned that, in many communities, no such facilities existed: "'Latrines for us!' they exclaimed in astonishment. 'We go and perform our functions out in the open. Latrines are for the big people.'"

Gandhi became increasingly concerned by the unhealthy conditions he observed throughout the country—and increasingly aware of the obstacles to improvement. One woman Gandhi spoke with explained her dilemma, saying, "The sari I am wearing is the only one I have. How am I to wash it? Tell Mahatmaji to get me another sari, and I shall then promise to bathe and put on clean clothes every day." After completing the home visit, Gandhi summarized his findings as follows: "This cottage was not an exception, but a type to be found in many Indian villages. In countless cottages in India people live without any furniture, and without a change of clothes, merely with a rag to cover their shame."

Gandhi's patience and perseverance in gathering first-hand information allowed him to make more fully informed decisions on behalf of those he served.

Likewise, Lincoln's frequent visits to the front lines, where he surveyed the troops and discussed strategy with his generals, provided invaluable information as he guided the war effort. Lincoln's hands-on approach sometimes involved travel into enemy territory. Along with his Secretary of War, Edwin Stanton, Lincoln explored the shoreline to select a landing spot for the troops. He was not afraid to set foot on Confederate soil, if necessary.

Like Gandhi, it was against Lincoln's nature to make decisions or pronouncements without first coming to a complete understanding of a situation. Lincoln waited to state his position until he knew his subject "inside and outside, upside and downside" and "he was remorseless in his analysis of facts and principles." As a lawyer, he spent countless hours in the library studying legal statutes. As the 16th President, Lincoln traveled countless miles to assess the situation "on the ground."

After his release from prison, Nelson Mandela made up for lost time. "During the first six months after my release," Mandela recalled, "I spent more time abroad than at home." He toured African countries, European countries, and traveled to the United States. In each location, Mandela was greeted by enthusiastic crowds, including nearly 500,000 people in Dar es Salaam, Tanzania. Mandela enjoyed the opportunity "to see new—and old—sights, taste different foods, speak with all manner of people."

After twenty-seven years of incarceration, travel forced Mandela to adjust "to a world radically different from the one [he] had left. With changes in travel, communication, and media, the world had accelerated; things now happened so fast it was sometimes difficult to keep up with them." An up-to-date knowledge of living conditions and world affairs was essential to Mandela's ability to lead his nation.

Listen

By the mid-1960s, Mother Teresa traveled with great frequency. The schedule was grueling, but "Mother Teresa acknowledged with girlish pleasure that she has 'an itch to travel.'" She was less interested in sight-seeing than spending time with her sisters and the people that they served.

Countless face-to-face meetings allowed Mother Teresa to listen to and learn from the poor. One observer commented on her "gift for giving her whole attention to every person she encountered." Mother Teresa's priest and biographer, Father Maasburg, spoke of "her warmth and the direct way in which she approached people," recalling that, "when she turned to speak to someone, she concentrated on them completely. It was as if she and that person, with their questions and concerns, were the only people there."

Mother Teresa "did not regard visitors as a bothersome disturbance." On one occasion, an impatient photographer paced outside the chapel, afraid to disturb his subject. After a sister motioned to the photographer, "He took off his shoes and went into the chapel but hesitated to kneel down beside Mother Teresa." Then, as Father Maasburg recalled, "She must have heard or sensed it when he knelt down beside her on the floor, for she looked up and welcomed him with a radiant smile. Her attention now belonged entirely to the photographer. He presented his business in a few words. She gave him an answer. He stood up and left the chapel. Before he was even outside, Mother Teresa was already completely and utterly immersed again in prayer."

This incident was typical. Mother Teresa responded similarly to countless interruptions and requests for her time. Mother Teresa often said, "if you don't have a smile, make a smile." Similarly, if she didn't have time for people, she made time. As Father Maasburg explained, "for that moment, whether it lasted seconds or minutes or even hours, that individual was, for Mother Teresa, the most important person in the world. Through this feeling of being accepted by her and, indeed, important to her, and through this intimacy, many people who met her felt that they were her best friend."

As Gandhi became increasingly famous, he spent less and less time alone. Each day, Gandhi received a steady stream of visitors who approached him with a variety of requests. Some requested an interview, some sought advice, some wanted a judgment on a religious matter, and some wished to engage him in political debate. Gandhi graciously made time for his visitors, often by asking them to join him at meals, on walks, or at the spinning wheel.

Likewise, Dr. King had many demands on his schedule but found time for people who wanted to speak with him. "If you wanted to talk to him, he was going to take time to talk to you. That's just the way he was, that was his nature," recalled one of his colleagues. Dr. King was often late for engagements because "It would literally take him forty-five minutes to an hour to walk one and a half blocks."

While attending a meeting at a hotel in Atlanta, a porter put down his broom and pulled Dr. King aside for a rather lengthy conversation. An impatient executive complained that he had not traveled "a thousand miles to sit and wait while he talked to a porter." A wiser and more patient executive admonished his colleague, "Well, when the day comes that he stops having time to talk to a porter—on that day I will not have the time to come one mile to see him."

Mandela valued punctuality but, like Dr. King, he would stop what he was doing and make time to greet visitors. He was eager to listen to people, whether conversations were spontaneous or scheduled. As a child, Mandela learned the importance of listening while observing his father—who was an advisor to the chief—at work in the Great Palace. Mandela learned an important lesson: "I have always endeavored to listen to what each and every person in a discussion had to say before venturing my own opinion. Oftentimes, my own opinion will simply represent a consensus of what I heard in the discussion."

Similarly, Dr. King was eager to hear from others. Before arriving at a decision, he would solicit the opinions of friends and colleagues. One of his advisors, Andrew Young, recalled that if he was not satisfied with the range of ideas offered, Dr. King would ask someone to "express as radical a view as possible and somebody to express as conservative a view as possible." By entertaining a wider variety of options, Dr. King felt that he had a better chance to discover the truth.

Before addressing crowds in public, Dr. King listened to people in private. Dr. King would often look outside of his inner circle for input from those who possessed relevant expertise. On one such occasion, Dr. King sought strategic advice at the dawn of the Montgomery Bus Boycott:

> *I remembered that some time previously my good friend Rev. Theodore Jemison had led a bus boycott in Baton Rouge, Louisiana. Knowing that Jemison and his associates had set up an effective private car pool, I put in a long-distance call to ask him for suggestions for a similar pool in Montgomery. As I expected, his painstaking description of the Baton Rouge experience was invaluable.*

Like Dr. King, Gandhi was quick to listen and slow to speak. When Gandhi observed that, "empty drums make the loudest noises," he pointed to an unfortunate reality: Too often, people who know the least speak the most. But heroes like Lincoln, Mother Teresa, Nelson Mandela, and Dr. King opened their ears before opening their mouths. They were more eager to hear the opinions of others than to share their own. It is not a coincidence that some of the most profound speeches are delivered by outstanding listeners.

For Gandhi, listening was a default setting. While reflecting on his natural inclination to listen rather than speak, Gandhi concluded that "beyond occasionally exposing me to laughter, my constitutional shyness has been no disadvantage whatsoever." Carrying his self-analysis further, Gandhi explained that,

> *On the contrary, it has been all to my advantage. My hesitancy in speech, which was once an annoyance, is now a pleasure. Its greatest benefit has been that it has taught me the economy of words. I have naturally formed the habit of restraining my thoughts. And I can now give myself the certificate that a thoughtless word hardly ever escapes my tongue or pen. I do not recollect ever having had to regret anything in my speech or writing. I have thus been spared many a mishap and waste of time. Experience has taught me that silence is part of the spiritual discipline of a votary of truth. Proneness to exaggerate, to suppress or modify the truth, wittingly or unwittingly, is a natural weakness of man, and silence is necessary in order to surmount it. A man of few words will rarely be thoughtless in his speech; he will measure every word...My shyness has been in reality my shield and buckler. It has allowed me to grow. It has helped me in my discernment of truth.*

Wise and prudent decisions are based on accurate information. Finding the truth takes time. Time to learn from experience and time to observe conditions on the ground. Time to listen to experts, advisors, and especially the people the hero serves. Along the way, these three modes of information-gathering—living among the people, observing their conditions, and listening to their concerns—help heroes build trusting relationships with those they serve.

When the hero has the humility to recognize their lack of understanding, the patience to delay important decisions until they have become more fully informed, and the perseverance to gather important information, they are able to make wise decisions on behalf of their followers.

Chapter 5

Finding Solitude

The best thinking has been done in solitude.
The worst has been done in turmoil.
-Thomas Edison

Mother Teresa was relentless. Even in her later years, despite several heart surgeries and other health challenges, Mother Teresa rarely stopped moving. When asked how she maintained such a frenetic pace, Mother Teresa would explain that "It is the joy of giving, the joy of bringing love into people's lives that keeps us all going."

Mother Teresa traveled between Missionaries of Charity homes, on average, every three days. On flights, she kept a tablet of paper on her seatback table, upon which she would write letters of gratitude and encouragement. Sometimes she would fall asleep mid-letter, then pick up right where she left off when she awoke.

Mother Teresa was sometimes short on sleep, but she found ways to rest and regain her strength. When Mother Teresa was exhausted from perpetual travel and endless meetings, she would escape to a chapel and re-emerge revitalized.

Prayer was Mother Teresa's way to retreat from the chaos of her daily routine. Even with endless requests for her time, Mother Teresa regularly sought out seclusion and silence. As Mother Teresa explained, "silence gives us a new outlook on life." This is why Mother Teresa prescribed silence to her sisters. Not just a lack of noise, but "true interior silence of the eyes, ears, tongue, mind, and heart."

Rest

Like Mother Teresa, Gandhi traveled extensively[1] and received a constant stream of visitors from around the world. And like Mother Teresa, Gandhi found ways to rest. Whether he was at home at the Ashram, or imprisoned[2], Gandhi began each day in meditation and prayer. Because Gandhi was so generous with his time and gracious with those who sought his council, he spent less and less time by himself. But when a friend apologized for disrupting a quiet moment alone, Gandhi replied. "You did not disturb my solitude. My solitude is taken in the midst of many."

During the Civil War, Lincoln would retreat to his big chair by the window, where he spent quiet moments reading and thinking. These times of silence and seclusion helped Lincoln maintain his composure in public appearances and private interactions (despite exhaustion brought on by persistent insomnia and constant stress).

Some people can get by on little sleep and still retain their patience, empathy, and sense of humor. But Lincoln was successful *despite* getting little sleep, rather than *because of* getting little sleep. Sleep is important to our physical and emotional health. Most of us lose our patience when we lose sleep.

Have you noticed that, as a society, we have a strange relationship with sleep? People talk about how much they can't wait to hit the pillow. But late nights are worn by self-made martyrs like badges of honor.

---

[1] After his return from South Africa, Gandhi spent 43% of his days traveling outside the Ashram in Ahmedabad.
[2] In total, Gandhi spent 18% of his time in prison, which amounts to nearly 6 years of his life.

Ironically, a misguided attempt to demonstrate an uncompromising commitment to the cause (or the corporation) leaves the individual less productive and more prone to make mistakes. Boasting about a lack of sleep due to long hours worked is a bit like a fisherman bragging that he spent two hours fileting a trout with a dull knife.

When we lose sleep, our minds become dull. Exhaustion welcomes a host of vices, including impatience, impulsivity, and insensitivity. These vices lead to poor decisions and collateral damage in the form of costly mistakes and broken relationships.

Under the weight of responsibility, Dr. King was reluctant to rest. He often paid the price. During his public life, Dr. King was in-and-out of the hospital with exhaustion and infections. The long days, constant travel, and ever-present threats to his safety weakened his immune system and took a toll on his mental health.

Dr. King finally surrendered to the reality that he needed rest. "The doctors tell me I can't get by on two or three hours of sleep a night," he wrote to a friend, "I try to do it, and I learn I just can't." At some point, even Nobel Laureates, beloved presidents, and civil rights icons need to recognize their physiological needs.

Gandhi understood the importance of sleep. When a friend from Germany criticized the residents at Gandhi's Ashram for sleeping away a third of their life, he responded playfully and presciently, "sleeping a third of your life adds a third to your life span!"

We all need sleep.

Recreation

From a 21st century vantage point, some of Gandhi's ideas about health seem a bit antiquated. But in many ways, he was well ahead of his time—especially regarding the importance of nutrition and exercise. In his 1927 autobiography, *The Story of My Experiments with Truth*, Gandhi wrote, "I believed then, and I believe even now, that, no matter what amount of work one has, one should always find some time for exercise, just as one does for one's meals. It is my humble opinion that, far from taking away from one's capacity for work, it adds to it." Gandhi developed a habit of taking daily walks long before the physical and mental health benefits of exercise had been confirmed by researchers.

Nelson Mandela was equally enthusiastic about exercise. Two decades before the term "jogging" was popularized by University of Oregon Track and Field Coach (and Nike Co-Founder) Bill Bowerman, Mandela jogged around Johannesburg. In his autobiography, *Long Walk to Freedom*, Mandela shared his long-held belief in the benefits of physical activity:

> *I have always believed that exercise is not only a key to physical health but to peace of mind. Many times in the old days I unleashed my anger and frustration on a punching bag rather than taking it out on a comrade or even a policeman. Exercise dissipates tension, and tension is the enemy of serenity. I found that I worked better and thought more clearly when I was in good physical condition, and so training became one of the inflexible disciplines of my life.*

While practicing as a young lawyer, Mandela also trained as a boxer. During his first years in prison, exercise took on a different form—walking to and from the quarry, where Mandela and his fellow prisoners crushed rocks.

After the political prisoners finally won the right to forgo mandatory labor, Mandela resumed his old boxing regimen. He summarized a typical workout in his autobiography: "stationary running in my cell in the morning for up to forty-five minutes…one hundred fingertip push-ups, two hundred sit-ups, fifty deep knee-bends, and various other calisthenics."

Exercise is not new—it was simply hidden within the daily activities of all but the most recent generations of human beings. As transportation, education, work, and entertainment became increasingly sedentary activities, the need to exercise deliberately to maintain physical and mental health emerged. In an ironic twist, for many people, exercise has become a form of rest—a break from a stationary life in which so much time is spent sitting in front of a screen. Making time to rest and exercise requires commitment and fortitude, especially when so many other things "need" to be done. But, as Stephen Covey explained in his classic self-help book, *The 7 Habits of Highly Effective People*, sometimes it is necessary to "sharpen your saw."

Once heroes have taken time to recover their strength and stamina, they find a way to let go of the things that are weighing them down.

Release

During the Civil War, roughly 1 in 50 Americans lost their lives as a direct or indirect result of combat. With the mounting weight of 620,000 deaths on his shoulders, Lincoln understood that to be at his best, he needed both rest *and* recreation. Lincoln spent evenings in the living rooms of his cabinet members, "where he was assured of good conversation and much-needed relaxation."

Lincoln was an expert at releasing stress. Even during the gravest moments of his Presidency, Lincoln found opportunities to laugh. When General Lee escaped with his Confederate army, Lincoln wrote a funny poem describing the incident. As Lincoln himself explained, "With the fearful strain that is on me night and day, if I did not laugh, I should die." Lincoln called laughter "the joyous, beautiful, universal evergreen of life."

Lincoln also released stress by attending theatrical performances—especially Shakespearian plays dealing with "the burdens of power, the nature of ambition, the relationship of leaders to those they governed"—at the local theatres. "People may think strange of it," Lincoln remarked, "but I must have some relief from this terrible anxiety, or it will kill me."

Nelson Mandela shared Lincoln's acute understanding of human nature. While on Robben Island, Mandela dealt with the stress of prison life by adopting a new hobby—gardening. Fellow soldiers joked that, since he returned from digging in the rock quarry only to dig in the little patch of ground the warden provided, he must be a miner at heart.

Mandela grew crops like tomatoes, chilies, and onions, which would survive the dry, rocky soil on Robben Island. His vegetable harvests supplemented his meager diet, provided additional nourishment for fellow prisoners, and were eventually offered as an olive branch to some of the guards. Gardening also provided Mandela with a means to deal with the frustrations of prison life. As Mandela explained, "A garden was one of the few things in prison that one could control…the sense of being the custodian of this small patch of earth offered a small taste of freedom."

Mandela understood that he could better lead his colleagues in prison—and better prepare to promote peace and reconciliation upon his release—if he was able to find a way to let go of frustration and anger. Likewise, Lincoln knew that, to make prudent decisions on behalf of those he was sworn to protect, he had to find a way to release the emotional weight that was upon him.

The solemn expression that so often appeared on Mother Teresa's wrinkled face in black-and-white photos hid the playfulness and sense of humor that those around her enjoyed so much. Father Maasburg recalled an incident for which the following piece of background information will be helpful: Mother Teresa described her network of volunteers as the "most disorganized organization in the world."

On this occasion, Mother Teresa asked Father Maasburg to travel downtown to the airline office to switch flights for her and a few of the sisters due to a last-minute change of plans. After navigating traffic to-and-from the travel office, where he pleaded with representatives to make an exception for Mother Teresa, Father Maasburg returned to the Missionaries of Charity home, only to find that plans had once again changed, and he would need to switch back to their original tickets.

Seeing his frustration, one of the Sisters turned to Father Maasburg and asked, "Father, do you know what the abbreviation MC after our name really stands for?"

"No, what?" he asked.

"Not just missionaries of Charity," she explained, "but also Much Confusion."

When Father Maasburg finally took his seat next to Mother Teresa on their re-rebooked flight, he turned to her and said, "Mother Teresa, I learned today what the abbreviation MC really means: not 'Missionaries of Charity' but 'Much Confusion.'"

With a twinkle in her eye, Mother Teresa responded to his slightly passive-aggressive comment: "But, Father, do you know what else it means? It also means: More Confusion, Mental Case, Multiple Change."

Like Lincoln, Mandela, and Mother Teresa, Gandhi retained his sense of humor while in danger. And Gandhi did not take himself too seriously as he faced serious challenges. As his grandson Arun Gandhi observed, "most of us think of important people as being serious and imposing, but my image of my grandfather is of a kind, funny man who liked to relax and play games." Arun recalled going on long walks with his "Bapuji" and another boy, who like Arun, was much taller than his 5'5" grandfather. Gandhi playfully referred to the boys as his "walking sticks." With his arms around their shoulders, the man known as Mahatma ("the Great Soul") would swing his legs off the ground with childlike joy.

Laughter is a great way to relieve the stress that comes with responsibility. Laughter is also a fantastic barometer, which reveals our current emotional and cognitive state. A sense of humor indicates clarity of mind that is needed to make prudent decisions in times of chaos. If a person can laugh, they have the impulse control to maintain restraint in the face of frustrations. The ability to laugh at *ourselves* also reveals the humility needed to put the needs of others ahead of our own.

Reset

There is an area of psychological research known as "embodied cognition," which has revealed how our posture and our gestures influence our thinking. For example, people smile because they are happy. But the relationship between the facial and emotional markers of happiness moves in both directions. When people smile on purpose—rather than as a natural reaction to some pleasing event—they feel happier.

You can recreate this phenomenon by holding a pencil in your mouth in two different ways. First, place the pencil between your teeth lengthwise. Then, pay attention to how you feel as your mouth is fixed into a smile. Second, bite the eraser tip end of the pencil with the pencil tip pointing out. Now that your face has taken the form of a scowl, pay attention to how you feel. A second demonstration goes like this: stand up and slouch with your shoulders rolled forward and look slightly down. How do you feel? Then, take a deep breath, roll your shoulders back, hold your head up high, and raise your arms up as far as they will go. Now how do you feel?

Some people use embodied cognition to "get big" before important performances through a muscle-to-mind pathway. Others, like Mother Teresa, prefer to get small through an actions-to-attitude pathway.

While flying to meet President Ronald Reagan in DC, one of the sisters noticed that Mother Teresa was spending an unusual amount of time in the lavatories. And not just one lavatory. Mother Teresa emerged from a lavatory in business class only to enter the adjacent lavatory. Then she proceeded to the back of the plane and visited each of the lavatories in economy. After Mother Teresa returned to her seat, the sister's curiosity and concern won over, and she asked for an explanation. "Exorcism," Mother Teresa explained.

On another trip to the United States, Mother Teresa was invited to address the General Assembly of the United Nations in New York City. That morning, after Holy Mass and prayers, Mother Teresa followed her normal cleaning routine in the Missionaries of Charity home—washing her sari, mopping the floors, and cleaning the toilets.

Cleaning was an essential part of her daily life, and the lives of the Missionaries of Charity. In addition to self-care, Mother Teresa and the Sisters would clean the bodies, the clothing, and the houses of the poorest of the poor. By removing the filth from each person, each garment, and each dwelling, Mother Teresa and her Sisters were protecting the health and dignity of the destitute.

Mother Teresa almost never called attention to her own talents, but when it came to cleaning toilets, she made an exception. "I am a specialist in that," she explained, "probably the world's best specialist in cleaning toilets."

For Mother Teresa, cleaning toilets had a profound spiritual significance. Before meeting world leaders, royals, and celebrities, Mother Teresa would spend extra time on her hands and knees. As Father Maasburg observed, "it was precisely in cleaning the toilets that she found an antidote to any hint of pride." Mother Teresa explained the significance of these simple acts by asking and answering her own question: "How do you learn humility? Only through humiliations!"

"To know oneself and not to be untrue," Mother Teresa suggested, "is the essence of living." By engaging in demeaning tasks, and experiencing humiliations, Mother Teresa was able to identify her shortcomings—to know herself more fully and more honestly. Cleaning toilets was a way for her to perform internal audits, so to speak.

Gandhi shared Mother Teresa's high regard for toilet cleaning. For Gandhi, cleaning toilets was an essential component of "self-care." Like Mother Teresa, Gandhi found spiritual significance in cleaning his own toilet and insisted that cleaning toilets would be a chore shared by every resident at the Ashram, regardless of their caste or social standing.

On one occasion, a young man returned to India with the hope of using his expertise to influence fiscal policy in his native country. His parents, who were close friends of Gandhi, suggested to their son that he travel to the Ashram to ask for Gandhi's blessing. But when the young man arrived, instead of offering his blessing, Gandhi gave him a chore: clean the toilets. The young man protested, "I have a PhD from the London School of Economics, and you want me to waste my time cleaning toilets?" Gandhi stood firm: "you will get my blessing when I am convinced that you clean the toilets as enthusiastically as you want to go out and change the economy of the country."

Gandhi saw a young man who wanted to solve problems. But he also saw a man whose lack of humility would prevent him from truly understanding the problem he intended to solve—a young man whose arrogance might even create greater problems. Before the prideful young man could put his education to good use, he would need to humble himself enough to truly understand the living conditions and the mindset of poor, outcast Indians who had no other option but to clean their own toilets.

As usual, Gandhi insisted that external change must begin with internal change. When people who are serious about serving others take a serious look at themselves, they are not searching for things to celebrate. They are looking for ways to improve.

A journalist once asked, "Mother Teresa, what is wrong with the church today?" Without hesitation, she responded, "you and me!" For Mother Teresa, self-assessments were not self-congratulatory exercises intended to boost her self-esteem. Quite the contrary. She was searching for her faults and flaws. "Self-knowledge puts us on our knees," she explained, "Sometimes the little pencil was a broken pencil. Sometimes it needed sharpening just a little more."

Mother Teresa believed that reform must begin in the heart of each person. She was intent on becoming a sharper pencil and a fuller vessel.

Mother Teresa followed the guidance of Augustine: "Fill yourself first and then only will you be able to give to others." She suggested her followers do the same. "Even God cannot fill something that is already full," Mother Teresa explained. Through prayer and ritual, Mother Teresa sought "personal interior contact with the fire of God's love," which she, in turn, radiated to those around her.

Total surrender of self to a higher power or higher ideals is a hallmark of heroism and a defining characteristic of extraordinary leaders. It is a bit paradoxical, but heroes often gain their power and influence by giving up control. There is freedom in surrender. And heroes are unencumbered by vanity and pride.

After resting their bodies and minds, releasing their frustrations and fears, and resetting their priorities and their focus, heroes take time to equip themselves for the battles ahead.

Chapter 6

Preparing for Battle

Failing to prepare is preparing to fail
-John Wooden

Heroes are known for what they do in public, but heroes prepare for battle in private.

For six decades, James Bond battled villains in houses, hotels, and casinos. He pursued criminals on mountaintops, beaches, and bayous. He foiled evil plots aboard boats, planes, trains, sports cars, helicopters, and submarines. After each mission, 007 returned to MI6 headquarters to prepare for the next mission. James Bond left MI6 headquarters ready to face any challenge, no matter how improbable.

James Bond's habit of retreating to a calm place where he can prepare for the next mission is an important part of the plot. Heroes don't show up for battle unprepared.

John Wooden taught his players to be prepared—meticulously prepared. His attention to detail is illustrated by a famous anecdote: At the beginning of each season, Wooden gathered his players (including upperclassmen who had won the NCAA national championship the previous season) to teach them how to put on their socks and shoes. Wooden's rationale was this: if his players can avoid blisters, they will be better able to focus on passing, dribbling, shooting, and rebounding. The fact that doing so *might* matter was enough reason to devote time to a topic that others might have considered insignificant.

If John Wooden had an antithesis, it would be Bob Knight. Wooden was stoic and self-controlled; Bob Knight berated players and threw chairs. But both coaches agreed on the importance of preparation. Bob Knight once observed that "the will to win is not as important as the will to prepare to win."[1] Basketball teams win because they prepare to win. Heroes succeed because they prepare to succeed.

Real-life heroes equip themselves with knowledge and understanding rather than gadgets and weapons. Real-life heroes spend their time reading and reasoning rather than testing fast cars and firearms. Real-life heroes prepare for battle by developing a clear understanding of the challenges they face, investigating potential solutions, and committing to the most promising course of action.

While serving as the chairman and CEO of Microsoft, Bill Gates regularly held "think weeks." At the beginning of each retreat, Gates brought a tote bag full of books to his waterfront cabin on Hood Canal, not far from his home in Medina, Washington. The solitude of his waterfront getaway allowed uninterrupted time to read, process, and prepare for the challenges ahead. As Gates transitioned from leadership of Microsoft to leadership of the Bill and Melinda Gates foundation, he increased the amount of time he spent reading, thinking, and preparing to address some of the most persistent global health challenges.

---

1 This is perhaps Coach Bob Knight's most famous quote, but in his biography, Knight revealed that he borrowed the saying from former University of Oklahoma football coach Bud Wilkinson.

Read

After meeting in 1991, two of the wealthiest men on the planet—Bill Gates and Warren Buffett—served together on several corporate boards. As their friendship developed, they found that they shared something else in common: prioritizing solitary time.

Warren Buffett explained, "I insist on a lot of time being spent, almost every day, to just sit and think. That is very uncommon in American Business." When asked about his work routines, Warren Buffett responded, "I just sit in my office and read all day." He advised others to do the same, explaining, "the most important investment you can make is in yourself." Buffett once recommended, "read 500 pages like this every day. That's how knowledge works. It builds up, like compound interest," then he added, "all of you can do it, but I guarantee not many of you will do it."

Reading is something that heroes do regularly and extensively. Gandhi spent much of his time away from home, either traveling throughout India or residing in one of "His majesty's hotels," as he playfully called the prison cells in which he was so often confined. Gandhi was a guest at Yeravda Prison so frequently that, when a British official asked for his address, he replied "Yeravda." The byline on many of his letters listed Yeravda Mandir ("Yeravda temple") as his place of residence.

Gandhi spent much of his time in prison reading—especially from the Bible and the *Bhagavad Gita*. Gandhi once remarked that, due to his busy schedule (and frequent incarcerations), "Most of my reading since 1893 has been done in jail."

Whether at home or at work, on a plane or on a train, in a hotel room or jail cell, heroes find time to read. As Harry Truman observed, "Not all readers are leaders. But all leaders must be readers." The biographies and autobiographies of the greatest leaders in any field confirm Truman's observation. Highly successful people tend to be avid readers.

Dr. King studied classic philosophers like Plato and Aristotle and contemporary philosophers like Kierkegaard, Lock, Rousseau, and Thoreau. He studied religions of the East (Hinduism, Buddhism, Confucianism, Taoism) and West (Christianity, Judaism). He considered ideas advocated by proponents of various political and economic systems, including capitalism and socialism. He read works by and about historical figures such as Caesar, Augustine, Aquinas, and Lincoln.

Dr. King was well-spoken *because* he was well-read.

Lincoln honed his habit of reading while traveling the legal circuit. His reading was motivated by curiosity and reinforced by the excitement of new discoveries. "I know of nothing so pleasant to minds as the discovery of anything which is at once new and valuable."

Heroes read to learn. They don't just *spend* time reading to enjoy themselves, they *invest* time reading to improve themselves.

Lincoln read to satisfy his "want of education" left by his lack of formal schooling. "Life was to him a school," fellow circuit rider Leonard Swett observed, "and he was always studying and mastering every subject which came before him." Lincoln remained in the state library studying until he understood an issue "inside and outside, upside and downside." Lincoln spent nights and weekends reading and studying mathematics, astronomy, politics, philosophy, and literature. His first law partner, John Stuart, recalled that "he read hard works—was philosophical—logical—mathematical—never reading generally."

Lincoln was especially fond of the 3 B's: "The Bible, Blackstone, and the Bard." As Lincoln explained, the Bible "answered all questions about God and man's purpose in life," Blackstone's Commentaries "were at the core of a lawyer's law practice," and Shakespeare "offered the most profound insight into human nature."

Lincoln advised others to "Get books, sit yourself down anywhere, and go to reading them yourself." He considered it "a loss to a man not to have grown up among books." Lincoln explained to an audience at the Wisconsin State Fair in 1859, "A capacity, and taste, for reading, gives access to whatever has already been discovered by others. It is the key, or one of the keys, to the already solved problems. And not only so. It gives a relish, and facility, for successfully pursuing the yet unsolved ones."

On another occasion, Lincoln described additional benefits for readers: "Books serve to show a man that those original thoughts of his aren't very new after all." Lincoln viewed humility as a cause and a consequence of reading. Humility—or a lack of humility—helps explain why some read while others refrain.

Some don't read due to a total lack of curiosity. Others refuse to read because they are hampered by the twin maladies of arrogance and ignorance—which converge at the prideful conclusion that, because they already know it all, the ideas written by others would be of little use. But John Wooden, who was a great admirer of Lincoln, observed, "it's what you learn after you know it all that counts."

Wooden agreed with Lincoln's emphasis on reading and Wooden lived by his father's recommendation to "drink deeply of good books, including The Good Book."

Those who read are often compelled by humility and responsibility—the realization that they have room for improvement and the recognition that they have a duty to prepare themselves to make wise decisions on behalf of their followers.

Heroes read not because they *will* find better answers to their most perplexing questions but because they *might* find answers. The possibility that they will find valuable new ideas provides plenty of motivation to maintain their habit of reading.

Lincoln's close study of the Bible, Blackstone's Commentaries, and the collected works of Shakespeare, along with countless other texts, proved invaluable throughout his political career. Long before he was elevated to high office, Lincoln had formed a repository of wisdom, knowledge, and quotations from which he could reliably draw upon in speeches, letters, and conversations. Whether writing to a procrastinating general, an obstinate political rival, or a mother grieving the loss of her young soldier, Lincoln was well equipped.

Dr. King suggested to his followers that, "When we go into action and confront our adversaries we must be as armed with knowledge as they." As Dr. King explained, "education gives us not only knowledge, which is power, but wisdom, which is control." Dr. King saw reading as a way of gathering ammunition *and* a way of developing the wisdom needed to know when and how to use the ammunition.

Reading is an important way in which leaders prepare for battle, both metaphorical and literal.

When the ANC decided to pursue more militant forms of resistance to apartheid in South Africa, Nelson Mandela poured through books to prepare for battle—literal battle. "I began the only way I knew how, by reading and talking to experts," he explained,

> *What I wanted to find out were the fundamental principles for starting a revolution. I discovered that there was a great deal of writing on this very subject, and I made my way through the available literature on armed warfare and in particular guerrilla warfare. I wanted to know what circumstances were appropriate for a guerrilla war; how one created, trained, and maintained a guerrilla force; how it should be armed; where it gets its supplies—all basic and fundamental questions.*

After Mandela was arrested, tried, and sent to prison on Robben Island, he became even more devoted to his studies. "As freedom fighters and political prisoners," Mandela recalled, "we had an obligation to improve and strengthen ourselves, and study was one of the few opportunities to do so."

Robben Island became known as "The University." As Mandela recalled, "at night, our cell block seemed more like a study hall than a prison." Several prisoners earned multiple degrees in a variety of subjects such as art, geography, and mathematics.

Mandela was curious. Mandela was diligent. Mandela studied meticulously. And Mandela insisted on understanding issues from multiple vantage points. Mandela understood that one does not truly understand their own beliefs unless they also understand competing viewpoints.

Though sentenced to life in prison, Mandela assumed that one day, he would be released. Mandela never wavered in his commitment to bringing about peace and equality for all South Africa. During his imprisonment on Robben Island, Mandela turned his attention to diplomatic and conflict-resolution skills needed to face the challenges ahead. Mandela studied the writings of Dr. King, who viewed reading as a way to "see the enemy's point of view" and to "learn and grow and profit from the wisdom of the brothers who are called the opposition."

In *The Art of War*, Sun Tzu famously suggested that "If you know the enemy and know yourself, you need not fear the result of a hundred battles. If you know yourself but not the enemy, for every victory gained you will also suffer a defeat. If you know neither the enemy nor yourself, you will succumb in every battle."

Forced solitude provided Nelson Mandela with time to engage in self-reflection. But Mandela was equally interested in understanding his adversaries. While in prison, Mandela learned to speak Afrikaans. He read Afrikaans poetry, studied Afrikaans military history, and familiarized himself with rugby—the most popular sport among Afrikaners. Once he was able to converse with the prison guards in their native language—on topics of interest to them—Mandela was able to better understand the hopes, fears, values, and beliefs of working-class Afrikaners. Mandela's fluency in Afrikaans language and culture would later prove invaluable as the first president of South Africa elected to power by a free and fair, one-person-one-vote, election. "When you speak Afrikaans," Mandela explained, "you go straight to their hearts."

Review

Abraham Lincoln was the most accessible president in American history. But shortly before delivering his second inaugural address, Lincoln announced that he would "not receive callers (except members of the Cabinet) for nay purpose whatsoever, between the hours of three and seven o'clock p.m." As his second term approached, Lincoln understood the gravity of the task before him. To prepare his address (which became one of the most famous speeches in American history), Lincoln needed silence and solitude to contemplate his message and to consider the words that he would speak to a war-weary population.

When Dr. King had an important decision to make, he would usually tell his colleagues, "I want to think it over." Then he would disappear for a while. Whether in his living room, hotel room, or jail cell, Dr. King made time to contemplate the many challenges that he faced as the face of the civil rights movement. Some contemporaries grew impatient as he mulled things over, but Dr. King was more interested in making correct decisions than quick decisions.

Dr. King observed that, "rarely do we find men who willingly engage in hard, solid thinking. There is an almost universal quest for easy answers and half-baked solution. Nothing pains some people more than having to think."

Dr. King lamented the gullibility of soft-minded people, as evidenced by the effectiveness of television and radio advertisements in persuading people to buy things they didn't need. Dr. King observed that, "Advertisers have long since learned that most people are soft minded, so they have developed special skill to create phrases and slogans that will penetrate the thin mind of the average reader or listener. This undue gullibility is also seen in the tendency of many to accept the printed word of the press as final truth. They fail to see that even facts can be slanted and truth can be distorted."

In comparison to weak minds that are impatient and lazy, Dr. King asked his followers to develop "a tough mind characterized by incisive thinking, realistic appraisal, and decisive judgment." As he explained, "The tough-minded person always examines the facts before he reaches conclusions. The tough mind is sharp and penetrating, breaking through the crust of legends and myths and sifting the true from the false."

President Lincoln also believed that there is no substitute for "cold, calculating, unimpassioned reason."

In the den of his apartment near the UCLA campus, John Wooden had a bookshelf devoted entirely to Abraham Lincoln books and biographies. Calling Lincoln his "favorite American," Wooden applied many of the lessons that he learned from Lincoln as he coached his UCLA Bruins basketball teams. Wooden quoted Lincoln so frequently that many of Abraham Lincoln's sayings are incorrectly attributed to John Wooden. John Wooden was a curator of wisdom who applied the lessons that he learned from the 16th President, including the importance of cold, calculating, unimpassioned reasoning.

John Wooden's unparalleled success as coach of the UCLA men's basketball program was a result of meticulous planning. Before each practice session, Wooden followed a tried-and-true procedure, which was designed to promote continuous improvement.

The procedure went like this: prior to each practice session, Wooden would reach in his files to find the practice plans corresponding to that practice session from the previous season. Each practice plan was written on a stack of notecards, which corresponded to 5-minute segments of a practice session.

Notecards from the previous season included modifications that he had noted after each practice, which he intended to implement during the following season. Each year, Wooden studied each practice plan to find ways to make practices more efficient—and provide each player with additional repetitions. After considering the strengths and limitations of the members of his current team, Wooden would update the practice plans with his assistant coaches so that every player, every coach, and every ball was in the right place during each 5-minute segment of practice.

Consider this: For each hour that his players practiced as a team, Wooden spent five hours preparing. Wooden's procedure for planning practice sessions required the patience and perseverance needed to sustain a time-intensive habit day after day, season after season. As a result of his incisive thinking and decisive judgment, Wooden was more prepared than the coaches he faced. So much so that Wooden often sat silently on the bench watching the game unfold and claimed that, because he had done *his* job in his office and on the practice court, he could have watched his players do *their* job while sitting in the bleachers with his wife Nell. Due to *his* preparation as their leader, Wooden's players were better prepared than the opponents that they faced.

By investing the time and energy needed to prepare for battle during a time of relative calm, heroes better situate themselves—and their followers—to perform at their best in times of chaos.

Resolve

Mother Teresa was affectionately called a "Benevolent Dictator." In explaining how she came to her decisions, Mother Teresa drew a distinction between "decision making" and "decision taking." In other words, "between the gathering of the different aspects and the final taking of the decision."

Heroes are neither introverts nor extroverts. They are omniverts. Heroes are comfortable—or, at least, willing—to spend time alone *and* spend time with others. Before taking decisions, heroes gather information "outdoors" by living, looking, and listening. Then, they head "indoors" to search for solutions by reading what has been written on the topic. Finally, they invest the time needed to carefully consider the information that they have gathered.

Mother Teresa "consulted many people, asked their advice, and studied the issues with great attention and concentration" on her way to a decision. After taking the decision, "Her decision then stood firm as a rock."

Leaders are sometimes praised as "bold" and "decisive" when they make decisions quickly. But decisiveness is sometimes a sign of lazy leadership. One telltale sign of poor leadership occurs when an individual makes decisions quickly and confidently before they have taken the time to learn. Too often, leaders do not even take the time to confirm (or even consider) their unverified assumptions before reaching a conclusion. Decisiveness is only a virtue when a leader takes the time to understand the problem before they try to fix it.

Nelson Mandela believed that the bold decision was often the slow decision. Mandela waited to make decisions until he had as much information as possible. He wanted to consider all options. He wanted to understand the big picture. He wanted to avoid hasty decisions. Mandela made decisions in the same way that he advised others to make decisions: "don't hurry; think, analyze, then act."

Lincoln, like Mother Teresa and Nelson Mandela, was diligent in the way he came to a decision. And equally firm in his resolve: "I think it cannot be shown that when I have once taken a position, I have ever retreated from it."

Record

After taking time to read, review, and resolve, heroes put their conclusions in writing. Before returning to the battlefield, they record their thoughts in some way, whether in a journal, a letter, a blog, or an autobiography.

Writing allows heroes to communicate across time and space—both to others and to their future selves. The act of writing ensures that a vision is clear. If a hero cannot articulate their vision in private, they will have difficulty sharing their vision in public.

If such an endeavor seems like an unnecessary use of time for a busy individual or organization, consider the importance of the Constitution to the United States. In addition to having abundant natural resources and a population of adventurous immigrants who wanted to be intentional about the way they lived, the founding documents deserve immense credit for helping the United States become the sort of place that people literally risk their lives to reach.

The Constitution was an open letter written to our future selves, which was created to remind us of who we are and how we will do things. The Constitution was written for good times and bad times—but *especially* for times of turmoil—so that, even when strong emotions are aroused, we can remember our priorities when tough decisions need to be made.

The Constitution recognizes the best and worst parts of human nature. The document assumes that, with freedom and liberty to pursue happiness, people would rise to new heights. But the writers recognized that absolute power corrupts absolutely. With less admirable elements of human nature in mind, the framers included a system of checks and balances between three separate but equal branches—the legislative, the executive, and the judicial—to ensure that the interests of the masses would not fall victim to the selfish desires of a few tyrants elected to public office.

The Constitution includes a preamble that spells out *why* the document was written and *why* the United States of America was brought into existence. The body of the Constitution—the Articles and Sections—lay out *how* the country would be governed, *who* would be responsible and accountable in various situations, and *what* each branch of the government would be responsible for. The Constitution articulates the rights and privileges afforded to members of the government and the citizenry. The Constitution also specified *when* certain actions of the Federal government would be taken.

To adapt to new challenges, the framers included provisions for changes to be made to the Constitution—but only with overwhelming consent of future citizens. The first ten amendments to the Constitution—known as the Bill of Rights—lay out the non-negotiable principles upon which this new nation would be governed. These principles included the right to free speech, the right to peaceful assembly, the right to keep and bear arms, and the right to be free from unlawful search and seizure. Each of these principles take precedence over any conflicting legislation subsequently passed into law, whether in calm or tumultuous times.

The Constitution was written during a time of relative calm to guide us during the most perilous storms to come. For more than two centuries, the U.S. Constitution has served as a reminder of who we are and who we want to be—even when anger, fear, and impatience might tempt us to violate these fundamental values.

To be successful, organizations and individuals need a set of non-negotiable principles so that decisions and behavior are guided by systematic thought and careful reflection rather than emotion and convenience. Values and processes should be amendable—but only during calm times of deep reflection.

Writing out a personal, a family, or an organizational constitution forces an individual, group, or leadership team to follow-through on the critically important job of deep reflection during a time of calm. Then, in tumultuous times, when emotions are aroused and patience is tested, decisions can be based on firm convictions rather than fickle emotions.

Engaging in what Dr. King called "hard, solid thinking" can be difficult in a world full of distractions. But the world needs patient, disciplined, tough-minded heroes who are willing to engage in disciplined thought in private so that they are worthy to lead others in public.

Heroes take time to read, reflect, resolve, and record. Then, with clarity of purpose and confident resolve, they are ready to return to battle.

Chapter 7

Disarming Opponents

Do I not destroy my enemies when I make them friends?
-Abraham Lincoln

In the aftermath of the Nicaraguan Revolution, which left nearly one in four citizens homeless, Mother Teresa traveled to Nicaragua to assess the situation. During the mid 1980's, the relationship between the Catholic Church and the Sandinista government—which was created in the image of Marx, Lenin, and Castro—was precarious at best. While traveling to a festival in Cuapa with a group of Catholic clergy members, Mother Teresa's police-led convoy stopped to eat lunch in a grassy meadow.

"Suddenly," as Father Maasburg recalled, "a hundred heavily armed soldiers emerged from the nearby woods." Although he felt "extremely uneasy," Father Maasburg marveled at the way "Mother Teresa took the Initiative." As he recalled,

> *The soldiers had just taken up a threatening position when she stood up and walked straight toward them. She stopped right in front of their machine guns, which were aimed at us. She rummaged in her bag and gave each soldier a Miraculous Medal, one by one. In order to take the*

medals, the soldiers had to sling their weapons round their necks. After Mother Teresa had given a medal to each and every soldier—and they had taken them—she invited them all to eat with us.

A few days later, Mother Teresa requested a meeting with Daniel Ortega, the president of Nicaragua, to ask his permission to establish a Missionaries of Charity home.

By international standards, Ortega did not take a conventional path to power. In the two decades prior to his election, Ortega spent several years in prison, received guerilla warfare training from Fidel Castro's Marxist-Leninist government in Cuba, promoted an uprising that deposed Nicaragua's former president, and became the head of Sandinista National Liberation Front's National Directorate.

Father Maasburg, who accompanied Mother Teresa to her meeting with the authoritarian leader, described the "rather scary armor-cracking incident" in detail:

> *We were led into a windowless room with a platform at one end. On the platform was a long desk, and behind the desk sat four masked men with big machine guns. In the middle, between the masked men, sat Daniel Ortega. He gave his three visitors—Mother Teresa, a Sister and me—a fiery, thirty-minute speech about the legitimacy of his guerilla war and the demonic character of his opponents. When he finally ended, trembling with rage, there was an embarrassed silence. Mother Teresa broke it with a single sentence: "yes, yes, works of love are works of peace."*
>
> *The tension mounted; the official translator obviously did not want to translate this sentence, which had been spoken in English, into Spanish for the president. Finally, the Sister took on this manifestly thankless task, though in a trembling voice. Not only was the room stifling, there was also a dangerous tension in the air.*

Suddenly, and without waiting for the dictator's reaction to her remark, Mother Teresa stood up, went forward and stepped quite close to the platform. Rummaging in her bag, she asked the dictator, "Do you have children?"

Clearly not understanding the implication of her question, he answered, "Yes."

"How many?"

"Seven."

Mother Teresa now brought seven Miraculous Medals out of her bag, one after the other, kissed each one and held it up as high as she could toward the platform. Ortega took them—one by one—leaning far across the desk each time so as to reach Mother Teresa's hand.

"Do you have a wife?"

"Yes!"

Another medal was found in the bag, which was kissed then held out.

"And here's one for you." With that Mother Teresa handed him the last medal. "You need it! But you must wear it round your neck, like this..."

Mother Teresa pointed to a cord around the dictator's neck and explained in sign language where the medal should hang.

With one stroke she had completely changed the mood. Then she offered the dictator another present: five of her Sisters to care for the poorest of the poor in the slums of Managua!

Mother Teresa responded to the threat of force with the force of tender love. Mother Teresa received the permission she sought the next day and the Missionaries of Charity home opened in Managua, Nicaragua on December 8, 1986.

Use Charm to Disarm

Mother Teresa was rarely confronted by armed opposition but her experiences in Nicaragua were not entirely unprecedented. In most cases, new Missionaries of Charity homes were established in places from which she had received invitations and urgent pleas for assistance. But in other places where Mother Teresa sought to establish new homes—especially in countries led by authoritarian leaders or communist regimes—she often faced resistance.

In 1973 Mother Teresa traveled to Addis Ababa with intentions to help victims of a severe drought in Ethiopia.

Mother Teresa was undeterred by the prevailing belief that Emperor Haile Selassie would not permit a Roman Catholic congregation to enter Ethiopia. Mother Teresa won the admiration of the emperor's daughter, Princess Tenagnework, who agreed to relay to her father Mother Teresa's offer of her Sisters to the suffering poor as a gift to honor the forty-third anniversary of his coronation.

Before meeting with the emperor, the Minister of the Imperial court interrogated Mother Teresa:

"What do you want from the Government?"

"Nothing. I have only come to offer my Sisters to work among the poor suffering people."

"What will your Sisters do?"

"We give whole-hearted free service to the poorest of the poor."

"What qualifications do they have?"

"We try to bring tender love and compassion to the unwanted and the unloved."

"I see you have quite a different approach. Do you preach to the people,

trying to convert them?"

"Our works of love reveal to the suffering poor the love of God for them."

After the pre-interview, Mother Teresa entered the court and had a very short face-to-face conversation with the Emperor, who delivered the surprising news: "I have heard about the good work you do. I am very happy you have come. Yes, let your Sisters come to Ethiopia."

When Mother Teresa was unable to get a meeting with the person who could say "yes," she charmed her way to the top. Mother Teresa won the approval of the Ethiopian Emperor by first touching the hearts of his daughter and Minister.

Then, Mother Teresa set her sights on China. Determined to enter the world's most populous country, Mother Teresa visited the Chinese Embassy in New Delhi to offer her sisters to the suffering poor. An initially reluctant official agreed to visit Nirmal Hriday. After seeing the home for the dying, he said to Mother Teresa, "If I can do anything to help you, please let me know."

Despite his support, Mother Teresa met further resistance from higher-level officials who explained that there were no poor people in China because the government provided for the needs of the Chinese people. Then, Mother Teresa suggested, "perhaps there might be some people who were disheartened and in need of a little encouragement. She and her Sisters would like to bring hope to the discouraged."

The Chinese government accepted Mother Teresa's offer of "tender love and care." They even provided a building for the Sisters to establish a home for the dying in Hong Kong. As the home was opened, Mother Teresa was asked if she had brought any message from the Vatican, to which she replied diplomatically, "No, I am coming from Calcutta."

Mother Teresa's experience entering the Soviet Union was similar. She was informed that poverty did not exist in "the worker's paradise." Adhering to Soviet doctrine, one official explained to Mother Teresa that, "We have no poor people here in our country. What could your Sisters do here? It is not like in the West; here the state provides people with everything that they need."

Mother Teresa responded in her usual kind but direct manner: "They will bestow tender love and care on those who have no one in their lives. The state cannot do that."

In 1987, Mother Teresa visited Moscow to accept the Soviet Peace Committee's Prize for Peace. "I have no silver and gold," she stated, "but my gift to the peoples of the Soviet Union are my Sisters, whom I am offering." Shortly after accepting the award, the legal prohibitions against charitable organizations were lifted, allowing the Missionaries of Charity to open a home in Moscow on December 22, 1988.

As she had done many times before, and would do many times after, Mother Teresa used her charm to disarm those who had previously opposed her. Due to Mother Teresa's gentle, apolitical approach, her sisters were not merely allowed in, but welcomed in, to new communities on both sides of the Iron Curtain. As one observer noted, Mother Teresa had "that charisma—that of opening doors which others cannot."

Mother Teresa's approach was gentle but powerful. Rather than gossiping about unscrupulous leaders, or criticizing them in the media, Mother Teresa greeted them directly, broke down barriers with kindness, received the concessions that she requested, and, in many cases, inspired them to join her cause.

Gandhi shared Mother Teresa's magnetism. Even Gandhi's avowed opponents were not immune to his charm. When new British administrators traveled to India to assume their duties, they were often warned by their predecessors: "Don't go near Gandhi. He'll get you."

Most of Gandhi's friends were people who had visited Gandhi "to observe and stayed to serve." One of these friends was Jawaharlal Nehru, a wealthy young man who returned to India after studying in Cambridge.

Initially, he agreed with revolutionaries who considered violence the antidote to colonialism. But when the young man visited Gandhi, his views began to change. "You are always talking about revolution," Gandhi observed. "I am making one. What is revolutionary about violence? If you really love your people, help me show them how to turn their backs on violence and throw off their fear." Gandhi's influence was inescapable. Unlike the rich young ruler of the Bible, this young man shunned his luxuries and joined Gandhi's movement.

The young man's father, Motilal Nehru, a wealthy lawyer from a prominent family, was unhappy with his son's decision. He traveled to see Gandhi and pleaded with him, "You have taken our only son. Give him back to us, and I will put my wealth at the disposal of your campaign." But Gandhi would do no such thing. He smiled back at his new friend and shook his head. "Not only do I want your son. I want you, and your wife, and your daughters, and the rest of your family too." Shortly thereafter, the entire Nehru family joined the cause.

Abraham Lincoln possessed a similar ability to charm and disarm. Long before he was elected president, Lincoln was working in his grocery store one day as two customers got in an argument that came to blows. When Lincoln attempted to intercede, one of the combatants, who didn't care for Lincoln's verdict, shouted "See here, Lincoln, I'll lick you!" The six-foot-four grocery store clerk looked upon his five-foot customer and replied, "all right, but let's fight fair. You are so small there isn't much of you for me to hit, but I am so big, you can't help hitting me. So you make a chalk mark on me that will show your size. When we fight, you must be sure to hit me inside this mark or it won't be fair." The absurdity of his proposed rules of engagement caused his opponent to laugh so thoroughly that the fight was immediately cancelled.

Lincoln displayed the same good-natured approach as a traveling lawyer. He was gracious with legal opponents. As one colleague observed, Lincoln "was remarkably gentle with young lawyers...no young lawyer ever practiced in the courts with Mr. Lincoln who did not in all his after life have a regard for him akin to personal affection."

When Lincoln turned to a career in politics, he was equally gracious with his political opponents. In the run-up to his re-election to the Illinois House of Representatives, Lincoln was walking to a debate when he noticed a carriage approaching. The carriage was owned by his Democratic challenger, who asked Lincoln to join him. As the incumbent, Lincoln spoke last at the event, telling his audience that, "As a poor man I don't have a carriage and my opponent kindly gave me a lift in his carriage. Now I'm here today to ask for your support for my re-election to the legislature. But if you can't vote for me, I wish you vote for my opponent who is a fine gentleman."

Lincoln's ceaseless ambition compelled him to campaign vigorously. Despite his exceptional ability as an orator, Lincoln sustained several election losses during his political career. But, due to his kindness in the face of disappointment, Lincoln was able to gain friends and supporters after each defeat.

Capture with Charisma

When Lincoln moved to Washington to serve in Congress, he "always attracted the riveted attention of the House when he spoke" and in social situations "he always kept his company in a roar of laughter." As a young congressman in DC, Lincoln lived in a boarding house. According to a fellow boarder, Samuel Busey,[1] Lincoln "was always ready with a story or anecdote to entertain, persuade, or defuse an argument." Busey admired Lincoln "for his simple and unostentatious manners, kind-heartedness, and amusing jokes, anecdotes, and witticisms." He fondly recalled how the future president would "lay down his knife and fork, place his elbows

---

1 Dr. Samuel Busey was later elected president of the Medical Society of the District of Columbia.

upon the table, rest his face between his hands, and begin with the words 'that reminds me,' and proceed. Everybody prepared for the explosion sure to follow."

Unfortunately, some of Lincoln's contemporaries (including fellow boarders) were not so genteel. Busey remembered one of their housemates as "a very offensive man in manner and conversation, and seemed to take special pleasure in ventilating his opinions and provoking unpleasant discussion." Lincoln, however,

> *Did not wish to introduce or discuss subjects that would provoke a controversy. When such conversations would threaten angry or even unpleasant contentions he would interrupt it by interposing some anecdote, thus diverting it into a hearty and general laugh, and so completely disarrange the tenor of the discussion that the parties engaged would either separate in good humor or continue conversation free from discord. This amicable disposition made him very popular with the household.*

Fame, power, and success did not change Lincoln. When Lincoln returned to Washington a decade later as the president-elect, a reporter from the New York Tribune, Henry Villard, witnessed Lincoln preparing for the presidency while entertaining a stream of callers. Villard concluded that Lincoln "is the very embodiment of good temper and affability. They will all concede that he has a kind word, an encouraging smile, a humorous remark for nearly everyone that seeks his presence, and that but few, if any, emerge from his reception room without being strongly and favorably impressed with his general disposition."

Villard was particularly impressed by Lincoln's ability to use a story or anecdote "to explain a meaning or enforce a point," which "helped many times to heal wounded feelings and mitigate disappointments." With a unique combination of kindness and charisma, Lincoln won the affection of his contemporaries, converted colleagues into friends, and former adversaries into admirers.

Nelson Mandela possessed a similar level of charisma. He was exceptionally charming. Mandela's charm was something that he honed over many years. He studied people before meeting them. He read articles written by journalists so that he could praise their work before sitting for an interview.

Mandela prided himself on his ability to persuade with a combination of logic and charm. Mandela honed his ability to influence people—rather than order people—to act.

Mandela's meeting with P. W. Botha was the first between an ANC political prisoner and the South African President. Botha's autocratic leadership and gruff manner had earned him the nickname Die Groot Krokodil (The Big Crocodile). Mandela "deliberately strode across the room, greeting Botha with a robust handshake and a wide smile. He disarmed the South African president with his own friendliness and informal manner, something that he had planned and practiced."

As Mandela recalled, "The meeting was not even half an hour, and was friendly and breezy until the end. It was then that I raised a serious issue. I asked Mr. Botha to release unconditionally all political prisoners, including myself. That was the only tense moment in the meeting, and Mr. Botha said that he was afraid that he could not do that." But Mandela and Botha built a relationship that would allow a productive dialogue between the ANC and the South African government, even after Botha was replaced by F. W. de Klerk in 1989.

Look For the Good In Others

During his first years in prison, Mandela was beaten, insulted, threatened, and intimidated by guards who called him "boy" and viewed him as a terrorist. Meanwhile, John Vorster, a Nazi-sympathizer who was busy expanding the system of Apartheid while serving as President of South African from 1966-1978, lamented the fact that Mandela had not been executed.

After 27 years in prison, Mandela had ample reason to become bitter and resentful. Yet he tried to find "something decent and honorable" in everyone he encountered, including people who had mistreated him personally. On Robben Island, Mandela's opinion of the boorish guards changed after he came to view them "as victims of the system as well as perpetrators of it." Mandela's benevolent view stemmed from a realization that the guards were "simple, uneducated men who had been inculcated in an unfair and racist system since they were children."

When asked about Vorster, Mandela was generous: "He was a very decent chap…he was very polite." Mandela recognized the darker side of people like John Vorster. But Mandela refused to only see the dark side. He understood that nobody is entirely evil or entirely good. As Aleksandr Solzhenitsyn wrote in the Gulag Archipelago, "The line separating good and evil passes not through states, nor between classes, nor between political parties either-but right through every human heart…even within hearts overwhelmed by evil, one small bridgehead of good is retained. And even in the best of hearts, there remains…un uprooted small corner of evil."

It can be difficult to view someone in a positive light, especially if they have acted shamefully in the past. But heroes find a way to see the good in others—even when the good lies hidden under layers of less attractive qualities.

Mandela followed a sort of "innocent until proven guilty" assumption about people. He assumed that others were acting in good faith unless their behavior proved otherwise. And he believed that people could change for the better. Mandela felt that "just as pretending to be brave can lead to acts of real bravery, seeing the good in other people improves the chances that they will reveal their better selves."

Mandela's tendency to trust endeared him to countless people. But his critics alleged that he was too trusting. "People will feel I see too much good in people," Mandela acknowledged, "So it's a criticism I have to put up with, and I've tried to adjust because whether it is so or not, it is something I think is profitable." Mandela went on to explain that "It's a good thing to assume, to act on the basis that others are men of integrity and honor, because you tend to attract integrity and honor if that is how you regard those with whom you work."

Coach John Wooden shared Mandela's inclination to trust—at least until someone proved themselves to be untrustworthy. When asked about corruption and recruiting violations in college basketball, Wooden refused to impugn the behavior of other coaches. He explained that "There's as much crookedness as you want to find." Wooden's approach was shaped by a lesson that he learned from Abraham Lincoln, who said that "he'd rather trust too much than distrust and be miserable all the time." John Wooden explained that treating people as if they were untrustworthy can create a self-fulfilling prophesy, saying "The coach who continually tells his players they are rotten is sure to make them so."

Mother Teresa was often asked to comment on the decisions and the actions of others. Amidst deep poverty in Calcutta, some blamed government officials—and invited Mother Teresa to do the same. When reporters attempted to bate Mother Teresa into saying something salacious, she would respond, "I know very well that there is corruption in Calcutta, but I also know that there is good, and I have decided to see the good."

When asked to comment on specific politicians, Mother Teresa "always insisted that she knew nothing about politics, and that political methods of bringing about change were for others." When asked about issues of concern to the countries that she visited, she would state that "she was not there to mix in politics but to support life."

Mother Teresa witnessed corruption as she traveled to homes around the world but "she, as a matter of principle, never said a negative word about anyone." Each time she returned to Calcutta, Mother Teresa was asked about her travels, with some wanting juicy details of betrayals and mistreatment along the way. But she would summarize her experiences by saying, "They were so good to us!" before listing ways in which local politicians had assisted in her work.

When pressed further, Mother Teresa would simply say, "I do not feel like judging or condemning." Mother Teresa modeled the advice that she gave to others: "never judge." She once remarked that, "One sin that I have never had to confess is that I judged someone." Mother Teresa explained that she would "rather excuse than accuse" because, "If you judge someone, then you have no time to love him."

Mother Teresa taught her Sisters that heads of countries knew their duty and that the role of the Missionaries of Charity was to pray that the leaders were faithful in fulfilling their duties. By remaining politically neutral, Mother Teresa was able to maintain friendships with people who held opposing political views, including countless world leaders whom she was able to influence.

Make Friends Before Making Your Case

While serving in the Illinois House of Representatives, Abraham Lincoln was invited to speak to the Springfield Washington Temperance society—a group of people that used disapproval and shame in an unsuccessful effort to persuade others to abstain from alcohol. On February 22, 1842, the 33-year-old Lincoln explained to his audience that condemning people who sell or consume alcohol in "thundering tones of anathema and denunciation" was both unkind and counterproductive.

Lincoln explained that, when members of the temperance society accused bar keepers of being "the authors of all the vice and misery and crime in the land; that they were the manufacturers and material of all the thieves and robbers and murderers that infested the earth; that their houses were the workshops of the devil; and that their persons should be shunned by all the good and virtuous, as moral pestilences," it was not surprising that the barkeepers "were slow, very slow, to acknowledge the truth of such denunciations, and to join the ranks of their denouncers in the hue and cry against themselves."

Rather than standing in judgment of the temperance society (who stood in judgment of barkeepers), Lincoln taught a master class on human nature and interpersonal influence:

If you would win a man to your cause, first convince him that you are his sincere friend. Therein is a drop of honey that catches his heart, which, say what he will, is the great highroad to his reason, and which, when once gained, you will find but little trouble in convincing his judgment of the justice of your cause, if indeed that cause really be a just one.

Lincoln explained to members of the temperance society that it is much easier to persuade a friend than to convince a foe. Therefore, he suggested, if they wanted to:

Assume to dictate to his judgment, or to command his action, or to mark him as one to be shunned and despised, he will retreat within himself, close all the avenues to his head and his heart; and though your cause be naked truth itself, transformed to the heaviest lance, harder than steel, and sharper than steel can be made, and though you throw it with more than Herculean force and precision, you shall be no more be able to pierce him, than to penetrate the hard shell of a tortoise with a rye straw. Such is man, and so must he be understood by those who would lead him, even to his own best interest.

Drawing upon his keen understanding of human nature, Lincoln provided actionable intelligence for members of his audience. During his political career, Lincoln followed his own advice. Lincoln disagreed with those who defended slavery, but "rather than upbraid slave owners," Lincoln tried to "comprehend their position through empathy" before trying to prove that their position was ultimately indefensible. Despite his personal convictions, Lincoln was careful not to "impugn the motives of anyone opposed" to his beliefs on slavery or any other issue.

Lincoln treated those who disagreed with him as friends to be converted rather than as enemies to be defeated. For Lincoln, losing an argument was usually preferable to losing a friend. As Lincoln observed, "the better part of one's life consists of friendships" and "The loss of enemies does not compensate for the loss of friends."

Lincoln valued his many friendships and sought to be at peace with those around him. When he felt that he had spoken or written too harshly or hastily to a subordinate, he was quick to ask forgiveness: "I want it said of me that I always plucked a thistle and planted a flower when I thought a flower would grow."

Extend Forgiveness and Grace

In the summer of 1855, Abraham Lincoln was asked to provide legal counsel in a patent dispute that was to be tried in Chicago. But after Lincoln agreed to share his local expertise with the high-powered firm from Philadelphia, the case was moved to Cincinnati. George Harding, the lead attorney for the defense, neglected to inform Lincoln that his services were no longer necessary. To prepare his briefing, Lincoln traveled from Springfield to Chicago to personally examine the mechanical reaping machine at the center of the dispute. Once Lincoln received word that the case had been transferred to Cincinnati, he set off to join the other members of the defense.

When Lincoln arrived at the boardinghouse, he found an astonished George Harding standing outside along with his distinguished colleague, Edwin Stanton, who immediately dismissed Lincoln as a "damned long armed ape." Unaware of the salacious words that Stanton whispered to Harding, Lincoln proposed the three men "go up in a gang" to the courthouse. However, Harding and Stanton turned their backs on Lincoln and walked toward the courthouse, leaving Lincoln standing alone and embarrassed.

Neither Harding nor Stanton took the time to examine Lincoln's meticulously prepared briefing. Lincoln relented to Stanton's passive aggressive signals and withdrew from the case. Nonetheless, Lincoln remained in Cincinnati to observe the trial. Each day, Lincoln walked alone to the courthouse and ate alone at the boarding house where he and the other two lawyers slept. When the case was closed, Lincoln returned to Springfield with a firm belief that he would never again return to Cincinnati.

As fate would have it, Lincoln returned to Cincinnati just six years later *en route* to Washington, DC. As the newly elected President of the United States, Lincoln was tasked with appointing his cabinet. When his attention turned to the selection of a Secretary of War, Lincoln offered the position to Edwin Stanton—the same Edwin Stanton who shunned him in Cincinnati.

Lincoln was quick to extend forgiveness and grace to those who wronged him. His generous act toward a man who had treated him so shamefully, revealed "a singular ability to transcend personal vendetta, humiliation, or bitterness." As Lincoln explained, "I choose always to make my statute of limitations a short one." Lincoln's generosity brought former adversaries and the friends of his former adversary into the ranks of his admirers.

Lincoln used forgiveness to build friendships.

Lincoln used friendships to build coalitions.

Lincoln used coalitions to accomplish his goals.

Lincoln's inclination to forgive those who had wronged him was sometimes criticized. Some wondered why he did not seek revenge against his "enemies." In a speech delivered during the Civil War, Lincoln referred to the Confederates as "erring human beings." After the reception, an elderly woman approached Lincoln and asked, "Mr. President, how can you lower yourself to refer to such slave holding rebels as merely 'erring human beings' who were sworn enemies to the Union and freedom?" Lincoln looked back at the woman and said, "Why, madam, do I not destroy my enemies when I make them friends?"

Chapter 8

Defeating Villains

It always seems impossible until it's done
-Nelson Mandela

In *Superman: The Movie*, Lex Luthor lures Superman to his underground hideout and subdues the Man of Steel by exposing him to kryptonite. With Superman detained, Luthor enacts an elaborate plan to enrich himself. After acquiring worthless land, Luthor reroutes a nuclear missile toward the desert in the hope of triggering an earthquake that would cause coastal California to fall into the ocean—thereby transforming Luthor's real estate into ocean front property. He sends another missile toward Hackensack, New Jersey to distract Superman.

Superman escapes and redirects the Hackensack-bound missile into outer space before flying toward California to intercept the other missile. Tragically, Superman is too late. The missile detonates, causing an expansive earthquake, which damages Californian landmarks like the Golden Gate Bridge and the Hollywood sign, destroys the Hoover Dam, and triggers massive flooding. Amidst the chaos, Lois lane's car falls into a crevice, where she suffocates under a pile of debris and dies.

But then, disregarding prior warnings from his father Jor-El not to meddle with the course of history, Superman flies around the earth so fast that he is able to rewind time—and save Lois Lane. Once he brings Lois to safety, Superman flies Lex Luthor and his assistant Otis into the prison's courtyard, where he delivers them to the warden.

Like most superhero films, *Superman: The Movie* is a melodrama. The story follows a tried-and-true formula: the hero defeats the villain and saves the city while protecting his love interest from the evil villain.

Superman also follows another formula. The seven rules that heroes—real and imagined—obey when battling villains:

Heroes Don't Start Fights
Heroes Counteract Aggression
Heroes Neutralize Aggressors
Heroes Wield the Weapons of Peace
Heroes Defeat Injustice, Not Individuals
Heroes Seek Redemption, Not Revenge
Heroes Complete Their Mission

Heroes Don't Start Fights

Abraham Lincoln was born in Kentucky 190 years after the first slave ship arrived on the shores of Virginia. In the 18th century alone, an estimated 6-7 million people were shipped from Africa to the New World, where most were forced to work as slaves in tobacco, rice, and indigo plantations on the Southern Coast. After the Revolutionary War, a growing anti-slavery sentiment emerged in the North. Between 1774 and 1804, each of the Northern states abolished slavery. But when Eli Whitney invented the cotton gin in 1793 (and selling cotton to the thriving textile industry in the United Kingdom became increasingly lucrative), the financial incentives for Southern plantation owners to retain their slaves increased.

In 1807, two years prior to Lincoln's birth, the United States Congress abolished the African slave trade. Nonetheless, the domestic trade flourished, and the slave population tripled during the five decades that followed. By the start of the Civil War, people of African descent accounted for nearly one third of the population in Southern states.

Meanwhile, with guidance from free blacks such as Fredrick Douglass and white supporters such as Harriet Beecher Stowe, the abolition movement gained momentum in the North. But despite their fervent efforts, the Fugitive Slave Act, which mandated that escaped slaves be caught and returned to their owners in the South, was passed in 1850. And the Kansas-Nebraska Act, which allowed the possibility that additional territories could join the union as slave states, became law in 1854.

Lincoln listened to pro-slavery arguments offered by his opponents but confessed, "Whenever I hear anyone arguing for slavery, I feel a strong impulse to see it tried on him personally." Lincoln believed that "if slavery is not wrong, nothing is wrong" because "the slave is a man who cannot be considered 'mere merchandise.'"

At the close of the 1858 Republican State Convention, Abraham Lincoln, then a senate candidate, delivered his "House Divided Speech," in which he declared, "A house divided against itself cannot stand."

"I believe," Lincoln argued, "this government cannot endure, permanently half *slave* and half *free*. I do not expect the Union to be *dissolved* - I do not expect the house to *fall* - but I do expect it will cease to be divided. It will become *all* one thing, or *all* the other."

Lincoln predicted that "Either the *opponents* of slavery will arrest the further spread of it, and place it where the public mind shall rest in the belief that it is in course of ultimate extinction; or its *advocates* will push it forward till it shall become alike lawful in *all* the States, old as well as new- *North* as well as *South*."

Lincoln was steadfast in his commitment to prevent the spread of slavery—and, ultimately, end the practice of slavery altogether. When Lincoln found that the opportunity to abolish slavery was finally within his powers as president, he issued the Emancipation Proclamation in 1863, freeing three million slaves with the stroke of his pen.

Lincoln did not start the fight. But, when given the opportunity, he fought on behalf of those who were less able to defend themselves.

Like Abraham Lincoln, Gandhi, Dr. King, and Nelson Mandela shared the common experience of being born and raised at a time and in a place where racial discrimination was commonly practiced *and* enshrined in law. But unlike Lincoln, Gandhi, Dr. King, and Mandela were themselves targets of racial discrimination.

Gandhi was born in India. He moved to Great Britain to earn his law degree, developed a legal practice in South Africa, and eventually returned to India. But no matter where Gandhi called home, he was a member of a marginalized social class.

Dr. King was born in the segregated South where he was not allowed to eat lunch, watch a movie, or ride a bus next to white children.

Mandela was raised under the system of apartheid in South Africa where, even while working as an attorney, he was not able to vote in national elections.

Each man felt the sting of prejudice. Each man developed a first-hand understanding of inequality. And despite their educational accomplishments—Gandhi and Mandela earned law degrees and Dr. King received a Ph.D. in Systematic Theology—each of these extraordinary men lived in communities in which they were not considered full citizens.

Nonetheless, Gandhi, Dr. King, and Mandela managed to attain some level of career success. Despite the prejudice they faced, each man could have chosen to enjoy a relatively quiet, comfortable, and prosperous life. But instead, Gandhi, Dr. King, and Mandela chose to forego their own comforts for the sake of those who were not so fortunate.

Gandhi, Dr. King, and Mandela chose to act. But it would be even more accurate to say that each man chose to react. They reacted to injustice. They responded to threats against the most vulnerable members of their societies.

They didn't start a fight. They joined a fight already in progress.

Heroes Counteract Aggression

When Martin and Coretta King moved to Montgomery in 1954, schools were segregated. Restaurants were segregated. Buses were segregated. White taxi operators were not allowed to serve black passengers, and vice versa. The median income for white citizens, who accounted for 58% of the population, was $1,730. The median income for black citizens, who comprised the remaining 42% of the population, was $970. Of the 30,000 black citizens who had reached adulthood, barely 2,000 were registered to vote.

Due to deep racial divisions in the city, coupled with what he described as "a threefold malady—factionalism among the leaders, indifference in the educated group, and passivity in the uneducated," Dr. King began to wonder if any "lasting social reform could ever be achieved in Montgomery."

Progress in the struggle for civil rights in the American South was hindered by the widespread acceptance of a false dichotomy—the idea that those who were oppressed had to choose between two equally undesirable options.

In his first book, *Strive Toward Freedom*, Dr. King described each option: "One way is acquiescence: the oppressed resign themselves to their doom. They tacitly adjust themselves to oppression, and thereby become conditioned to it." But, Dr. King argued, acquiescence was unacceptable:

> *To accept passively an unjust system is to cooperate with that system; thereby the oppressed become as evil as the oppressor. Noncooperation with evil is as much a moral obligation as is cooperation with good.*

> *The oppressed must never allow the conscience of the oppressor to slumber. Religion reminds every man that he is his brother's keeper. To accept injustice or segregation passively is to say to the oppressor that his actions are morally right. It is a way of allowing his conscience to fall asleep. At this moment the oppressed fails to be his brother's keeper. So acquiescence—while often the easier way—is not the moral way. It is the way of the coward.*

Others responded to oppression in a second way—by resorting to "physical violence and corroding hatred." Dr. King acknowledged that "Violence often brings about momentary results. Nations have frequently won their independence in battle," but argued that "in spite of temporary victories, violence never brings permanent peace. It solves no social problem; it merely creates new and more complicated ones."

While some in the "black power" movement advocated armed confrontations, Dr. King maintained that:

> *Violence as a way of achieving racial justice is both impractical and immoral. It is impractical because it is a descending spiral ending in destruction for all. The old law of an eye for an eye leaves everybody blind. It is immoral because it seeks to humiliate the opponent rather than win his understanding; it seeks to annihilate rather than to convert. Violence is immoral because it thrives on hatred rather than love. It destroys community and makes brotherhood impossible. It leaves society in monologue rather than dialogue. Violence ends by defeating itself. It creates bitterness in the survivors and brutality in the destroyers.*

Dr. King then proposed that there was an alternative—a third way. A way in which oppressed people could avoid acquiescing to injustice or responding to violence with violence. Dr. King called this third option "nonviolent resistance." As Dr. King explained,

> *The nonviolent resister agrees with the person who acquiesces that one should not be physically aggressive toward his opponent but he balances the equation by agreeing with the person of violence that evil must be resisted. He avoids the nonresistance of the former and the violent resistance of the latter. With nonviolent resistance, no individual or group need submit to any wrong, nor need anyone resort to violence in order to right a wrong.*

Prior to the Montgomery Bus Boycott, nonviolent resistance was more theoretical than practical. But when Rosa Parks refused to give up her seat, Dr. King and local leaders were able to organize a successful protest, which culminated in the integration of city busses. Dr. King was emboldened by the realization that change was possible. He was convinced that nonviolent resistance would be the most effective means to enact additional change.

Five months after bus lines were integrated in Montgomery, Dr. King marched on Washington among 25,000 demonstrators. Standing in front of the Lincoln Memorial, Dr. King delivered his "Give Us the Ballot" speech, in which he stated that, "Our most urgent request to the President of the United States and every member of Congress is to give us the right to vote." Dr. King continued his plea: "Give us the ballot and we will transform the salient misdeeds of mobs into the good deeds of orderly citizens." He closed his remarks with the timeless refrain, "Give us the ballot…Give us the ballot…Give us the ballot…"

Dr. King repeated this same demand several months later, while speaking to an audience in Miami: "We want the right to vote now," he stated. "We do not want freedom fed to us in teaspoons over another 150 years. Under God, we were born free. Misguided men robbed us of our freedom. We want it back."

With the demand for the right to vote clearly stated, but not yet realized, Dr. King led a direct-action campaign in Alabama. The Birmingham campaign involved a boycott of local merchants, lunch counter sit-ins, mass meetings, and marches on City Hall. City officials received a court injunction against the protests, but Dr. King persisted. He was arrested and put in jail. During his incarceration, Dr. King wrote his "Letter from Birmingham Jail,"[1] in which he stated, "injustice anywhere is a threat to justice everywhere."

When Dr. King was released a week later, he rejoined the protest. Shortly thereafter, Dr. King's colleague, James Bevel, suggested that they should invite children to participate in the demonstrations (because their availability was less hindered by work commitments). The involvement of children set the stage for a gruesome scene when Bull Connor, who held the sardonically ironic title of "Commissioner of Public Safety," ordered police officers to use clubs, cattle prods, fire hoses, and dogs on the unarmed protestors. On May 7, 1963, news images of the disproportionate aggression sanctioned by Bull Connor were viewed by millions of citizens throughout the United States. Dr. King found a way to use excessive force—and gruesome images—to the advantage of the civil rights movement.

Heroes Neutralize Aggressors

As a student at an English-speaking boarding school in Tokyo, Kanō Jigorō was the victim of bullying. Hoping that martial arts could provide a solution, Kanō wanted to find a Jujitsu master who could teach him methods of close combat that would help him defeat his bullies. But as Japan became increasingly modernized in the late nineteenth century, martial arts had fallen out of fashion and many of the old masters were so disillusioned that they refused to teach a new generation of students. Undeterred, Kanō eventually found a teacher, then another, and another, from whom he learned the techniques of Jujitsu. Jigorō went on to earn

---

1   Dr. King's "Letter from a Birmingham Jail" inspired his 1964 memoir, *Why We Can't Wait*.

Menkyo ("mastery") status.

When Kanō opened his own 12-mat *Kodokan* ("a place for expanding the way"), he emphasized defensive rather than offensive techniques. Kanō came to the realization that his approach went beyond *jutsu* ("art") to provide a more encompassing *do* ("way"), with broad applications to the lives of its practitioners.

Kanō's philosophy was guided by the concepts of seiryoku zen'yo (maximum efficiency, minimum effort), *jita kyōei* (mutual welfare and benefit), and *ū yoku gō o seisu* (softness controls hardness). This gentler approach, which Kanō taught as a route to self-improvement and the betterment of society, became known as *jūdō*.

In practice, Judo is based on the notion that, by using the attacker's aggression against him, a weaker *judoka* ("practitioner") could defeat a stronger opponent.

Dr. King never studied martial arts, but in his fight for freedom, he was a judo master.

On March 7, 1965, with the incidents in Birmingham seared into the public consciousness, James Bevel (head of the Southern Christian Leadership Conference) and Amelia Boynton (local civil rights leader) led a procession across the Edmund Pettus Bridge in Selma, Alabama en route to Montgomery. The Marchers were met by state troopers whom Governor George Wallace had positioned on the county line. Armed with billy clubs and tear gas, and backed by a posse of "irregulars," state troopers attacked the unarmed protesters.

A widely publicized photograph of Boynton lying unconscious came to symbolize the brutality of the police response on "Bloody Sunday." Violence toward protestors displayed the ugliness of segregation and discrimination. The country looked on in horror as national news media replayed the disturbing footage.

Dr. King immediately headed to Selma to join his colleagues. On March 9th, he led 2,000 marchers in a second attempt to cross the bridge, but aborted the effort when he and the marchers were again confronted by state troopers. Six days later, President Lyndon Johnson spoke to the nation in a televised address, where he expressed support for the marchers and called upon Congress to pass voting rights legislation.

Johnson then federalized the Alabama National Guard and directed the guardsman to escort the marchers. On March 21, Dr. King led 2,000 people from Selma to Montgomery, flanked by police officers—who were there to protect them as they marched rather than prevent them from marching. In Montgomery, the protesters were welcomed by 50,000 supporters.

With a limited budget and organizational capacity, Dr. King was able to use his high profile—and the mass media—to shine a more intense light on an ugly situation. Increased exposure of injustice influenced public opinion and put additional pressure on politicians to address the underlying reasons for the march. The voting rights act was passed five months later.

While maximizing the efficiency of the resources available to him (*seiryoku zen'yo*), Dr. King marched for the mutual welfare and benefit of all Americans (*jita kyōei*). He demonstrated the principle of *ū yoku gō o seisu,* that softness, can in fact, control hardness.

Heroes Wield the Weapons of Peace

Eleven years prior to his birth in 1869, Gandhi's native land experienced a popular uprising known to Indians as the First Indian War of Independence and to the British as the Indian Rebellion of 1857. Grievances had been accumulating for decades but the conflict came to a boil when soldiers mutinied against the East India Company shortly after the introduction of the Enfield P-53 rifle. Soldiers were required to bite open the cartridges of the new firearm to release the gunpowder inside. Their objection was based on a rumor that cartridges were greased with beef and pork tallow, which offended the convictions of Hindu and Muslim soldiers, respectively.

Shortly thereafter, civilians joined the rebellion against the East India

Company, which had maintained control of India since 1612. In just seven months, tens of thousands of soldiers and hundreds of thousands of civilians—mostly on the Indian side—were killed. Ultimately, the British crown claimed direct control of India. Great Britain established the India Office, appointed a Viceroy of India, and left the bureaucracy of the East Indian Company mostly intact.

When wronged, the natural human inclination is to meet evil with evil, to respond to force with force, and to demand an eye for an eye. But violence failed to free India from centuries of colonization.

That is why Gandhi chose a different approach.

During his time in South Africa, Gandhi's triumphs on behalf of fellow Indians living in the Transvaal and Natal regions earned him widespread recognition back home. When Gandhi returned to India after two decades in diaspora, he was swarmed by a cheering crowd as he and his family disembarked the S. S. Arabia. Gandhi's reception was similar as he arrived at train stations throughout India during his year-long fact-finding mission.

Before returning to India, Gandhi devoted time to reading, conversation, and contemplation. Gandhi became increasingly interested in religious texts. One work by a Gugarati poet Shamal Bahtta gripped Gandhi's "mind and heart" and the idea of returning good for evil became his "guiding principle." The "wonderful lines" Gandhi referred to read as follows:

> *For a bowl of water give a goodly meal;*
> *For a kindly greeting bow thou down with zeal;*
> *For a simple penny pay thou back with gold;*
> *If thy life be rescued, life do not withhold.*
> *Thus the words and actions of the wise regard;*
> *Every little service tenfold they reward.*
> *But the truly noble know all men as one,*
> *And return with gladness good for evil done.*

Gandhi found similarities between the words written by Shamal Bhatt and the Sermon on the Mount delivered by Jesus. Gandhi said the Sermon on the Mount "went straight to my heart." He was particularly engrossed by verses that called for returning good for evil:

> *You have heard that it was said to the people long ago, 'You shall not murder, and anyone who murders will be subject to judgment.' But I tell you that anyone who is angry with a brother or sister will be subject to judgment.*
>
> *You have heard that it was said, 'Eye for eye, and tooth for tooth.' But I tell you, do not resist an evil person. If anyone slaps you on the right cheek, turn to them the other cheek also.*
>
> *You have heard that it was said, 'Love your neighbor and hate your enemy.' But I tell you, love your enemies and pray for those who persecute you,*

Gandhi found in the Sermon on the Mount—as well as Battha's poetry, and the *Bhagavad Gita*—a call to abandon human inclinations, including the urge to retaliate against those who have done wrong. Gandhi's thinking was also shaped by the Hindu ideal of Ahimsa, which refers to an all-encompassing commitment to nonviolence.

Ahimsa sustains life. To commit himsa is to cause destruction. As Gandhi explained:

> *Man cannot for a moment live without consciously or unconsciously committing outward himsa. The very fact of his living, eating, drinking and moving about necessarily involves some himsa, destruction of life, be it ever so minute. A votary of ahimsa therefore remains true to his faith if the spring of all his actions is compassion, if he shuns to the best of his ability the destruction of the tiniest creature, tries to save it, and thus incessantly strives to be free from the deadly coil of himsa. He*

will be constantly growing in self-restraint and compassion, but he can never become entirely free from outward himsa.

Gandhi wrote in his autobiography that the idea "that renunciation was the highest form of religion appealed to me greatly." Gandhi put the idea of renunciation into practice in his own life, disavowing pleasures like eating meat, engaging in sexual intercourse, and succumbing to passions like anger and judgment.

Adherence to a growing list of vows was one way in which Gandhi developed the strength necessary to "turn the other cheek" when wronged by others. Self-restraint allowed Gandhi to resist his oppressors without giving into the temptation to respond with anger and hostility.

While searching for a way to explain his philosophy and strategies to others, Gandhi "found that the term 'passive resistance' was too narrowly construed." To Gandhi, "passive resistance" seemed like "a weapon of the weak, that it could be characterized by hatred, and that it could finally manifest itself in violence." At a loss for a more suitable term, Gandhi offered a cash prize to readers of his *Indian Opinion* publication. The winning submission was "Sadagraha" (Sat = truth, Agraha = polite but firm insistence), which Gandhi revised slightly to "Satyagraha."

Satyagraha (polite but firm insistence on truth) inspired Gandhi's first acts of civil disobedience in South Africa.

Around the time Gandhi arrived in South Africa in 1893, an effort was made in some regions (e.g., Transvaal, Natal) to rid the country of Asian immigrant—or to at least make sure they felt thoroughly unwelcome. In 1896, people of non-European descent were stripped of their right to vote. In 1907, the Transvaal Asiatic Registration Act was passed by the white government, mandating that all Asian men be fingerprinted and carry a pass in public. The "Black Act," as it became known, represented an existential threat to the continued existence of Indian communities in South Africa.

Indians gathered at the Empire Theater in Johannesburg to come up with a response. Most arrived at the theater expecting some type of violent reprisal. But Gandhi suggested a different solution. A nonviolent solution. Gandhi's solution was radical. As a group, they would simply refuse to obey the law and they would accept the consequences.

Gandhi believed that, without cooperation, injustice cannot endure. And Gandhi hypothesized that, if they remained a united group, they could defeat violence with love. Gandhi considered love to be the root of nonviolence. He taught his followers that the object of Satyagraha "should not be to punish the opponent or to inflict injury upon him." Instead, Gandhi explained that "even while noncooperating with him, we must make him feel that in us he has a friend" and "we should try to reach his heart by rendering him humanitarian service wherever possible."

Under Gandhi's leadership, thousands of Indians defied the mandates and accepted punishment for their civil disobedience—including floggings and incarceration—without retaliation. Those who had gathered at the theater in Johannesburg remained true to their vows of nonviolence.

With the nonviolent campaign in its infancy, Gandhi met with General Jan Smuts, the leader of the Transvaal government. In a calm, quiet voice, Gandhi made his intensions clear: "I've come to tell you that I am going to fight against your government."

> *"You mean you have come here to tell me that?, he asked with a chuckle, "Is there anything more you want to say?"*
>
> *"Yes," replied Gandhi. "I am going to win."*
>
> *"Well," replied the dumbfounded general, "and how are you going to do that?"*
>
> *With a broad smile, Gandhi replied: "With your help."*

Tensions increased in 1912 after the government banned Asian immigrants and levied a £3 tax on indentured Indian workers. The situation escalated further in 1913 when the Supreme Court refused to recognize Indian marriages. In response to anti-Indian laws, Gandhi led a march across the Natal-Transvaal border. Gandhi was arrested, along with thousands of others involved in the civil disobedience campaign.

Due to public outcry over the violent treatment of peaceful protestors, General Smuts invited Gandhi to a meeting in January, 1914. As a gesture of good faith, Gandhi called off the mass marches. Five months later, the Indian Relief Act was passed, abolishing the £3 tax and legalizing Indian marriages. Satyagraha had won—with the help of General Smuts.

Then, as an experienced Satyagrahi, Gandhi returned to his native India determined to apply Satyagraha in the quest for equality, self-reliance, and self-rule.

After returning from his year-long fact-finding tour of India, Gandhi focused his initial efforts on the plight of farmers and laborers in Champaran, Ahmedabad, and Kheda. Gandhi led strikes, protests, and advocated nonpayment of excessive taxes. He organized face-to-face negotiations with landlords and mill owners. Gandhi won increased autonomy for oppressed workers—and the respect of an entire nation.

During each campaign, Gandhi taught local leaders and laborers the ways of Satyagraha, insisting that they adhere to the four conditions of a successful protest:

1. Never to resort to violence,
2. Never to molest blacklegs (workers who crossed the picket lines)
3. Never to depend upon alms, and
4. To remain firm, no matter how long the strike continued, and to earn bread, during the strike, by any other honest labour.

Gandhi worked tirelessly to counteract the temptation to respond with retaliation and violence. He considered violence both immoral and impractical: "However much I may sympathize with and admire worthy motives, I am an uncompromising opponent of violent methods even to serve the noblest of causes," Gandhi stated, "Experience convinces me that permanent good can never be the outcome of untruth and violence." Though violence sometimes "appears to do good, the good is only temporary; the evil it does is permanent."

Heroes Defeat Injustice, Not Individuals

On January 1, 1930, the Indian Congress party raised a new national flag to symbolize their commitment to gaining complete independence. After such a brazen political statement, all eyes were focused on Gandhi, and every ear awaited his instructions. As he searched for an appropriate next step toward self-rule, Gandhi received his inspiration in a dream.

After the passage of the British Salt Act of 1882, it was illegal for Indians to collect or sell salt. Therefore, to protest the Salt Act and the heavy taxation of salt, Gandhi marched with 78 of his most loyal followers from Ahmedabad to Dandi, where they planned to harvest salt from seawater.

An enormous crowd gathered at his ashram to see the sixty-one-year-old off on his journey. Throughout the Salt March, streets were lined with supporters who cheered his steps and laid flowers in his path. Gandhi stopped in towns along the way to share his vision. He told the large, attentive crowds that, "this is a struggle of not one man, but millions of us."

From March 12-April 6, thousands of Indians joined Gandhi during the 241-mile trek. The march inspired hundreds of thousands of others to defy the salt laws, with coastal residents gathering salt from atop the sand and selling the salt to those in cities, whose purchase served as their contribution to the protest. Open defiance of salt laws, which had protected the British monopoly for decades, resulted in 80,000 incarcerations.

The 24-day Salt March was observed by global news media, whose coverage increased Gandhi's international profile and helped foster sympathy for the Indian quest for independence. Gandhi was named Time

Magazine's "Man of the Year" in 1930.

Shortly after the march, several British officials, who were accompanied by thirty well-armed police officers, arrived at Gandhi's work camp around midnight. One of the officials awoke Gandhi with a flashlight, declaring that he had "come to arrest Mr. M. K. Gandhi." The suspect, by then known as "Mahatma," responded, "I am Mohandas Karamchand Gandhi. I am at your service."

The officer asked Gandhi to gather his belongings, adding "we will give you the time you need." As he picked up a small bundle off the floor, Gandhi replied, "I am ready now. This is all I need." Gandhi then brushed his teeth, recited a short prayer, and walked to the car outside, all while exchanging pleasantries with his captors.

Willingness to comply with the arrest was not a mark of a fearful or feeble man. Gandhi demonstrated that "nonviolence is the weapon of the brave" and that Satyagraha "has no room for cowardice or even weakness." Gandhi suggested that those who used or threatened violence were the true cowards: "I can imagine a fully armed man to be at heart a coward. Possession of arms implies an element of fear, if not cowardice. But true nonviolence is an impossibility without the possession of unadulterated fearlessness."

Even when taken into custody, Gandhi displayed calm, compassion, and kindness towards his oppressors. "Satyagraha is gentle," Gandhi explained, "it never wounds. It must not be the result of anger or malice. It is never fussy, never impatient, never vociferous" and "It is never the intention of a satyagrahi to embarrass the wrongdoer." "Man and his deed are two distinct things," Gandhi explained,

> Whereas a good deed should call forth approbation and a wicked deed disapprobation, the doer of the deed, whether good or wicked, always deserves respect or pity as the case may be. 'Hate the sin and not the sinner' is a precept which, though easy enough to understand, is rarely

practiced, and that is why the poison of hatred spreads throughout the world.

Gandhi taught his followers that, while resisting an oppressor, "The appeal is never to his fear; it is, must be, always to his heart. The satyagrahi's object is to convert, not to coerce, the wrongdoer."

During the railway strike in South Africa, one of the leaders of the protest recruited Gandhi, saying "let's join forces. A strike is a legitimate nonviolent campaign, and we are fighting a common enemy." Gandhi responded by explaining, "I don't consider anyone to be my enemy. They are all my friends. I want to educate them and change their hearts." Shortly thereafter, Gandhi led another peaceful protest, which was designed to gain "the sympathy of everyone—including the police—not to hurt or embarrass them." Gandhi taught his followers that nonviolent resistance "does not seek to destroy the opponent" but to "wean him from his error… to liquidate antagonisms but not the antagonists themselves."

Dr. King was inspired by Gandhi to follow a similar path.

Dr. King felt that "segregation is totally un-Christian, and that it is against everything the Christian religion stands for" but suggested that this "does not at all cause me to hate those who believe in segregation." For Dr. King, the civil rights movement was not a conflict between white people and black people, but "a conflict between justice and injustice" and a struggle between "the forces of light and the forces of darkness."

Dr. King constantly reminded his followers to love those who persecuted them: "If we are arrested every day, if we are exploited every day, if we are trampled over every day, don't ever let anyone pull you so low as to hate them." Dr. King suggested to his followers that they "should seek to persuade the perpetrators of segregation through love, patience, and understanding."

Heroes Seek Redemption, Not Revenge

Upon his release from prison, many assumed that Nelson Mandela would seek revenge against those who were responsible for his 27-year imprisonment. "I knew that people expected me to harbor anger toward whites," he explained, "But I had none. In prison, my anger towards whites decreased, but my hatred for the system grew. I wanted South Africa to see that I loved even my enemies while I hated the system that turned us against one another."

As a child, Mandela learned an important lesson from an unruly donkey, which he summarized as follows:

We had been taking turns climbing up and down its back and when my chance came I jumped on and the donkey bolted into a nearby thorn bush. It bent its head, trying to unseat me, which it did, but not before the thorns had pricked and scratched my face, embarrassing me in front of my friends... Even though it was a donkey that unseated me, I learned that to humiliate another person is to make him suffer an unnecessarily cruel fate. Even as a boy, I defeated my opponents without dishonoring them.

In defeating apartheid, Mandela went out of his way to allow adversaries—who had defended the detestable practice of apartheid—to save face. In promoting freedom for all South Africans, Mandela pursued redemption and reconciliation rather than retaliation and revenge.

After commencing secret negotiations with the apartheid government, Mandela was asked about his plans for the white minority. Mandela directed their attention to the ANC Freedom Charter, which stated that "South Africa belongs to all who live in it, black and white." He reassured his opponents that, "I do not want to drive you into the sea."

While speaking to the media, Mandela "wanted to impress upon the reporters the critical role of whites in any new dispensation." He explained that "Whites are fellow South Africans…and we want them to feel safe and to know that we appreciate the contribution that they have made toward the development of this country." Mandela stated that seeking revenge rather than reconciliation would be, not only immoral, but counterproductive: "We did not want to destroy the country before we freed it, and to drive the whites away would devastate the nation."

Mandela found "a middle ground between white fears and black hopes" and worked diligently to persuade his "white compatriots that a new, nonracial South Africa will be a better place for all." Mandela continually repeated his promise that "Any man or woman who abandons apartheid will be embraced in our struggle for a democratic, nonracial South Africa."

Heroes Complete Their Mission

On July 2, 1940, ten months into WWII, Gandhi sent an open letter from his residence in Delhi addressed "To Every Briton." The letter contained a bold claim: "I have been practicing with scientific precision non-violence and its possibilities for an unbroken period of over fifty years. I have applied it in every walk of life, domestic, institutional, economic and political. I know of no single case in which it has failed."

While some sought to evaluate Satyagraha in philosophical or academic terms, Gandhi asked his critics to focus on the fruits it bore rather than the structure of the tree, so to speak.

With strictly nonviolent methods, Gandhi convinced the government to reverse discriminatory laws and restore basic rights for immigrants in South Africa. With these same nonviolent methods, Gandhi won autonomy and civil liberties for farmers and laborers in India. Nonviolent methods allowed Gandhi to diminish faith in the idea that some people were born "untouchable."

Gandhi was never elected to political office and had no official role in the British or Indian governments. But while leading armies of nonviolent protestors, the 5'5" Gandhi earned the title of Mahatma ("Great Soul"), gained the loyalty of a nation, and won the respect of many of his former opponents. In a few short decades, Gandhi proved that "there is no force in the world that is so direct or so swift in working." Gandhi demonstrated that with nonviolent methods, "you can bring the world to your feet."

And that is exactly what Gandhi did.

On August 8, 1942, Gandhi delivered his "Quit India" speech at the Gowalia Tank Maidan park in Bombay. Gandhi reaffirmed his belief in peaceful protest and reminded his followers that, "Our quarrel is not with the British people, we fight their imperialism."

Gandhi demanded Great Britain relinquish control of India voluntarily and observed that, "in the history of the world, there has not been a more genuinely democratic struggle for freedom than ours." He believed that, because the French Revolution and the Russian Revolution "were fought with the weapon of violence, they failed to realize the democratic idea."

Gandhi then shared his vision for India: "In the democracy which I have envisaged, a democracy established by non-violence, there will be equal freedom for all. Everybody will be his own master." Then, speaking to all Indians, Gandhi issued a call to action that infuriated the British: "It is to join a struggle for such democracy that I invite you today."

Within 24 hours of his speech, Gandhi, along with nearly all Indian National Congress leaders—both at the national and state level—were arrested and imprisoned under the "Defense of India Rules." The press was forbidden from reprinting any portion of Gandhi's speech or supporting his call to action. British authorities were unable to subdue the rebellion. Approximately 1,000 protestors were killed and 100,000 were imprisoned. Although the British were able to win the battle, they did not win the war.

India gained Independence on August 15, 1947. And Gandhi was the runner-up to Albert Einstein as Time Magazine's Person of the Century.

Einstein held Gandhi in high esteem, saying "generations to come will scarcely believe such a man as this ever walked upon this earth."

The historian J. B. Kripalani, who counted himself amongst Gandhi's most loyal friends, initially doubted the potential of nonviolent resistance. Early in their friendship, Kripalani confronted Gandhi: "Mr. Gandhi, you may know all about the Bible or the *Bhagavad Gita*, but you know nothing at all about history. Never has a nation been able to free itself without violence." With a fatherly smile, Gandhi gently corrected the historian: "You know nothing about history. The first thing you have to learn about history is that because something has not taken place in the past, that does not mean that it cannot take place in the future."

When others thought something was difficult, improbable, or impossible, Gandhi found a way to get it done.

That is what heroes do.

Chapter 9

Uniting the Village

*If you want to make peace with your enemy,
you have to work with your enemy.
Then he becomes your friend.*
-Nelson Mandela

Having served exactly four years in office, Abraham Lincoln stood in front of the Capitol Building on March 4, 1865, to deliver his second inaugural address. With the Civil War in its 48th month, yet bolstered by hope that the end of the war was near, Lincoln focused the attention of his citizens on the future of their reunited nation.

The 16th President cited slavery as the cause of the war and pondered the role of divine will in its continuance. "More than any of his other speeches," observed Doris Kearns-Goodwin, "the Second Inaugural fused spiritual faith with politics—a feeling of religious reverence, and belief in God—his justice and overruling power—increased in him." Lincoln alluded to three verses from the Old Testament and four verses from the New Testament. In quoting scripture, Lincoln pointed to beliefs held in common by the Union and the Confederacy—and the tragic irony of their conflict: "Both read the same Bible and pray to the same God, and each invokes His aid against the other."

Lincoln expressed an intense desire to see a cessation of conflict while reaffirming his resolve to preserve the union:

> *Fondly do we hope, fervently do we pray, that this mighty scourge of war may speedily pass away. Yet, if God wills that it continue until all the wealth piled by the bondsman's two hundred and fifty years of unrequited toil shall be sunk, and until every drop of blood drawn with the lash shall be paid by another drawn with the sword, as was said three thousand years ago, so still it must be said 'the judgments of the Lord are true and righteous altogether.'*

Lincoln pleaded with his fellow Americans to enter a new season of healing and reconciliation:

> *With malice toward none, with charity for all, with firmness in the right as God gives us to see the right, let us strive on to finish the work we are in, to bind up the nation's wounds, to care for him who shall have borne the battle and for his widow and his orphan, to do all which may achieve and cherish a just and lasting peace among ourselves and with all nations.*

Forty-three days later, General Lee surrendered to U. S. Grant at Appomattox, Virginia, signaling the end of the Civil War.

When the news reached Washington, a crowd gathered outside of the Whitehouse. Not wanting to steal his own thunder from a speech he planned to give the following evening, Lincoln was reluctant to address the spontaneous assembly. But as the crowd grew, Lincoln stepped onto the balcony, where he acknowledged their jubilation. As the crowd settled down, he spoke extemporaneously:

> *I am very greatly rejoiced to find that an occasion has occurred so pleasurable that the people cannot restrain themselves…I have always thought 'Dixie' one of the best tunes I have ever heard. Our adversaries over the way attempted to appropriate it, but I insisted yesterday that*

we fairly captured it.

As the crowd roared in approval, Lincoln continued:

I presented the question to the Attorney General, and he gave it as his legal opinion that it is our lawful prize. I now request the band to favor me with its performance.

In requesting the patriotic song of the South, Lincoln believed that "it is good to show the rebels that with us they will be free to hear it again." The band followed "Dixie" with "Yankee Doodle," and "the crowd went off in high good-humor."

A similar display of heroism, reconciliation, and musical diplomacy transpired 130 years later in South Africa. At his inauguration, Nelson Mandela reaffirmed his vision for a rainbow nation in a speech he delivered in Cape Town:

Today we are entering a new era for our country and its people. Today we celebrate not the victory of a party, but a victory for all the people of South Africa.

Our country has arrived at a decision. Among all the parties that contested the elections, the overwhelming majority of South Africans have mandated the African National Congress to lead our country into the future. The South Africa we have struggled for, in which all our people, be they African, Colored, Indian or White, regard themselves as citizens of one nation is at hand.

The next day, on May 10, 1994, Mandela delivered a second speech in Pretoria, where he echoed Lincoln's calls for healing, reconciliation, and peace:

The time for the healing of the wounds has come. The moment to bridge the chasms that divide us has come. The time to build is upon us. We have, at last, achieved our political emancipation. We pledge ourselves to liberate all our people from the continuing bondage of poverty, deprivation, suffering, gender and other discrimination. We succeeded to take our last steps to freedom in conditions of relative peace. We commit ourselves to the construction of a complete, just and lasting peace...

We are both humbled and elevated by the honour and privilege that you, the people of South Africa, have bestowed on us, as the first President of a united, democratic, non-racial and non-sexist South Africa, to lead our country out of the valley of darkness.

We understand it still that there is no easy road to freedom. We know it well that none of us acting alone can achieve success. We must therefore act together as a united people, for national reconciliation, for nation building, for the birth of a new world.

Let there be justice for all. Let there be peace for all. Let there be work, bread, water and salt for all. Let each know that for each the body, the mind and the soul have been freed to fulfill themselves.

Never, never and never again shall it be that this beautiful land will again experience the oppression of one by another and suffer the indignity of being the skunk of the world.

Let freedom reign. The sun shall never set on so glorious a human achievement!

God bless Africa!

As Mandela closed his remarks, the cheering crowd looked up "in awe as a spectacular array of South African jets, helicopters, and troop carriers roared in perfect formation over the Union Buildings."

Amidst the pomp and circumstance, and the profound significance of the momentous occasion, Mandela recalled that, "The day was symbolized for me by the playing of our two national anthems, and the vision of whites singing "*Nkosi Sikelel' iAfrika*" and blacks singing "*Die Stem*," the old anthem of the republic." Mandela remarked that, "Although that day neither group knew the lyrics of the anthem they once despised, they would soon know the words by heart."

Like Lincoln, Mandela used the *de facto* national anthems of two previously opposing factions to symbolize his message that all were welcome, all were valued, and all were equal in the reunited nation.

Everyone Is Welcome

As the first democratically elected president of South Africa and the unofficial father to his country, Nelson Mandela's great task was to reunite a bloodied and battered nation.

As he assumed the presidency, Mandela made it clear that everyone would be welcome in the Rainbow nation. This was a message that he conveyed even while in prison.

On Robben Island, Mandela saw himself "not just as the leader of the ANC, but as a promoter of unity, an honest broker, a peacemaker." Mandela was careful to never give the impression that he was prejudice against or more favorable toward any group. Mandela tried to unify the various factions on Robben Island by reminding them that, despite differences in ideology and strategy, their "struggle was indivisible."

When some of the prisoners played soccer on weekends, Mandela "always chose an Indian or a Colored prisoner to walk with to show that he did not believe in grouping people by race." During games, Mandela refused to choose a side, as he felt that it was "a tactless thing for a leader to do." When asked whom he was supporting, Mandela would tell them that he supported all of them—that he supported the best in them.

Many of Mandela's fellow prisoners viewed Afrikaners as the enemy to be defeated. But Mandela explained to his colleagues that "Afrikaners were Africans too. They were people of Dutch, German, and other European ancestry who had immigrated to Africa, cutting their ties with Europe. The Afrikaner no longer had a homeland elsewhere. He was a transplant now firmly rooted in Africa, just like the hardy and beautiful Jacaranda tree, which had come from Europe and had long since become a symbol of South African culture." Therefore, their enemy was not the Afrikaner, but an unjust political system.

Upon his release from prison, Mandela reaffirmed his pledge that "no man or woman who has abandoned apartheid will be excluded from our movement toward a nonracial, united, and democratic South Africa based on one-person one-vote on a common voters' roll."

Mandela spoke kindly of his jailers at his first press conference. His generosity helped lay to rest fears that he was a bitter man who harbored grievances that he would avenge as President. In the run-up to the election, Mandela stayed on-message, constantly pleading with his fellow South Africans to "forget the past."

When election results confirmed that Mandela was victorious, he considered his mission to be "one of preaching reconciliation, of binding the wounds of the country, of engendering trust and confidence." He "reminded people again and again that the liberation struggle was not a battle against any one group or color, but a fight against a system of repression." Each time he spoke publicly, Mandela declared that "all South Africans must now unite and join hands and say we are one country, one nation, one people, marching together into the future."

As Mandela celebrated his election victory, a special guest joined the president-elect on the podium—Mrs. Coretta Scott King. While speaking to those gathered, Mandela glanced at Dr. King's widow as he echoed her late husband's famous words: "Free at last! Free at last!"

Coretta Scott King's attendance was no accident. Mandela had studied the tactics that her husband used to unify a divided country.

Whereas Dr. King promoted reconciliation and integration, other leaders in the civil rights movement, including the more militant Malcolm X, promoted a more isolationist approach and suggested that violence might be necessary. But Dr. King reminded his audiences that they would be "living tomorrow with the very people against whom [they are] struggling today." Therefore, Dr. King suggested, "Let us remember that as we struggle, we must have love, compassion and understanding goodwill for those against whom we struggle."

After the Supreme Court declared segregation on Montgomery busses unconstitutional, Dr. King addressed the crowd: "I would be terribly disappointed if any of you go back to the buses bragging…We must not take this as a victory over the white man but a victory for justice and democracy." Dr. King asked his followers to "respond to the decision with an understanding of those who have oppressed us and with an appreciation of the new adjustments that the court order poses for them."

To promote "integration based on mutual respect," Dr. King asked his followers to "act in such a way as to make possible a coming together of white people and colored people on the basis of a real harmony of interests and understanding" and to "go back to the buses in all humility and with gratitude to Almighty God for making this decision possible."

As the civil rights movement gained momentum, the involvement of white supporters increased exponentially—especially in the aftermath of the Selma to Montgomery March. Dr. King was quick to welcome white Americans—who were "just as determined to see us free as we are to be free ourselves"—into the family. To impress upon his followers that all should be welcome in an integrated society, he created an organization that reflected this objective. As Dr. King explained, "I always have in the past and will in the future insist that my staff in the SCLC be interracial. By insisting on racial openness in our organizations, we are setting a pattern for a racially integrated society toward which we work."

Dr. King was eager to include all who were willing to help the cause.

Everyone Is Valued

At the time of Mother Teresa's death in 1997, there were 3,842 sisters serving in 594 houses across 120 countries. The work of the Missionaries of Charity was accomplished, first and foremost, by the Sisters, who received their vocations after taking formal vows. But Mother Teresa and her Sisters received substantial help from an army of lay volunteers called "coworkers."[1]

When fresh faces showed up to help, Mother Teresa usually walked them to Nirmal Hriday, the House for the Dying. Upon their arrival, she would delegate a special assignment. Mother Teresa "would take each volunteer by the hand, one at a time, and lead him through the rows of sick and dying people, lay the volunteer's hand on one person's forehead, and tell him exactly what to do next: Give the dying person something to eat, or just sit by him, pray beside him, or shave him."

After Mother Teresa "had put the volunteers physically in touch with the dying," she would "position herself on the slightly raised door rest at the entrance, from which she could oversee everything. Then she would smile broadly and contentedly."

The first volunteers included neighbors who were inspired to help with the good work that Mother Teresa was doing. Being "pragmatic and very practical by nature," Mother Teresa often received assistance for her work and her plans through chance meetings. Father Maasburg recalled one fortuitous misunderstanding:

> *An elegantly dressed man came into the House for the Dying and asked to speak with Mother Teresa. The Sisters informed him that Mother Teresa was at the back of the house cleaning the toilets. So he walked*

---

[1] After Mother Teresa's passing, the Missionaries of Charity continued to grow. As of 2020, there were 5,191 sisters serving in 762 houses in 139 countries.

in the direction they had indicated and found Mother Teresa literally scrubbing the toilets. She saw him come in, evidently took him for a volunteer, and immediately explained to him how to hold the toilet brush correctly and how to clean the toilet so as to conserve water. Then she put the brush in his hand and left him standing there. After fifteen minutes the man came back from the room, went straight up to Mother Teresa and said, "I have finished; may I speak with you now?" "Yes, certainly," Mother Teresa replied. He took an envelope out of his pocket and said, "Mother Teresa, I am the director of the airline, and here are your tickets. I just wanted to bring them to you personally."

The airline director found joy in the humble task assigned to him, and later spoke of his time at the home for the dying as "the most important twenty minutes of my life—cleaning toilets."

Mother Teresa welcomed everyone who came to help—whether intentionally or accidentally—into her family of coworkers.

Some of the coworkers were, like Mother Teresa, compelled by their Catholic faith. But most served for other reasons. Among the early volunteers were a Buddhist woman who lent a truck for picnics and retreats, a Jewish doctor who repaired cleft palates of children, and Hindu university students who spent weekends shaving dying men.

Everyone was welcome in Mother Teresa's community. "Doesn't matter race, doesn't matter religion, Christian or Communist doesn't matter," Mother Teresa explained, "We are all children of God, created to love and to be loved." Her army of Co-Workers, which included men and women of all ages, races, creeds, and castes, was a tangible reminder of the degree to which she welcomed everyone, regardless of background.

Mother Teresa was always recruiting, but not always for the Missionaries of Charity in particular. She wanted to encourage people to see the needs around them and to perform small acts with great love. To not just provide the means to help but to get their hands dirty helping. "It is not your money but your time we need," she told the attendees at the seventy-second Rotary International Convention, "we want all of you to donate YOURSELVES to the poor people."

Mother Teresa found special joy in connecting people across social classes. "She did not want to set people against each other but to be a bridge between them. She wanted the rich to save the poor and the poor to save the rich."

Mother Teresa was known for having many friends in high places. She developed particularly close, personal relationships with Princess Diana and Pope John Paul II. Nonetheless, Mother Teresa "spoke no differently with the president of a nation than with a prostitute, no differently with a Carmelite nun than with Muhammad Ali, the world champion boxer who visited her in Calcutta." When rumors of Princess Diana's marital difficulties emerged, Mother Teresa expressed the same concern that she would have offered to any of her closest friends, saying, "I am praying so much for her happiness…she and her husband should pray too. Prayer can help them through their troubles."

In 1980, Prince Charles visited Calcutta where he observed Mother Teresa and her Sisters provide meals for more than seven thousand people. Seeing the Prince's concern for a baby that had been found in a gutter, Mother Teresa promised to pray for the Prince "so that the love and compassion you have for the poor and the needy grows and you are able to serve them better." Three years later, Mother Teresa received the Insignia of the Honorary Order of Merit from the mother of Prince Charles, Queen Elizabeth II. At a ceremony held in Delhi. Mother Teresa was not particularly concerned with protocol. After the Queen handed the award to its recipient, Mother Teresa thanked the Queen for the "beautiful gift." Then, speaking to Queen Elizabeth as she would an old friend, inquired, "and how is your grandson, Prince William?"

Mother Teresa—a reluctant celebrity in her own right—was unimpressed by celebrity and status. "The great and the humble were treated alike for in

Mother Teresa's eyes they were all children of God and worthy of respect." Every person was equal in value. This wasn't just a glib saying, but a logical deduction from a bible verse that had a particularly strong influence on Mother Teresa's life: "what you do unto the least of these you do unto me." Having taken the words of Jesus literally, Mother Teresa "always saw a child of God above all else, even in mayors, ministers and presidents."

Time spent with dignitaries and world leaders "did nothing to alter the interest, respect and love she had for individuals, regardless of nationality, standing or creed." In Mother Teresa's eyes, everyone she encountered was Jesus—literally. As such,

> *When Mother Teresa picked a human being out of the gutter, when she gave the poor something to eat or bestowed attention and tender love on the dying, she never made a distinction with regard to religious affiliation. Hindus and Muslims, Christians and people without God, could all count just the same on her love and care.*

Gandhi shared Mother Teresa's concern for 'the least of these" in India. Members of the lowest caste were known by a Sanskrit name that translates to "those who cannot be touched." Gandhi objected to the idea of untouchability in no uncertain terms: "I hate from the bottom of my heart the hideous system of untouchability for which millions of Hindus have made themselves responsible." To ease their feelings of inferiority, and recognize their inherent dignity and worth, Gandhi renamed these people Harijans, "the children of God."

Gandhi worked to unify the people of India, regardless of caste or class. "All of us are one. When you inflict suffering on others, you are bringing suffering on yourself. When you weaken others, you are weakening yourself, weakening the whole nation." Gandhi refused to enter Hindu temples that barred Harijans from entering, saying "There is no God here. If God were here, everyone would have access." Gandhi was the undisputed spiritual leader of India and his words made an impact. Many of the great Hindu temples began allowing all Hindus to worship within their walls.

Everyone Is Part of The Team

When Dr. King began his pastorate in Montgomery, Dexter Baptist had a reputation as a silk-stocking church catering only to elites. But the newly appointed pastor wanted Dexter to shake its reputation as a "big folks" church. Dr. King believed that worship should be "a social experience with people of all levels of life coming together to realize their oneness and unity under God." He feared that, if members came only from the upper class, the church would be "in danger of becoming little more than a social club with a thin veneer of religiosity."

As his involvement in Montgomery increased, Dr. King joined several organizations, including the NAACP (which focused on legislation) and the Council on Human Relations (which focused on education). He noticed that leaders of various organizations often did not get along and were mutually unsupportive. The NAACP, for example, refused to assist with any civil rights activity that did not originate from their office.

Dr. King was deeply troubled by "factionalism among the leaders" in Montgomery. He noticed that their differences were more often personal than philosophical. Instead of working together, leaders were vying for prominence. Dr. King explained this phenomenon by observing that, "deep down within all of us," [we have] an instinct. It's a kind of drum major instinct—a desire to be out in front, a desire to lead the parade, a desire to be first." But Dr. King tried to convince them that "the ability of Negroes to enter alliances is a mark of our growing strength, not of our weakness."

To impress upon his colleagues the gravity of the situation, Dr. King drew a parallel between the book of Exodus and the civil rights struggle: "Whenever Pharaoh wanted to keep the slaves in slavery, he kept them fighting among themselves." Therefore, Dr. King worked to convince fellow leaders that "there is amazing power in unity" and suggested that "where there is true unity, every effort to disunite only serves to strengthen the unity."

While some leaders tried to elevate their positions or fight for prominence, Dr. King spent time with people on the ground.

Dr. King had earned a doctoral degree and came from a relatively privileged upbringing, but the people of Montgomery identified closely with Dr. King. They knew that he had been "the victim of the deferred dreams, of blasted hopes." Dr. King walked the walk rather than just talk the talk. That is why people followed his lead, allowed him to speak for them, and permitted him to make decisions on their behalf.

As Dr. King emerged as the face of the civil rights movement, he "was met with all the natural human emotions of jealousy, apprehension, and distrust—even in his own hometown." However, because Dr. King was deliberate in nurturing friendships, and listening to and consulting with his fellow leaders, he was able to "orchestrate a group of individuals that probably pretty much approached egomania." Dr. King defused disagreements with his "remarkable facility for sitting through long, contentious meetings and then summarizing what everybody had said and synthesizing" their perspectives into a conclusion that everyone could agree upon.[2]

Maintaining unity was an ongoing task. As Dr. King explained, "The biggest job in getting any movement off the ground is to keep together the people who form it."

Disputes and disagreements are inevitable in social groups, large and small. In some cases, group members find a resolution. In others, conflicts can linger or grow to the point that they threaten the continued existence of a group or movement. When divisions become entrenched, they tend to

---

2   Dr. King often applied this Hegelian method of thesis-antithesis-synthesis, which he learned in graduate school.

perpetuate themselves until a unifier emerges—someone who possesses the humility and quiet confidence required to truly lead. Fortunately, the civil rights movement found a unifier in Dr. King.

Dr. King brought Americans of all races and creeds together in previously segregated communities. His work in the civil rights movement helped return long-withheld rights to marginalized citizens. Dr. King joined the ranks of those who unified *their* villages. Abraham Lincoln restored unity to a nation in the aftermath of a civil war. Mandela unified a nation after decades of apartheid. And Gandhi brought fellow Indians together as their nation approached independence.

But sadly, unity is often fragile and impermanent. In fact, none of the heroes described above were completely or permanently successful in unifying their communities or their countries. India's fracture resulted in two separate, bitterly divided countries (India and Pakistan). In the United States and South Africa, race relations remain imperfect, to say the least. Too often, people forget—or refuse to heed—the words of the heroes they celebrate. The problem is not that the ideals of Lincoln, Gandhi, Dr. King, and Nelson Mandela did not work. The problem is that too many people stopped working on behalf of their ideals.

History has proven that unity is a process, not a destination.

Chapter 10

Disregarding Speed Limits

*There is a higher court than courts of justice
and that is the court of conscience.
It supersedes all other courts.*
-Gandhi

Just before sunrise on Thursday, November 8, 2018, Capt. Matt McKenzie of the California Department of Forestry and Fire Protection looked beyond his station in Jarbo Canyon and immediately knew there was trouble. Due to intense winds, a forest fire that had ignited across the canyon was building fast. Unable to reach the fire, Capt. McKenzie radioed an evacuation order for the sparsely populated town of Pulga: "This has got potential for a major incident. Still working on access."

As the fire was driven West by 50mph winds, children began to arrive at school in nearby Paradise, CA. With the flames moving closer, a text alert was seen only by residents who had previously chosen to opt-in to the early notification system. Firefighters started going door-to-door. Unable to prevent the blaze from entering the town, fire crews in Paradise focused on evacuating residents in a zone-by-zone basis.

Marc Kessler, a science teacher at Paradise Intermediate School, saw the cloud of smoke moving closer as a sheriff's deputy arrived in the school's parking lot. An officer got out of his squad car and said, "seat belt laws don't apply!" He instructed teachers to "stuff as many kids as you can in the cars" and evacuate to the nearby city of Chico.

The so-called "Camp Fire" continued to burn for the next two weeks. Having destroyed nearly 19,000 structures and claiming 85 lives, the Camp Fire became the most destructive and the deadliest wildfire in California state history. Schools were destroyed but, thankfully, none of the children who were evacuated in their teacher's cars through the flames, smoke, and debris, were listed among the fatalities.

The Rule of Law

In 1838, at 28-years-old, Abraham Lincoln addressed the Young Man's Lyceum—a local society that "contained all the culture and talent" in Springfield, IL. Lincoln's remarks—some of his first to be published—were delivered against the backdrop of a rising tide of mob rule throughout the country.[1] Prior to his speech, a black man in St. Louis was the victim of a ruthless burning. Lincoln opened his remarks, saying,

> *There is, even now, something of ill-omen, amongst us. I mean the increasing disregard for law which pervades the country; the growing disposition to substitute the wild and furious passions, in lieu of the sober judgment of Courts; and the worse than savage mobs, for the executive ministers of justice.*

Lincoln then explained the relationship between liberty and the rule of law and offered a remedy for the nation's rising problem. Lincoln sought to promote, not just respect for the law, but reverence for the law:

> *Let every American, every lover of liberty, every well wisher to his posterity, swear by the blood of the Revolution, never to violate in the least particular, the laws of the country; and never to tolerate their*

---

[1] Lincoln's Address was titled "The Perpetuation of Our Political Institutions."

violation by others. As the patriots of seventy-six did to the support of the Declaration of Independence, so to the support of the Constitution and Laws, let every American pledge his life, his property, and his sacred honor;—let every man remember that to violate the law, is to trample on the blood of his father, and to tear the character of his own, and his children's liberty. Let reverence for the laws, be breathed by every American mother, to the lisping babe, that prattles on her lap—let it be taught in schools, in seminaries, and in colleges; let it be written in Primers, spelling books, and in Almanacs;—let it be preached from the pulpit, proclaimed in legislative halls, and enforced in courts of justice.

Twenty-three years later, Lincoln took the oath of office as President of the United States. He was charged with upholding the rule of law during one of the most tumultuous times in American history. Meanwhile, across the Atlantic Ocean, the French poet and novelist Victor Hugo was busy finishing his literary masterpiece set during one the most tumultuous times in French history.

A Duty to The Law

In 1862, Victor Hugo published *Les Misérables*, a historical novel set amidst the French Revolution. *Les Misérables* is considered one of the most important literary works of the 19th century and is the basis for countless stage and screen adaptations. In *Les Misérables,* Hugo explored the relationship between justice and mercy through the interactions of thief-turned factory owner Jean Valjean and the chief of police, Inspector Javert.

As the story begins, Valjean is paroled after nineteen years in prison. Valjean travels to the town of Digne where he looks for shelter. But due to his criminal past, Valjean is unsuccessful—until he knocks on the door of a monastery, where Bishop Myriel and his fellow contemplatives live in humble circumstances. Their only extravagance is a set of silverware and a pair of silver candlesticks. The benevolent bishop welcomes Valjean as his honored guest, providing him with food and shelter.

Despite the bishop's act of compassion, Valjean steals the silverware and leaves the monastery in the dark of night. After Valjean is apprehended and returned to the monastery, Bishop Myriel tells a merciful lie. The Bishop explains to the police officers that the silverware was a gift and scolds Valjean for forgetting to also take the candlesticks. After the police release their suspect, Bishop Myriel implores Valjean to use the precious silver to become an honest man.

Valjean is transformed by Bishop Myriel's grace and forgiveness and keeps his vow to leave behind his criminal past. Valjean reinvents himself as Monsieur Madeleine in the town of Montreuil, becomes a prosperous factory owner, and is eventually elected mayor.

When some of Madeleine's employees find out that their coworker, Fantine, has an illegitimate daughter named Cossette, Madeleine's unscrupulous foreman fires her. In an act of desperation, Fantine turns to prostitution and is arrested by Montreuil's police chief, inspector Javert. Madeleine offers to care for Cossette after he learns of Fantine's legal troubles and failing health. But his attempts to help are thwarted when Inspector Javert suspects that Madeleine is in fact Jean Valjean. When an innocent man is wrongly accused of Valjean's parole violation, the real Valjean confesses that it is he who is guilty.

Years later, Valjean and Cossette move to Paris. When Javert learns of their arrival, he remains intent on recapturing the escaped prisoner. Meanwhile, Cossette falls in love with a young revolutionary named Marius. When Valjean learns that Marius is in grave danger on the front lines, he heads to the barricade to save the life of the man Cossette loves.

Upon his arrival, Valjean finds Javert, who has been discovered as a double agent. Valjean volunteers to execute the inspector, but when the two men are alone, Valjean releases Javert unharmed. Valjean then escapes with an injured Marius through the sewer system, but shortly after, Javert once again catches him. Valjean pleads with the inspector to let him deliver his would-be son-in-law to Marius' grandfather so that he can receive life-saving medical care. Javert permits his detainee to escape but feels tormented after forsaking his duty to the law. In a moment of anguish, Javert jumps to his death in the river below.

Javert's sense of duty to the law blinds him to all other considerations.

A Singular Focus

In the 1920's, a Swiss philosopher, zoologist, and psychologist named Jean Piaget developed an interest in the intellectual development of children. Piaget's theory of intellectual development set a course that the field of child development would take for most of the 20th century.

After moving from Zurich to Paris to study under Alfred Binet[2], Piaget honed his theories of intellectual development by closely observing the development of each of his three children.

Piaget came to view young children as not simply shorter, less knowledgeable adults, but organisms whose thought processes were qualitatively different than full-grown humans. Piaget viewed intelligence as a way in which humans adapt to their environment through the acquisition of increasingly complex "schemes."

In Piaget's language, a "scheme" (pronounced "skeem-ah") is an organized pattern of thought or action that a child uses to understand and respond to his or her experiences. Children develop behavioral schemes for actions like grasping or walking and operational schemes for mental activities like adding or multiplying two sums.

Piaget described the intellectual development of children in a series of four stages—each of which is a prerequisite for the next—that follow a predictable order. The "Sensorimotor Stage" (birth to age 2), the "Preoperational Stage" (age 2 to 7), the "Concrete-Operational Stage" (age

---

[2] Who developed what later became the Stanford-Binet IQ Test

7 to 11), and the "Formal Operational Stage" (age 11 into adulthood).

Preoperational Stage children tend to think from their own egocentric perspective. When a preschooler is asked by someone on the other end of the phone call where they are, the preschooler will simply say, "here." Preoperational children are unable to consider things from different points of view.

Preoperational Stage children are also prone to "centered thinking," meaning they focus on only one aspect of a situation. Until a child moves beyond centered thinking, she is unable to understand what Piaget called "conservation," or the recognition that an object retains its fundamental properties when manipulated in some superficial way. In one of his most famous demonstrations of preoperational thinking, Piaget instructed children to watch him poor water from a tall skinny glass to a shorter and wider glass. Then, Piaget asked each child, "now is there more water, less water, or the same amount?" Because children at this stage "center" on the height of the water (and lack the conservation skills to realize that the amount of water remains the same), they almost always say "less water." Then, when the water is poured back into the tall, skinny glass, the children conclude that there was "the same amount," once again centering on a single factor—the height of the water.

Preoperational stage children tend to think in concrete, black *or* white, terms. They view the world from their own perspective. They are not yet equipped to see more than one aspect of a situation at the same time. Preoperational children see the height of the water but miss the breadth.

Lives > Laws

Bruce Wayne's relationship with Gotham's police force is, shall we say, complicated. When Batman jumps into the Batmobile, he doesn't seem to obey speed limits. While pursuing a villain, Batman has dozens of police cars pursuing him. Batman's actions are sometimes misunderstood by local law enforcement, but his motives are understood by readers and viewers. The Caped Crusader disregards speed limits to defend the people of Gotham from immediate threats.

When Superman emerges from the phone booth to save Lois, he doesn't file a flight plan. His flights may violate restricted airspace above Metropolis. But to save lives, Superman is willing to break a few laws. Similarly, it probably isn't legal to swing from building-to-building in New York City, but Spiderman does nonetheless. Saving Mary Jane is more important than obeying New York City ordinances. When seconds count in life-or-death situations, completing the proper paperwork isn't always feasible.

Superheroes are celebrated rather than scorned for their disobedience. When superheroes disregard the law, their motivations are noble, and their violations are necessary. They disregard the law to defeat villains, protect the vulnerable, and defend the village from imminent threats. Superheroes need to move fast. Heroes focus on safeguarding others. Rules and regulations are less important than the lives they were meant to protect.

Les Misérables is the story of a criminal, Jean Valjean, who was transformed by forgiveness and grace offered by Bishop Myriel. The Bishop demonstrates that the man who entered his monastery was more important than the possessions housed within its walls. Even after betraying the Bishop's trust, Valjean was still not beyond redemption. Valjean was transformed by forgiveness and grace. He became an honest man who was driven to care for and protect those who were suffering.

Les Misérables is also the story of a law enforcer, Javert, who was unable to receive forgiveness and grace. Javert remained obsessed with capturing and prosecuting those who, in desperation, turned to petty theft and prostitution. Javert failed to realize that laws exist to protect people, not vice versa. By mechanically applying the letter of the law—without regard for the lives involved—Javert was unable to uphold the true purpose of the law. He chose to die rather than change. Javert centered on the height of justice but missed the breadth of mercy.

Thankfully, Javert was not present on that terrible morning in Paradise, CA. By directing teachers to break multiple laws, the law enforcement officers in Paradise saved the lives of hundreds of children.

Heroes obey the spirit of the law, but heroes don't always obey the letter of the law. Nonetheless, people are quick to forgive those who break the rules for the right reasons. In some cases, we admire people (like the police officers and teachers in Paradise, CA) *because* they were willing to break the rules.

John Wooden became one of the most admired coaches in the history of American sports, in part, because he was willing to disregard a few rules and regulations on certain occasions.

As the men's basketball coach at UCLA, John Wooden did things by the book. He never swore and he exercised unusual self-control on and off the court. Referring to Wooden's reputation as a strait-laced Indiana farm boy with no apparent vices, one commentator quipped, "John Wooden is so square you could divide him by four." But John Wooden was not a thoughtless rule follower. As Wooden confessed,

> *While I never violated a recruiting rule while I was coaching, I did ignore a few rules after players arrived at UCLA, but only in extending a kindness—love and concern—to those under my leadership. At UCLA during holidays such as Thanksgiving and Christmas, my wife, Nell, and I would invite them for dinner when they could not make it home to be with their immediate families. We knew this was a violation of NCAA rules; however, it was a rule I was willing to ignore. A young person should be with family on an important day.*

John Wooden also "bailed players out of jail for minor traffic violations on occasion even though, it violated rules. There was just no sense in letting a young man spend the weekend in jail for something like that. It was no different than what I would do for my own children." While Wooden was generally a stickler for rules, he maintained a balance between justice and care. And when the two came into conflict, he put people ahead of policies. And he never placed laws above the lives they were meant to protect.

The Letter of The Law

As Lincoln continued his speech at the Young Men's Lyceum in Springfield, he reaffirmed his belief in the importance of adhering to the rule of law, while at the same time reinforcing his condemnation of the mob mentality:

> *When I so pressingly urge a strict observance of all the laws, let me not be understood as saying there are no bad laws, nor that grievances may not arise, for the redress of which, no legal provisions have been made—I mean to say no such thing. But I do mean to say, that, although bad laws, if they exist, should be repealed as soon as possible, still while they continue in force, for the sake of example, they should be religiously observed. So also in unprovided cases. If such arise, let proper legal provisions be made for them with the least possible delay; but, till then, let them, if not too intolerable, be borne with.*

Lincoln wanted to impress upon his audience that, for the sake of liberty, the rule of law *must* be upheld. And to do so, citizens should obey the law—even laws that they consider to be "bad law." He also suggested that, if they object to a law, they should seek to change it "as soon as possible." However, if a bad law is "not too intolerable," they should obey it.

Although Lincoln advocated an uncompromising respect for the rule of law and strict adherence to even the most obscure statutes, he left open the possibility that, in some cases, a government might pass a law that is, in fact, too intolerable to bear.

In April 1963, amidst the protests in Birmingham, Alabama, Dr. King responded to his "dear fellow clergymen" who suggested that the direct-action protests were "unwise and untimely." In his "Letter from a Birmingham Jail," Dr. King explained the rationale for his selective obedience to the law:

> *You express a great deal of anxiety over our willingness to break laws. This is certainly a legitimate concern. Since we so diligently urge people to obey the Supreme Court's decision of 1954 outlawing segregation in the public schools, at first glance it may seem rather paradoxical for us consciously to break laws. One may well ask: "How can you advocate breaking some laws and obeying others?" The answer lies in the fact that there are two types of laws: just and unjust. I would be the first to advocate obeying just laws. One has not only a legal but a moral responsibility to obey just laws. Conversely, one has a moral responsibility to disobey unjust laws.*

Dr. King then explained how he reached the conclusion that certain laws were so unjust that, in Lincoln's words, they were "too intolerable" to bear.

> *Now, what is the difference between the two? How does one determine whether a law is just or unjust? A just law is a man made code that squares with the moral law or the law of God. An unjust law is a code that is out of harmony with the moral law. To put it in the terms of St. Thomas Aquinas: An unjust law is a human law that is not rooted in eternal law and natural law. Any law that uplifts human personality is just. Any law that degrades human personality is unjust. All segregation statutes are unjust because segregation distorts the soul and damages the personality. It gives the segregator a false sense of superiority and the segregated a false sense of inferiority. Segregation, to use the terminology of the Jewish philosopher Martin Buber, substitutes an "I it" relationship*

for an "I thou" relationship and ends up relegating persons to the status of things. Hence segregation is not only politically, economically and sociologically unsound, it is morally wrong and sinful. Paul Tillich has said that sin is separation. Is not segregation an existential expression of man's tragic separation, his awful estrangement, his terrible sinfulness? Thus it is that I can urge men to obey the 1954 decision of the Supreme Court, for it is morally right; and I can urge them to disobey segregation ordinances, for they are morally wrong.

Dr. King went on to explain that, by disobeying unjust laws, he is honoring the spirit of the law.

I hope you are able to see the distinction I am trying to point out. In no sense do I advocate evading or defying the law, as would the rabid segregationist. That would lead to anarchy. One who breaks an unjust law must do so openly, lovingly, and with a willingness to accept the penalty. I submit that an individual who breaks a law that conscience tells him is unjust, and who willingly accepts the penalty of imprisonment in order to arouse the conscience of the community over its injustice, is in reality expressing the highest respect for law.

After citing famous acts of disobedience from Hebrew, Roman, Greek, and American history, Dr. King reminded his fellow clergy that sometimes defying the law is simply unavoidable for a person with a conscience and some common sense:

We should never forget that everything Adolf Hitler did in Germany was "legal" and everything the Hungarian freedom fighters did in Hungary was "illegal." It was "illegal" to aid and comfort a Jew in Hitler's Germany. Even so, I am sure that, had I lived in Germany at the time, I would have aided and comforted my Jewish brothers. If today I lived in a Communist country where certain principles dear to the Christian faith are suppressed, I would openly advocate disobeying that country's antireligious laws.

Mother Teresa sometimes found herself in such a position.

When Mother Teresa sought to "bring tender loving care" to the people of her native Albania, she approached Ramiz Alia—who was the second and, ultimately the last, leader of the People's Socialist Republic of Albania—to ask permission. A twenty-three-year ban on religion had recently been lifted, but certain laws were still in effect.

President Alia informed Mother Teresa that, to open a house in Albania, she would have to break the law. With "mischievous satisfaction," Mother Teresa declared, "then I am ready to break the law." As one biographer noted, "the idea of being a law-breaker for God was one which obviously amused her." Shortly thereafter, Mother Teresa received permission to bring her sisters to Albania.

On another occasion, Mother Teresa met with Fidel Castro, who allowed Mother Teresa to bring four Sisters to care for the poor in Havana. However, the sisters were only allowed to care for patients inside one area of the hospital and were prohibited from visiting those in need of tender loving care nearby. When a priest alerted Mother Teresa to the situation, she responded, "Then the Sisters should visit as many families as possible; they cannot lock them all up."

Civil Disobedience Must Be Civil

The realization that "they cannot lock them all up" became a central part of Dr. King's strategy during the civil rights movement.

With no sign of an end to the Montgomery Bus Boycott, a city attorney found an obscure state law, which specified that when two or more people interfere with lawful business, they shall be guilty of a misdemeanor. The Montgomery County Grand Jury found those involved in the bus boycott to be in violation of Title 14, Section 54. Over 100 people were indicted, including Dr. King.

When the indictments were issued, Dr. King was in Nashville. Not wanting to be away from the action—or avoid his lawful punishment—Dr. King cut short his lecture series at Fisk University. He boarded an early morning flight to Atlanta, met his family, and continued on to Montgomery to turn himself in. When he arrived, "an almost holiday atmosphere prevailed" outside the jail. A jubilant Ralph Abernathy, who had been arrested the previous day, explained to Dr. King what had happened:

> *People had rushed down to get arrested the day before. No one, it seems, had been frightened. No one had tried to evade arrest. Many Negroes had gone voluntarily to the sheriff's office to see if their names were on the list, and were even disappointed when they were not. A once fear-ridden people had been transformed. Those who had previously trembled before the law were now proud to be arrested for the cause of freedom.*

Dr. King and his fellow protesters courted arrest several years later in Birmingham. A week into the Birmingham Campaign, a court injunction was issued, which banned all demonstrations until disagreements between the protesters and the city's leadership could be heard in court. After Dr. King huddled with colleagues, they chose to not abide by the injunction. Dr. King convened a press conference to make their intentions clear. He reaffirmed his message at a mass meeting the following evening: "Injunction or no injunction, we're going to march. Here in Birmingham, we have reached the point of no return. Now they will know that an injunction can't stop us."

Dr. King remained firm in his position, saying "I don't know what will happen...But' I'm going to jail." In response, Bull Connor raised the price of bail bonds from $200 to $1,500 and vowed that he would "fill the jail full of any persons violating the law as long as I'm at City Hall." With over 3,000 arrests, Connor kept his promise to fill the jails, but he quickly ran out of space. Dr. King later remarked that, "For the first time in the civil rights movement, we were able to put into effect the Gandhian principle: 'Fill up the jails.'"

Dr. King acknowledged on many occasions that the Birmingham Campaign in particular, and the civil rights movement in general, were in fact, "patterned after the Gandhian movement in India." In a press conference held on July 5, 1963, Dr. King reflected on the inspiration for his direct-action campaigns:

> *Some years ago, when I first studied the Gandhian philosophy and the method of nonviolent resistance, I came to the conclusion that it was the most potent weapon available to oppressed people in their struggle for freedom and human dignity. And I would say that this overall direct-action movement with it's sit-ins and its stand-ins, it's wade-ins, it's kneel-ins, it's mass marches and pilgrimages, and all of the other elements that enter the struggle, have been patterned a great deal after Gandhi.*

As Gandhi put Satyagraha into practice and refined his methods of civil disobedience, he implored his followers to obey certain rules of engagement, so to speak. First, he taught that civil disobedience does not mean total disregard for the law. In fact, Gandhi stated that:

> *A Satyagrahi obeys the laws of society intelligently and of his own free will, because he considers it to be his sacred duty to do so. It is only when a person has thus obeyed the laws of society scrupulously that he is in a position to judge as to which particular rules are good and just and which unjust and iniquitous. Only then does the right accrue to him of the civil disobedience of certain laws in well-defined circumstances.*

Second, Gandhi taught that, while engaging in civil disobedience, one must remain disciplined. As he explained,

Civility is the most difficult part of Satyagraha. Civility does not here mean the mere outward gentleness of speech cultivated for the occasion, but an inborn gentleness and a desire to do the opponent good.

Third, before a people could be fit for offering civil disobedience, "they should thoroughly understand its deeper implications." They must realize that civil disobedience must have "its roots not in hatred, but in love." Gandhi believed that, to remain civil, disobedience:

Must be sincere, respectful, restrained, never defiant, must be based upon some well-understood principle, must not be capricious and, above all, must have no ill will or hatred behind it.

Gandhi taught his followers to refrain from any public display of anger. However, Gandhi considered anger to be a sort of fuel: "I have learnt through bitter experience that one supreme lesson to conserve my anger, and as heat conserved is transmuted into energy, even so our anger controlled can be transmuted into a power which can move the world."

If Gandhi saw that his followers were not completely faithful to the tenants of Satyagraha, he discontinued protests. Prior to starting a new campaign, Gandhi taught that "Satyagraha is essentially a weapon of the truthful" and that "A Satyagrahi is pledged to non-violence." Therefore, "unless people observe it in thought, word, and deed," he would terminate the protest, even if there were signs that success was imminent.

Following Gandhi's example, Dr. King invited followers to obey similar rules of engagement. In 1963, demonstrators in Birmingham attended workshops on nonviolent protest sponsored by the Southern Christian Leadership Conference (SCLC). Attendees were asked to sign a commitment card that came to be known as the Birmingham Pledge, which read as follows:

> I hereby pledge myself—my person and body—to the nonviolent movement. Therefore, I will keep the following ten commandments:
>
> 1. Meditate daily on the teachings and life of Jesus
> 2. Remember always that the non-violent movement seeks justice and reconciliation—not victory
> 3. Walk and talk in the manner of love, for God is love
> 4. Pray daily to be used by God in order that all men might be free
> 5. Sacrifice personal wishes in order that all men might be free
> 6. Observe with both friend and foe the ordinary rules of courtesy
> 7. Seek to perform regular service for others and for the world
> 8. Refrain from the violence of fist, tongue, or heart
> 9. Strive to be in good spiritual and bodily health
> 10. Follow the directions of the movement and of the captain on the demonstration

Gandhi's influence can be seen in the "commandments" that protesters were asked to affirm. The pledge emphasized love and prohibited violence. The pledge also reflected Dr. King's beliefs that: "we must pursue peaceful ends through peaceful means" and the "Means we use must be as pure as the ends we seek."

In a speech delivered in Leavenworth, KS in December, 1859, Lincoln suggested that a noble cause could never justify ignoble means: "Old John Brown has been executed for treason against a State. We cannot object, even though he agreed with us in thinking slavery wrong. That cannot excuse violence, bloodshed, and treason."

Lincoln's speech in Leavenworth echoed a sentiment that he had expressed two decades prior. In his Lyceum speech, Lincoln arrived at a conclusion with which Gandhi and Dr. King, both pioneers in nonviolent civil disobedience, would have surely agreed:

> *There is no grievance that is a fit object of redress by mob law. In any case that arises, as for instance, the promulgation of abolitionism, one of two positions is necessarily true; that is, the thing is right within itself, and therefore deserves the protection of all law and all good citizens; or, it is wrong, and therefore proper to be prohibited by legal enactments; and in neither case, is the interposition of mob law, either necessary, justifiable, or excusable.*

Heroes don't always obey the rules. But not all disobedience is heroic. There is a fundamental difference between a violent protester who disobeys just laws for *selfish* reasons and a hero who disobeys unjust laws for *selfless* reasons. Marching peacefully to draw attention to injustice is not the same as joining an angry mob to express discontent through destruction and violence.

When heroes disobey, they do so for the right reasons, which are invariably selfless.

Chapter 11

Defending Values

The greatest of all virtues is love
-Martin Luther King, Jr.

In the 1940s, Clayton "Bud" Collyer's deep baritone heralded the start of each episode of the radio drama with the iconic words,

"Faster than a speeding bullet! More powerful than a locomotive! Able to leap tall buildings at a single bound!"

"Look! Up in the sky!"
"It's a bird!"
"It's a plane!"
"It's Superman!"

"Yes, it's Superman - strange visitor from another planet who came to Earth with powers and abilities far beyond those of mortal men. Superman—defender of law and order. Champion of equal rights, valiant, courageous fighter against the forces of hate and prejudice, who disguised as Clark Kent, mild-mannered reporter for a great metropolitan newspaper, fights a never-ending battle for truth, justice and the American way."

Those iconic lines, written by Allen Ducovny and Robert Maxwell, revealed Superman's powers—and his principles. Superman used his extraordinary abilities, not for his own selfish gain, but to prevent hate and prejudice. Superman used his super powers to ensure law, order, and equal rights—to promote truth, justice, and the American way. His might made him a super man. But his motives made him a super hero.

A Noble Cause

In his speeches, sermons, and writings, Dr. King focused on the themes of freedom, justice, and equality. On August 28, 1963, Dr. King wove these threads together in his most iconic speech. Standing in front of the Lincoln Memorial, Dr. King delivered his "I Have a Dream" speech to the 250,000 gathered at the "March on Washington for Jobs and Freedom." Quite appropriately, he began his speech with a focus on freedom:

> *Five score years ago, a great American, in whose symbolic shadow we stand today, signed the Emancipation Proclamation. This momentous decree came as a great beacon light of hope to millions of Negro slaves who had been seared in the flames of withering injustice. It came as a joyous daybreak to end the long night of their captivity.*

> *But one hundred years later, the Negro still is not free; one hundred years later, the life of the Negro is still sadly crippled by the manacles of segregation and the chains of discrimination; one hundred years later, the Negro lives on a lonely island of poverty in the midst of a vast ocean of material prosperity; one hundred years later, the Negro is still languished in the corners of American society and finds himself in exile in his own land.*

He then shifted to the theme of justice:

So we've come here today to dramatize a shameful condition. In a sense we've come to our nation's capital to cash a check. When the architects of our republic wrote the magnificent words of the Constitution and the Declaration of Independence, they were signing a promissory note to which every American was to fall heir. This note was the promise that all men, yes, black men as well as white men, would be guaranteed the inalienable rights of life, liberty, and the pursuit of happiness.

It is obvious today that America has defaulted on this promissory note in so far as her citizens of color are concerned. Instead of honoring this sacred obligation, America has given the Negro people a bad check, a check which has come back marked "insufficient funds." But we refuse to believe that the bank of justice is bankrupt. We refuse to believe that there are insufficient funds in the great vaults of opportunity of this nation. And so we have come to cash this check, a check that will give us upon demand the riches of freedom and the security of justice.

We have also come to this hallowed spot to remind America of the fierce urgency of now. This is no time to engage in the luxury of cooling off or to take the tranquilizing drug of gradualism. Now is the time to make real the promises of democracy; now is the time to rise from the dark and desolate valley of segregation to the sunlit path of racial justice; now is the time to lift our nation from the quicksands of racial injustice to the solid rock of brotherhood; now is the time to make justice a reality for all of God's children.

Then, Dr. King focused on equality:

I say to you today, my friends, so even though we face the difficulties of today and tomorrow, I still have a dream. It is a dream deeply rooted in the American dream. I have a dream that one day this nation will rise up and live out the true meaning of its creed, "We hold these truths to be self-evident, that all men are created equal."

I have a dream that one day on the red hills of Georgia, sons of former slaves and the sons of former slave-owners will be able to sit down together at the table of brotherhood. I have a dream that one day even the state of Mississippi, a state sweltering with the heat of injustice, sweltering with the heat of oppression, will be transformed into an oasis of freedom and justice. I have a dream that my four little children will one day live in a nation where they will not be judged by the color of their skin but by the content of their character.

Dr. King concluded his remarks by returning to the theme of freedom:

With this faith we will be able to work together, to pray together, to struggle together, to go to jail together, to stand up for freedom together, knowing that we will be free one day. And this will be the day. This will be the day when all of God's children will be able to sing with new meaning, "My country 'tis of thee, sweet land of liberty, of thee I sing. Land where my father died, land of the pilgrim's pride, from every mountainside, let freedom ring." And if America is to be a great nation, this must become true.

So let freedom ring from the prodigious hilltops of New Hampshire; let freedom ring from the mighty mountains of New York; let freedom ring from the heightening Alleghenies of Pennsylvania; let freedom ring from the snow-capped Rockies of Colorado; let freedom ring from the curvaceous slopes of California. But not only that. Let freedom ring from Stone Mountain of Georgia; let freedom ring from Lookout Mountain of Tennessee; let freedom ring from every hill and mole hill of Mississippi. From every mountainside, let freedom ring.

And when this happens, and when we allow freedom to ring, when we let it ring from every village and every hamlet, from every state and every city, we will be able to speed up that day when all of God's children, black men and white men, Jews and Gentiles, Protestants and Catholics, will be able to join hands and sing in the words of the old Negro spiritual: "Free at last! Free at last! Thank God Almighty, we are free at last!"

As Dr. King left the podium, he left no one wondering where he stood. Dr. King was devoted to seeing Freedom, Justice, and Equality for all citizens.

Principles Over Precedent

During the Montgomery Bus Boycott, Dr. King, along with fellow leaders from the Montgomery Improvement Association, met with opposing leaders to broker a settlement. After representatives from the city and bus company refused to yield, a white Methodist minister spoke against the boycott and in favor of segregation.

When it was his turn to speak, Dr. King observed that many in attendance had "been talking a great deal this morning about customs." Then, Dr. King affirmed his belief that principles must take precedence over precedent:

It has been affirmed that any change in the present conditions would mean going against the 'cherished customs' of our community. But if the customs are wrong we have every reason in the world to change them. The decision, which we must make now is whether we will give our allegiance to outmoded and unjust customs or to the ethical demands of the universe. As Christians we owe our ultimate allegiance to God and His will, rather than to man and his folkways.

A few months later, Dr. King addressed his congregation at Dexter Ave Baptist Church. In his "When Peace Becomes Obnoxious" sermon, Dr. King noted that some community members blamed the boycott for "peace being destroyed in the community, the destroying of good race relations."

Dr. King acknowledged that tensions had, in fact, increased since the protest began, but maintained that the protests were necessary because "peace is not merely the absence of this tension, but the presence of justice." Dr. King recognized that "it is true that if the Negro accepts his place, accepts exploitation and injustice, there will be peace, but," Dr. King continued, "it would be a peace boiled down to stagnant complacency, deadening passivity, and if peace means this, I don't want peace."

Then, employing the literary device of anaphora, which he so often used to great effect, Dr. King proclaimed:

> *If peace means accepting second-class citizenship, I don't want it.*
>
> *If peace means keeping my mouth shut in the midst of injustice and evil, I don't want it.*
>
> *If peace means being complacently adjusted to a deadening status quo, I don't want peace.*
>
> *If peace means a willingness to be exploited economically, dominated politically, humiliated and segregated, I don't want peace.*
>
> *So in a passive, non-violent manner, we must revolt against this peace.*

For Dr. King, peace was an important objective. But seeking peace was secondary to—and contingent upon—establishing freedom, justice, and equality for all. Dr. King insisted on a "permanent, positive peace," saying, "You have never had real peace in Montgomery. You have had a sort of negative peace in which the Negro too often accepted his state of subordination. But this is not true peace."

For Dr. King, the ideals of freedom, justice, and equality were not arbitrarily chosen aspirations to strive toward. They were means to even more important ends. By promoting freedom, justice, and equality, Dr. King sought to promote human dignity, prevent human suffering, and protect human life. Nelson Mandela fought for these same principles.

In his defense at the Rivonia Trial, Mandela provided context for his crimes, which were aimed at improving living conditions for Africans. Mandela explained how apartheid policies and racist norms robbed Africans of their self-respect:

> *The lack of human dignity experienced by Africans is the direct result of the policy of white supremacy. White supremacy implies black inferiority. Legislation designed to preserve white supremacy entrenches this notion. Menial tasks in South Africa are invariably performed by Africans. When anything has to be carried or cleaned the white man looks around for an African to do it for him, whether the African is employed by him or not.*

He then described the conditions in which many Africans lived:

> *Poverty and the breakdown of family life have secondary effects. Children wander about the streets of the townships because they have no schools to go to, or no money to enable them to go to school, or no parents at home to see that they go to school, because both parents (if there be two) have to work to keep the family alive. This leads to a breakdown in moral standards, to an alarming rise in illegitimacy and to growing violence which erupts, not only politically, but everywhere.*

Mandela affirmed the ideals that he and his ANC colleagues were fighting for:

> *Africans want a just share in the whole of South Africa; they want security and a stake in society. Above all, we want equal political rights, because without them our disabilities will be permanent...this then is what the ANC if fighting for. Their struggle is a truly national one. It is a struggle of the African people, inspired by their own suffering and their own experience. It is a struggle for the right to live.*

Stand for Principles, Not Against People

As Mother Teresa became internationally known, "Crowds came to meet her wherever she went. Churches were so packed that special bodyguards had to be appointed to prevent her from being crushed." Members of the international media followed Mother Teresa like the Whitehouse press pool follows the President of the United States. She once remarked that "I only have to cough and the world knows about it."

Mother Teresa offered up her loss of privacy as a sacrifice to God. She often joked that, for every picture taken of her, a soul should be released from purgatory. Photos, interviews, and constant attention were a small price she was willing to pay.

Mother Teresa knew that "her presence alone was enough now to focus the eyes of the world on a particular need, that sometimes she could tread where other leaders in the Roman Catholic Church could not, and that the high public profile, however personally painful, gave her a capacity to influence."

Mother Teresa was not shy about using her influence when she felt she could intervene. Across the globe, she was held in such high regard that it was almost taken for granted that "her intervention alone would be enough to resolve a problematic situation."

As war drums beat prior to Operation Desert Storm, Mother Teresa wrote a letter to the leaders of Iraq and the United States of America:

Dear President George Bush and President Saddam Hussein,

I come to you with tears in my eyes and God's love in my heart to plead to you for the poor and those who will become poor if the war that we all dread and fear happens. I beg you with my whole heart to work for, to labor for God's peace and to be reconciled with one another. You both have your cases to make and your people to care for but first please listen to the One who came into the world to teach us peace. You have the power and the strength to destroy God's presence and image, his men, his women and his children. Please listen to the will of God. God has created us to be loved by his love and not destroyed by our hatred. In the short term there may be winners and losers in this war that we all dread, but that never can, nor ever will justify the suffering, pain and loss of life which your weapons will cause.[1]

Mother Teresa's tender concern for those who would become collateral damage—expressed boldly to the leaders of two feuding nations—was not enough to prevent the first Gulf War. But this letter illustrates a central feature of Mother Teresa: she was never afraid to confront iniquity where she saw iniquity or to stand up for the most vulnerable—even when the odds were against her. Neither was she timid when expressing opinions with which she knew her audiences might disagree—or take offense.

On February 3, 1994, Mother Teresa addressed the National Prayer Breakfast in Washington, DC. In her speech (which she uncharacteristically wrote and revised beforehand), Mother Teresa asked her audience to love until it hurts. Those who assumed that Mother Teresa would focus only on the suffering experienced by the poorest of the poor in developing nations were surprised to find that her speech was more focused on the suffering experienced by people living in wealthy countries in the West.

She recalled visiting "a home where they kept all these old parents of sons and daughters who had just put them into an institution and forgotten them." As members of her audience began to shift in their seats, Mother Teresa continued: "I saw that in that home these old people had everything—good food, comfortable place, television, everything—but everyone was looking toward the door. And I did not see a single one with a smile on the face. I turned to Sister and I asked: "Why do these people who have every comfort here, why are they all looking toward the door? Why are they not smiling?"

---

1 As usual, Mother Teresa signed her letter, "God bless you. M. Teresa, MC."

The Sister responded, "This is the way it is nearly every day. They are expecting, they are hoping that a son or daughter will come to visit them. They are hurt because they are forgotten."

With a simple story, Mother Teresa focused the attention of her audience on spiritual poverty that stems from a "neglect of love." Throughout her speech, her words became increasingly personal:

> *Maybe in our own family we have somebody who is feeling lonely, who is feeling sick, who is feeling worried. Are we there? Are we there to be with them, or do we merely put them in the care of others? Are we willing to give until it hurts in order to be with our families, or do we put our own interests first?*

Mother Teresa pointed to the reality that, in the West, so many children used illicit drugs. She concluded that this societal affliction started at home:

> *Why is it like that, when those in the West have so many more things than those in the East? And the answer was: 'Because there is no one in the family to receive them.' Our children depend on us for everything - their health, their nutrition, their security, their coming to know and love God. For all of this, they look to us with trust, hope and expectation. But often father and mother are so busy they have no time for their children, or perhaps they are not even married or have given up on their marriage. So the children go to the streets and get involved in drugs or other things. We are talking of love of the child which is where love and peace must begin. These are the things that break peace.*

Then, after asking her audience to consider how well they were loving their parents and children—and the degree to which their selfishness and unwillingness to love until it hurt caused their loved ones to suffer—Mother Teresa managed to become even more provocative. While addressing a room full of politicians, she addressed the most polarizing political issue:

But I feel that the greatest destroyer of peace today is abortion, because it is a war against the child, a direct killing of the innocent child, murder by the mother herself.

And if we accept that a mother can kill even her own child, how can we tell other people not to kill one another? How do we persuade a woman not to have an abortion? As always, we must persuade her with love and we remind ourselves that love means to be willing to give until it hurts. Jesus gave even His life to love us. So, the mother who is thinking of abortion, should be helped to love, that is, to give until it hurts her plans, or her free time, to respect the life of her child. The father of that child, whoever he is, must also give until it hurts.

By abortion, the mother does not learn to love, but kills even her own child to solve her problems.

And, by abortion, the father is told that he does not have to take any responsibility at all for the child he has brought into the world. That father is likely to put other women into the same trouble. So abortion just leads to more abortion.

Any country that accepts abortion is not teaching its people to love, but to use any violence to get what they want. This is why the greatest destroyer of love and peace is abortion.

Many people are very, very concerned with the children of India, with the children of Africa where quite a few die of hunger, and so on. Many people are also concerned about all the violence in this great country of the United States. These concerns are very good. But often these same people are not concerned with the millions who are being killed by the deliberate decision of their own mothers. And this is what is the greatest destroyer of peace today - abortion which brings people to such blindness.

Rather than simply lamenting a problem and assigning blame, Mother Teresa offered herself and her sisters as a solution to the problem,

> *I will tell you something beautiful. We are fighting abortion by adoption - by care of the mother and adoption for her baby. We have saved thousands of lives. We have sent word to the clinics, to the hospitals and police stations: "Please don't destroy the child; we will take the child." So we always have someone tell the mothers in trouble: "Come, we will take care of you, we will get a home for your child." And we have a tremendous demand from couples who cannot have a child.*

Then, she appealed directly to each member of her audience:

> *Please don't kill the child. I want the child. Please give me the child. I am willing to accept any child who would be aborted and to give that child to a married couple who will love the child and be loved by the child. From our children's home in Calcutta alone, we have saved over 3,000 children from abortion. These children have brought such love and joy to their adopting parents and have grown up so full of love and joy.*

Mother Teresa expressed her aversion to abortion as directly and as forcefully as one possibly could. Many in the audience disagreed with her position, but nobody could question her courage or her consistency. Mother Teresa worked tirelessly to prevent human suffering and to protect human life—whether in the form of a fetus not yet born or in the form of a convicted felon on death row. By offering her sisters as a solution, nobody could question her willingness to provide a solution to the problem of unwanted pregnancies.

Anyone can see problems. Anyone can complain. But heroes don't just see problems. Heroes find solutions.

In her Prayer Breakfast speech, Mother Teresa made members of her audience feel uneasy. But not because she was uncharitable or unkind.

Mother Teresa did not vilify those who disagreed with her, including women who had sought abortions. In fact, women who had experienced abortion "belonged to a little circle of privileged persons whom Mother Teresa embraced with heartfelt love and in a special way." Despite their decision, Mother Teresa considered these women to be no less worthy—and in even greater need—of the tender love of Jesus. After meeting with her, "many young women with tear-stained faces…were once again each able to trust in the love and forgiveness of God that Mother Teresa had just shown her so tangibly."

The tender love of Mother Teresa touched the hearts of individuals and audiences. Tender love allowed Mother Teresa to confront them with tough love—and, in some cases, to influence their beliefs—without losing their affection or admiration.

In standing up for some people, Mother Teresa did not stand against other people. Heroes stand for principles, not against people.

Consistency

Abraham Lincoln and Dr. King prepared their speeches meticulously. Gandhi and Mother Teresa almost never prepared remarks in advance. But each of these exceptional individuals could enchant an audience—even when called upon to deliver extemporaneous remarks. Why? Because they had spent a lifetime honing their beliefs and clarifying their thinking.

On one occasion, Gandhi spoke for over two hours. After Gandhi was done speaking, a reporter from London approached Gandhi's secretary, Mahadev Desai, and inquired, "How is it that he is able to speak so well for such a long time without any preparation, without any prompting, without even any notes?" Desai responded that, "What Gandhi thinks, what he feels, what he says, and what he does are all the same. He does not need notes. You and I, we think one thing, feel another, say a third, and do a fourth, so we need notes and files to keep track."

Gandhi was consistent in his principles and clear in his convictions. He was able to speak, not just from the heart, but from his mind and soul, which were perfectly aligned. As Gandhi said,

> *At the time of writing I never think of what I have said before. My aim is not to be consistent with my previous statements on a given question, but to be consistent with truth as it may present itself to me at a given moment. The result has been that I have grown from truth to truth; I have saved my memory an undue strain; and what is more, whenever I have been obliged to compare my writing even of fifty years ago with the latest, I have discovered no inconsistency between the two.*

Likewise, Lincoln claimed, "I think it cannot be shown that once I have taken a position, I have ever retreated from it." In Lincoln's last public address, delivered April 11, 1865, he reaffirmed his belief that "Important principles may and must be inflexible." Lincoln urged his fellow Republicans to stick to their principles because "No party can command respect which sustains this year, what it opposed last."

Like Lincoln and Gandhi, it is easier to find instances where Dr. King repeated himself—whether those words were delivered in sermons, speeches, press conferences or were written in letters, articles, or books—than to find any statement he made, which contradicts another.

Dr. King's "brand," so to speak, is so consistent and so clear that it would be easy to imagine what he would have to say about current social issues—even issues that had not yet emerged during his lifetime. Likewise, the adherence of Gandhi, Mandela, and Mother Teresa to core principles allows us to confidently answer questions like "what would Gandhi do?" "What would Mandela advise?" "What would Mother Teresa say?"

Heroes are principled. And heroes are consistent in their principles.

Clarity

Mother Teresa left her teaching post to serve the poorest of the poor, but she never stopped teaching. She simply moved to a much larger classroom. As one biographer noted, "Mother Teresa had a gift of putting complicated theological concepts into very simple short sentences and slogans that were easy to remember." Her writing was usually succinct and poetic:

Life is opportunity, avail it
Life is beauty, admire it
Life is bliss, taste it,
Life is a dream, realize it
Life is a challenge, meet it
Life is a duty, complete it
Life is a game, play it
Life is costly, care for it
Life is a wealth, keep it
Life is love, enjoy it
Life is mystery, know it
Life is a promise, fulfill it
Life is sorrow, overcome it
Life is a song, sing it
Life is a struggle, accept it
Life is a tragedy, brace it
Life is an adventure, care it
Life is life, save it!
Life is luck, make it
Life is too precious, do not destroy it.

Mother Teresa found practical ways to share her wisdom, even in brief contacts with countless people who approached her. Mother Teresa would often take a person by the hand and point to each of their five fingers as she repeated the words of Jesus, "you did it to me." Mother Teresa also handed out "business cards," on which was printed:

> *The fruit of silence is prayer, the fruit of prayer is faith, the fruit of faith is love, the fruit of love is service, the fruit of service is peace.*

Her name didn't appear on her business cards. But the nature of her business was clear. When Mother Teresa handed out the cards, she would smile and tell recipients that "this is good business."

Mother Teresa's ability to make important ideas simple, memorable, and actionable is a characteristic that she shared with other heroes.

Gandhi communicated his vision with short, simple, memorable phrases like "Be the change you wish to see in the world" and "An eye for an eye leaves the whole world blind."

Nelson Mandela's name is synonymous with the power of forgiveness. He asked his fellow South Africans to "Forget the past" because "Resentment is like drinking poison and then hoping that it will kill your enemies." Dr. King's name is synonymous with his dream: "not by the color of their skin but by the content of their character…free at last, free at last, thank God almighty, we are free at last!" And Abraham Lincoln's immortal words revealed the better angels of *his* nature: "With malice toward none and generosity toward all."

Heroes have a message. And heroes deliver their message clearly, concisely, and with conviction.

Conviction

On March 1, 1859, Lincoln implored his fellow Republicans to remain steadfast in the conviction that slavery should not be extended beyond its current borders. Lincoln concluded his speech in Chicago with reassurances that his party would ultimately prevail:

All you have to do is to keep the faith, to remain steadfast to the right, to stand by your banner. Nothing should lead you to leave your guns. Stand together, ready, with match in hand. Allow nothing to turn you to the right or to the left. Remember how long you have been in setting out on the true course; how long you have been in getting your neighbors to understand and believe as you now do. Stand by your principles; stand by your guns; and victory complete and permanent is sure at last.

As Mandela concluded his Rivonia Defense, he set his notes down on the table before him and looked directly at Judge de Wet. In the quiet courtroom, Mandela recited the final words of his defense:

During my lifetime I have dedicated myself to this struggle of the African people. I have fought against white domination, and I have fought against black domination. I have cherished the ideal of a democratic and free society in which all persons live together in harmony and with equal opportunities. It is an ideal which I hope to live for and to achieve. But if needs be, it is an ideal for which I am prepared to die.

Nelson Mandela was prepared to die to uphold his ideals and Gandhi was prepared to die to defend *his* ideals. Gandhi was under constant threat as he traveled to certain parts of his native India. He noted that, some people "even went the length of threatening me with assassination if I went to the Punjab." These were not empty threats. There were eight attempts on his life. Yet, Gandhi never cowered in the face of danger. Prior to the final, fatal assassination attempt, Gandhi remarked that he "never liked to live for the sake of living."

Dr. King also lived with the grim possibility of assassination. But Dr. King believed that a man who won't die for something is not "fit to live." He explained to his followers that, "there comes a time when one must take a position that is neither safe nor politic nor popular, but he must take it because his conscience tells him it is right." He pleaded with his followers to "stand up for some great principle, some great issue, some great cause." Dr. King asked his congregants to live for something worth dying for—and admonished those who were unwilling to take the necessary risk.

> *You refuse to do it because you are afraid. You refuse to do it because you want to live longer. You're afraid that you will lose your job, or you are afraid that you will be criticized or that you will lose your popularity, or you're afraid that somebody will stab you or shoot at you or bomb your house. So you refuse to take a stand. Well, you may go on and live until you are ninety, but you are just as dead at thirty-eight as you would be at ninety. And the cessation of breathing in your life is but the belated announcement of an earlier death of the spirit. You died when you refused to stand up for right. You died when you refused to stand up for truth.*

Despite persistent threats, Dr. King continued to appear publicly with minimal security. He faced the possibility of assassination with reassurance that "The quality, not the longevity, of one's life is what is important." As a Christian, Dr. King held firm to his belief that "The end of life is not to be happy, nor to achieve pleasure and avoid pain, but to do the will of God, come what may."

Dr. King found solace in the realization that, even if he were assassinated, his courageous stand for people and principles would not be in vain because "you can kill the dreamer, but you can't kill the dream."

Chapter 12

Noah's Character Arc

*One of the most difficult things is not
to change society but to change yourself*
-Nelson Mandela

In the Biblical story of the flood, Noah is chosen by God to build an Ark. The world had become filled with unfaithful people whose thoughts were "only evil all the time." Noah was seen as a righteous man living among an unrighteous generation. After Noah was called, he was faithful in building the ark, faithful in loading the ark, and faithful in staying on the ark until the water receded. Noah started out faithful and Noah remained faithful.

In some ways, the Noah's Ark story follows the story arc summarized by the Hero's Journey. The hero received a call to action, entered the belly of the whale, and returned victorious. But unlike the prototypical protagonist who embarks on the hero's journey, Noah was not a reluctant commoner who rejected the call. Noah was a faithful servant who immediately obeyed. And unlike most epic tales, in the story of the flood, there is no character arc. As the world was transformed, Noah's character remained unchanged.

In his 1949 book, *The Hero with 1,000 Faces*, Joseph Campbell suggested that most of the world's great myths share a common formula—regardless of where and when each myth originated. Campbell summarized the hero's journey plot structure as follows:

> *A hero ventures forth from the world of common day into a region of supernatural wonder: fabulous forces are there encountered and a decisive victory is won: the hero comes back from this mysterious adventure with the power to bestow boons on his fellow man.*

The hero's journey is the plot structure of nearly all epic stories. The hero's journey *also* depicts the transformation of the protagonist from common villager to triumphant hero.

At the beginning of the hero's journey, the hero initially rejects the call. Why? Usually, out of fear for himself or a lack of concern for others. In short, the soon-to-be-hero starts out as an uncaring coward.

As the hero's journey begins, the protagonist undergoes a series of trials and challenges, which result in initial failure but eventual success. After descending into the abyss, the hero forsakes his desire for safety and comfort and takes responsibility for the wellbeing of others. His care and courage grow to the extent that he is willing to face an enormous test—often in the form of a monstrous villain—to save the world.

By letting go of his old self, the protagonist undergoes a metamorphosis. In protecting the village, he acquires a new identity. The common villager becomes the triumphant hero.

Multiple Pathways

There is a special group of scientists called embryologists, who study the development of embryos. Embryologists have jobs because embryos *don't* always follow the same developmental pathway. From the same starting point, a set of embryos can reach different destinations. Embryologists call this phenomenon "multifinality."

Sometimes, an embryo is affected by a "teratogen." The term teratogen, which literally means "monster forming," refers to anything—such as a drug, virus, or bacteria—that can disrupt the development of an embryo.

In the late 1950s, a drug called Thalidomide was prescribed to expectant mothers in 46 countries for morning sickness. If taken within the first 42 days of a pregnancy, thalidomide had devastating consequences on the developing child, including severe birth defects to the brain. Thalidomide was never approved by the FDA. In the United States, the drug was only distributed to a few women participating in clinical trials. But sadly, before the terrible consequences were discovered, between 10,000-20,000 children worldwide were born with severe birth defects from Thalidomide.

More recently, the Zika virus, which was discovered in the Zika Forest in Uganda in 1947, re-emerged as a threat to public health in the Americas around 2015. Most adults infected by the virus displayed minor symptoms such as fever, headache, joint pain, and rash. But the virus had devastating effects *in utero*, leading to severe birth defects, including neurocognitive disorders and microcephaly (meaning a child's head circumference is much smaller than expected).

In these two incidents, which occurred sixty-five years apart, babies were born with profound brain impairments, which were attributed to two different teratogens. When a similar destination—such as the maldevelopment of the brain—is reached from different starting points, embryologists call this phenomenon "equifinality."

The concepts of multifinality and equifinality, which originated in embryology, have been used to describe phenomena in other fields of study, including child development. These two concepts—multifinality and equifinality—can also help us see how ordinary people become heroes.

Two Saints

In the late nineteenth century, a boy in Western India listened intently for a bell, which would signal the end of each school day. Then, he would run home, afraid that if he were to talk to anyone, they would tease him. He was "very shy and avoided all company." His books and school lessons were his "sole companions." He went to bed each night with the light on because he was terrified of the dark; he "would imagine ghosts coming from one direction, thieves from another and serpents from a third."

He got married at the "preposterously early" age of thirteen years old. A warm, loving husband he was not. By his own admission, he "took no time in assuming the authority of a husband." He tried to control the activities of his child bride and made baseless accusations of infidelity. Consequently, his wife made a point to go out as often as she wished. This infuriated him. He and his young wife often refused to speak to one another. Due to their poor relationship, and his inability to express himself, he felt ashamed that he could not disclose his fears even to the girl sleeping by his side.

As a young man, he traveled to England to continue his studies. But while living in London, he was terribly homesick, suffered from insomnia, and cried often while thinking of his mother back home.

Both in the classroom, and in social situations, he was at a loss for words. Even when he "felt tempted to speak," he was unable to express himself. On one occasion, he was asked to deliver a few words at a social event. Speaking extemporaneously was "out of the question" for him, so he took time to write down his speech. But when he arose, his "vision became blurred and [he] trembled." A friend stepped in to read the speech, leaving the embarrassed young man "sad at heart for [his] incapacity."

The young man completed his law degree, but his fearful disposition remained. After returning to India to practice law, he agreed to represent his first defendant in Small Cases Court. But when it came time to cross-examine the witnesses, he froze. In his own words:

> *I stood up, but my heart sank into my boots. My head was reeling and I felt as though the whole court was doing likewise. I could think of no question to ask…I hastened from the Court, not knowing whether my client won or lost her case, but I was ashamed of myself, and I decided*

not to take up any more cases until I had courage enough to conduct them.

Why dwell on the failures of someone who was painfully shy as a child, harsh as a husband, and ineffectual as a defense attorney? To demonstrate that Gandhi was not always Gandhi. Before the title of "Mahatma" was bestowed upon him by millions of admirers, Mohandas Gandhi was nothing like the bold leader revered throughout the world. Before Gandhi moved to South Africa and witnessed the oppression of his fellow Indians, he lacked both the compassion that stimulated his public work and the courage that allowed him to press on despite increasing threats to his wellbeing. It was only when he answered the call to help that Mohandas (an ordinary name for a boy growing up in Western India) began his transformation into Mahatma ("great soul").

Gandhi shared many things in common with a woman who, in 1948 (the year Gandhi was assassinated), left the Loreto Sisters to devote her life to serving the oppressed poor of India. Both Gandhi and Mother Teresa were citizens of India, albeit one by birth and the other by choice. They dressed like the poor, ate like the poor, lived like the poor, and worked with powerful leaders to benefit the poor. Like Gandhi, Mother Teresa called her associates "co-workers."

Mother Teresa followed Gandhi's example and often expressed great respect for him. So much so that she named the leprosy center in Titlagarh "Gandhiji Prem Nivas," meaning "Gandhi Centre of Love." But Mother Teresa differed from Gandhi in other ways.

Growing up in Skopje, Agnes Bojaxhiu was "a popular child with an appealing sense of fun and plenty of female friends, although shy with boys and inclined at times to be somewhat withdrawn and introverted." She was an above average student who was especially fond of music and writing. Agnes was "a born organizer" and "something of a driving force in all the activities she undertook."

Agnes' early life was shaped by her mother, Dranafile Bojaxhiu, who brought her children to morning mass and prayed the Rosary with them each day. She introduced her children to the rituals of Catholicism and modeled the practical tenants of their Christian faith. The Bojaxhiu home became "a gathering place for the poor for whom she cared with a gentle warmth." When Agnes's brother Lazar asked their mother where the visitors came from, she replied, "some of them are our relations but all of them are our people." Agnes accompanied her mother on countless visits to sick and poor members of their community. Dranafile tried to impress on Agnes the importance of humble service: "When you do good, do it quietly, as if you were throwing a stone into the sea."

When Agnes decided to pursue a religious vocation, Dranafile withheld her blessing, but only to test the strength of her daughter's commitment. When Agnes kept her resolve, Dranafile supported her decision to pursue a life in ministry. After joining the Sisters of Loreto, Agnes lived anonymously for about 20 years, working as a teacher, administrator, and nun. Fellow nuns remembered Agnes as unusually prayerful but "in other respects she was in the most part unremarkable, not particularly educated, not particularly intelligent."

Leaving the safe confines of the school to show tender love to the poorest of the poor was a pivotal moment in her transformation from "Agnes" to "Mother Teresa." Agnes was a villager who, through small acts of kindness done with great love, became a hero.

Despite reaching a similar destination, Gandhi and Mother Teresa followed different paths to prominence. Gandhi was a tyrant at home and a coward in the living room, classroom, and courtroom. Mother Teresa was a likeable but unremarkable person who became a remarkable leader.

Like embryos, people sometimes reach similar destination from different starting points. What makes a hero a hero is not where they begin, but where they arrive.

Self-Love

Growth is not possible without change. Some people don't think they can change. Some people don't want to change. But no matter how much we resist, we can't prevent change. At best, we can influence the speed and the direction in which we change.

Interestingly, the one thing that prompts us to improve or prevents us from improving is the same: love.

The Greek language includes multiple words for love because there are multiple kinds of love. Some of the Greek words for love are —*philía* (brotherly love), *érōs* (romantic love), *storgé* (familial love), and *agápē* (unconditional love). There are also words for distortions of love—*lūdus* (game-playing love), *manía* (obsessive love), and *prágma* (checklist love). Each of these types of love are *inter*personal. But there is another type of Greek love that is *intra*personal.

The rise of social media "influencers" has paralleled a rise in recommendations to "love yourself." Self-love isn't a new idea. Self-love was discussed by the ancients. In fact, there is a special Greek word for self-love—*philautía*.

Philautía can be healthy or unhealthy, depending on whether the self-love is characterized by concern or conceit. Healthy self-love is based on concern for one's own wellbeing—caring for oneself in a way that you would care for a loved one. Unhealthy self-love, on the other hand, involves conceit—a prideful, arrogant, selfish appraisal of one's flawlessness.

There is a difference between love *for* self and love *of* self. Concern prompts change. Conceit prevents change.

A person who is truly concerned about their wellbeing—and the wellbeing of their future self—is motivated to improve. Why remain weak when you can grow strong? Why stay ignorant when you can learn? Why maintain bad habits when you can replace them with good ones? Why remain miserable when you can change your circumstances or mindset?

A person who is conceited, on the other hand, sees no reason to improve, to learn, or to grow. In fact, they have a compelling reason not to change. They are already perfect! Any change would simply introduce imperfections.

The distinction between concern and conceit parallels the difference between what Carol Dweck calls the "growth mindset" and the "fixed mindset." A person with a growth mindset is focused on becoming better; a person with a fixed mindset is focused on how good (or bad) they already are. A growth mindset is focused on improving oneself whereas a fixed mindset is focused on comparing oneself to others.

Someone with a growth mindset believes they *can* change whereas someone with a fixed mindset believes that "they are who they are." Each belief can become a self-fulfilling prophecy. In the words of Henry Ford, "If you think you can or if you think you can't, you are probably right."

People with a healthy form of *philautia* care for their own wellbeing. People with healthy self-love focus less on self-acceptance and more on self-improvement when it comes to the things they can and should control.

Social media influencers bastardize love by proclaiming their "love" to millions of anonymous "followers." Many of their followers feel a personal connection that does not actually exist. Social psychologists call these one-sided relationships "parasocial relationships."

Some social media influencers are walking, talking embodiments of self-conceit. It's not about their audience. It's about their image. They don't care about their followers. They care about their brand. They don't want love (a 2-way relationship). They want worship (a 1-way relationship). Their business model is built on accumulating as many parasocial relationships as possible. Their success is measured by the number of "likes" they receive, which translate to commissions on sales of products they endorse. They profit from strangers who mistake them for friends.

Social media influencers too often encourage "friends" and "followers" to celebrate flaws rather than fix them. But when people are encouraged to maintain unhealthy lives in the name of "positivity" or "being kind to yourself," the advice is both dangerous to followers and cowardly on the part of influencer.

Heroes do not celebrate fixable flaws. Heroes do not avoid interpersonal *or* intrapersonal conflict. Inner conflicts create cognitive dissonance, which prompts us to change. And change we must. Characters in movies need to change because if they don't change, they don't seem real. Real people need to change because growth and improvement are not possible without change.

Heroes are eager to become the best they can be.

Starting Within

Transformation—or the lack of transformation—in fictional characters helps us recognize character. Transformations cause us to admire, relate to, and cheer for heroes. A lack of transformation, on the other hand, causes us to detest villains.

As we saw earlier, Victor Hugo's *Les Misérables* is the story of a desperate villager, Jean Valjean, who (a) became a criminal by stealing a loaf of bread, then (b) became a wealthy industrialist and mayor, and finally, (c) became a hero by protecting the orphan daughter of one of his former factory workers. *Les Misérables* is also the story of Inspector Javert, who refused to change.

The transformation of Val Jean from bitter criminal to father figure was initiated by forgiveness and grace offered by Bishop Myriel, from whom Val Jean stole a set of silver. By asking a police officer to release Valjean, Bishop Myriel's act of mercy caused Valjean to repent of his criminal ways, which led to a restoration of his social standing and the redemption of his soul. But Valjean's offer of forgiveness and grace was refused by Javert, who chose to die rather than change.

Even though Val Jean was a convicted criminal and an escaped prisoner, it is Javert, not Valjean, who emerges as the villain of *Les Misérables*. A willingness to change demonstrates courage. Resistance to change reveals cowardice. As Blake Snyder[1] explains:

> *Stories are about change. And the measuring stick that tells us who succeeds and who doesn't is seen in the ability to change. Good guys are those who willingly accept change and see it as a positive force. Bad guys are those who refuse to change, who will curl up and die in their own juices, unable to move out of the rut their lies represent. To succeed in life is to be able to transform. That's why it's the basis not only of good storytelling but also the world's best-known religions. Change is good because it represents re-birth, the promise of a fresh start.*

To improve, a person must be able to see their faults and flaws. And they must be willing to modify their beliefs and behavior. Both require humility. Humility is difficult without surrendering to something or someone. In fiction, the hero must surrender to something greater than himself before he is able to step up to the final challenge. Joseph Campbell calls this phase "Atonement with the Father." By discarding vices and relinquishing flaws, a hero gains the ability to improve and the freedom to lead.

Lincoln, Gandhi, Dr. King, and Nelson Mandela expected more of themselves than from those around them. Mother Teresa was "strict and disciplined with herself, but at the same time kindly, considerate and extremely patient with others." In seeking to better serve those around them, heroes are relentless in their quest for self-improvement. As Lincoln stated, "Whether I shall ever be better I cannot tell; I awfully forebode that to remain as I am is impossible; I must die or be better."

Heroes influence people. But heroes start by influencing themselves. One reason influencing people is difficult is that it is impossible to change *their* behavior without first changing *your* behavior. This is a lesson that

---

[1] Author of the best-selling book on screenwriting, *Save the Cat!*

parents of toddlers can understand. The same is true when attempting to influence older children and adults. *Their* change must begin with *our* change. And our change must begin within. This timeless truth is the basis of Gandhi's iconic call to action: "Be the change you wish to see in the world."

Chapter 13

Fool's Gold

Must one kill to ensure there are no evildoers?
That makes two evildoers instead of one.
-Blaise Pascal

In comic books and superhero movies there are two types of protagonists: heroes and antiheroes.

Heroes are heroic.

Antiheroes are not.

Anti-heroes are, in fact, *anti-hero*. They are against heroism.

Unfortunately, we live in an age of antiheroes.

The world needs less antiheroes and more heroes. And we all need to do a better job of recognizing the difference.

Martin and Malcolm

Malcolm X once remarked that, "Dr. King wants the same thing I want. Freedom." But Malcolm X advocated a much different approach to gaining freedom. Ten months after Dr. King's "I have a dream" speech in front of the Lincoln Monument in August, 1963, Malcolm X delivered his "The Ballot or the Bullet" speech at King Solomon Baptist Church in Detroit,

Michigan.[1]

While addressing the lively crowd, Malcolm X stated—again and again—that the white man was the enemy. The white government was the enemy. White business owners were the enemy. African Americans who cooperated with the white establishment were aiding and abetting the enemy. Malcolm X tried to unite African Americans by dividing them against other Americans.

Malcolm X advocated separation and segregation rather than integration and cooperation. Malcolm X mocked the nonviolent strategies advocated by Dr. King. He considered peaceful protests like sit-ins and marches to be useless, or even harmful, to black communities:

> *As long as you got a sit-down philosophy you'll have a sit-down thought pattern. And as long as you think that old sit-down thought, you'll be in some kind of sit-down action. They'll have you sitting in everywhere. It's not so good to refer to what you're going to do as a sit-in. That right there castrates you. Right there it brings you down. What goes with it? What – think of the image of someone sitting. An old woman can sit. An old man can sit. A chump can sit, a coward can sit, anything can sit. Well, you and I been sitting long enough and it's time for us today to start doing some standing and some fighting to back that up.*

Malcolm X continued his critique of nonviolent approaches by mocking the protest songs that became the soundtrack to civil rights marches:

> *Part of what's wrong with you, you do too much singing. Today it's time to stop singing and start swinging. You can't sing up on freedom. But you can swing up on some freedom. Cassius Clay can sing. But singing didn't help him to become the heavyweight champion of the world. Swinging helped him.*

---

1 Malcolm X also delivered "The Ballot or the Bullet" speech at Cory Methodist Church on April 3, 1964 in Cleveland, Ohio.

Malcolm X sought freedom for African Americans "by any means necessary"—including violence or the threat of violence. But Malcolm X suggested that violence could still be avoided if the government acted quickly to reverse course.

> *This is why I say it's the ballot or the bullet. It's liberty or it's death. It's freedom for everybody or freedom for nobody. America today finds herself in a unique situation. Historically, revolutions are bloody, oh yes they are. They have never had a bloodless revolution. Or a nonviolent revolution. That don't happen even in Hollywood. You don't have a revolution in which you love your enemy. And you don't have a revolution in which you are begging the system of exploitation to integrate you into it. Revolutions overturn systems. Revolutions destroy systems. A revolution is bloody, but America is in a unique position… this country can become involved in a revolution that won't take bloodshed. All she's got to do is give the black man in this country everything that's due him, everything.*

The "Ballot or the Bullet" speech was a testament to Malcolm X's exceptional skill as a writer and as an orator. The loud cheers and laughter of the receptive crowed affirmed the attractiveness of his message. Members of his audience were desperate for change and were willing to consider an alternative to the nonviolent approach advocated by Dr. King.

Malcolm X was angry. The anger that he felt was understandable. The anger that his followers felt was understandable. The desire for change by any means necessary, including violence, was understandable. But his tactics were self-defeating. In viewing white Americans as the enemy, seeking to divide people rather than unite people, and justifying violence as an acceptable response to violence, Malcolm X established himself as the anti-hero of the civil rights movement and set himself up for failure.

Similarly, the anti-Apartheid movement in South Africa had a hero

(Nelson Mandela) and an anti-hero—a charismatic leader named Chris Hani. At the age of 15, Hani joined the ANC youth league. After graduating from Rhodes University, Hani joined, *uMkhonto we Sizwe*, the militant wing of the ANC, which was co-founded by Nelson Mandela in 1961. From 1963 to 1990, Hani lived in exile, received military training in the Soviet Union, participated in the Zimbabwean War of Liberation, and organized gorilla activities targeting South Africa's apartheid government. Shortly after his return from exile, Hani became head of the South African Communist Party.

When Nelson Mandela was released after 27 years in prison, South Africa was at the precipice of disaster. President de Klerk implemented a series of changes, which began to dismantle the system of apartheid. But after three centuries of white domination, black South Africans were anxious for change. Violence increased and a race war seemed increasingly inevitable. Some saw Mandela—now the elder statesman—as their deliverance from evil. Others—especially young South Africans—preferred the more militant approach of Chris Hani.

Mirroring the dynamic between Dr. King and Malcolm X, the two most prominent leaders of the anti-Apartheid movement in South Africa shared the same objective but differed greatly in style and tactics. Mandela wore the bespoke suits of an elder statesman while asking black South Africans to forgive and forget. Hani wore army fatigues and a beret while rallying crowds in preparation for a violent overthrow of the Apartheid government. In a calm voice, Mandela advocated negotiations and reconciliation; with fiery rhetoric, Hani promised retaliation and revenge.

Codes of Conduct

In the social sciences there are certain names that can stand-in for an entire field of study. Freud and Jung are synonymous with psychoanalysis. Piaget and Vygotsky are synonymous with child development. Adam Smith and

John Maynard Keynes are synonymous with economics. And Lawrence Kohlberg's name is synonymous with moral development.

After working with the Haganah[2] to evacuate Jews out of Romania during WWII, Kohlberg participated in nonviolent activism during the 1948 fighting that established the state of Israel. These experiences increased Kohlberg's interest in moral reasoning. When he was able to return to the United States, Kohlberg completed a bachelor's degree in one year by testing his way out of most of his classes. Shortly after graduation, Kohlberg began his doctoral work at the University of Chicago, where he studied Jean Piaget's research on intellectual and moral development.

Kohlberg focused his dissertation on moral reasoning in 10-16-years-olds. He presented a series of moral dilemmas and asked participants to explain (a) what they believed was the right thing to do in the situation and (b) the reasoning they used to reach their conclusion. Kohlberg found that adolescents reason from one of six perspectives.

The least mature forms of moral reasoning are based on the "pre-conventional" morality of punishments and rewards. The first stage is characterized by a belief that something is wrong only if the perpetrator gets caught and is punished for his action. The second stage is based on naïve hedonism, which means people should behave in a way that will benefit them—to "look out for number one."

The third and fourth stages of "conventional" moral reasoning are based on gaining approval from others and maintaining social order. In the third stage, people reason that if an action pleases or is approved by others (based on the actor's intent), then the action is right. The fourth stage is based on the belief that rules and laws prohibiting or allowing the action is what makes something right or wrong.

The fifth and sixth stages of "post-conventional" morality represent the most mature forms of moral reasoning. The fifth stage suggests that people are obligated to adhere to an implicit social contract and they should obey

---

2   A precursor to the Israeli Defense Forces

laws which reflect the will of the majority. Finally, the most mature form of reasoning, according to Kohlberg, involves self-chosen principles of conscience, which prioritize the wellbeing of others.

Kohlberg's findings can help us understand the moral reasoning that is implicit in hero and anti-hero characters. Anti-heroes pursue their objectives through any means necessary—which might include violence. Their pursuit of vigilante justice is motivated by a thirst for revenge and their rationalization that, if nobody is going to stop them, their actions are justified. Anti-heroes act with reckless disregard for the wellbeing of others.

The actions of heroes, on the other hand, represent Kohlberg's more advanced stages of moral reasoning. Superman stood for the values of "truth, justice, and the American way" and followed self-chosen principles of conscience while making decisions on behalf of those he vowed to protect. In defeating villains, he did not compromise his principles. Heroes pursue just ends only through just means. Heroes remain above reproach.

The Revenge Reflex

In *The Merchant of Venice*, the moneylender Shylock asks, "If you prick us, do we not bleed? If you tickle us, do we not laugh? If you poison us, do we not die? And if you wrong us, shall we not take revenge?"

Shakespeare recognized that, when people feel they have been wronged, the revenge reflex is natural. But, ultimately, seeking revenge is often self-defeating. Revenge tends to occur in cycles rather than isolated events. Those who take revenge put their own safety, and the safety of those close to them, at greater risk. Those who give into the temptation to seek revenge sometimes end up paying for a few minutes of satisfaction with decades of regret.

What prompts the self-destructive urge to retaliate? Often, revenge is motivated by a type of thinking that psychologists call "affect forecasting." The person who contemplates revenge estimates that, after retaliating for a supposed wrong, they will feel better because the target of their revenge will feel worse. These estimates usually turn out to be inaccurate. People don't feel better—at least not for long. The person who takes revenge experiences a very short burst of satisfaction via reward centers in the dorsal striatum, but the brief high is followed by a much longer low, characterized by an unceasing cycle of negative ruminations.

In trying to understand when and why people seek revenge, the nature of the perceived slight is relevant. People are more likely to take revenge when they feel that their rights have been violated, when someone close to them broke a commitment, or when they view an authority figure as abusive or uncaring. Intention matters as well. People are more likely to take revenge against those they believe to have been intentional and willful in their efforts to harm them. In assessing the intentionality of transgressions, people are more forgiving of children, disabled people, and animals, than able-bodied adults.

But the most powerful predictor of revenge can be summarized in one word: Anger. When people become angry—*really* angry—their attention narrows and brain resources are so busy processing the anger that the person becomes unable to process information that is not directly related to the event that initiated the anger. An angry mind becomes fixated on the anger and thoughts begin to ruminate on the source of the anger. Unlike sadness and fear, which motivate people to retreat, anger is an "approach emotion," which propels people toward the perpetrator.

Especially in cases when people are convinced that their anger is righteous and justified, anger can initiate a chain of events that increases the likelihood that a person will act on their impulses. As the perfect storm continues to form, anger reduces self-control and a person's ability to consider the benefits of other courses of action, including forgiveness. The ability to maintain self-control is especially difficult when cognitive resources are already depleted by hunger, tiredness, life stress, or a noisy, chaotic, stressful environment.

When people feel that they have been slighted, wronged, mistreated, or oppressed, anger is understandable. When anger narrows focus to a short-term goal, people are unable to differentiate between heroes and antiheroes. And when the dam of anger breaks, the natural inclination is to seek revenge.

Antiheroes are champions of revenge. Angry people identify with antiheroes in the hope that the antihero will avenge perceived wrongs against themselves or members of their tribe. Reduced self-control—and a sense of righteous anger—compels people to justify the antisocial actions of antiheroes. During tumultuous times, some people look for an enemy to defeat. Then, they look for an antihero to lead them into battle.

Two Paths

Although Mandela eventually became the hero that South Africa needed, he began his career in the anti-apartheid movement as a different sort of character. As a young leader within the ANC, Mandela was sympathetic to those who insisted that nonviolent protests were the best course of action. But he soon changed his mind.

Manilal Gandhi[3] helped Mandela and his ANC colleagues develop a two-stage plan for peaceful protests. First, they recruited volunteers to break apartheid laws by disobeying curfews and entering restricted areas without permits, including whites-only railway compartments, post office entrances, and bathrooms. The second phase involved nationwide strikes and work stoppages.

However, by the second day of the stay-at-home protest, Mandela began to question the efficacy of nonviolent resistance. As some repeated the refrain, "nonviolence has not failed us, we have failed nonviolence," Mandela concluded that a more militant approach was necessary. In

---

3   Manilal Gandhi was a prominent advocate of nonviolence and editor of the *Indian Opinion* newspaper, which his famous father, Mohandas Gandhi, founded.

an interview with the *Rand Daily Mail*, Mandela suggested that, if the government could simply crush peaceful protests with brute force, the ANC would need to pursue a different course of action. Manilal Gandhi believed in nonviolence on principle; but Nelson Mandela saw nonviolence as merely tactical. Like Malcolm X, the younger, pre-prison Mandela was willing to pursue freedom "by any means necessary." Mandela *was* an antihero.

In preparation for a new chapter in the anti-apartheid struggle, Mandela studied the tactics of guerilla warfare and sabotage. The armed wing of the ANC—*uMkhonto we Sizwe*—bombed government buildings, power facilities, and machinery. As a fugitive from justice, Mandela became known as the Black Pimpernel, in reference to the elusive Scarlet Pimpernel character created by Baroness Orczy. His colleagues within the ANC—and black South Africans who supported any effort to end apartheid—viewed Mandela as a freedom fighter. But from the perspective of the South African government, Mandela was a terrorist.

Iron Pyrite

The metallic luster of Iron Pyrite can lead to short-lived excitement among prospectors who do not realize that their discovery is merely "fool's gold." As a poor substitute for a more precious medal, pyrite serves as a valuable metaphor. In a certain light, iron pyrite can be mistaken for gold. Similarly, when vision is obscured by anger and vengeance, anti-heroes start to look a lot like heroes.

In truth, the younger, more radical, pre-prison Mandela was not a hero or a villain. Nelson Mandela was an antihero. He pursued a noble end—freeing black South Africans from the chains of apartheid—with morally questionable tactics. In his legal defense at the Rivonia trial, Mandela admitted that he planned and conducted acts of sabotage directed at the apartheid government's infrastructure. "I did not plan it in a spirit of recklessness nor because I have any love of violence," Mandela explained, "I planned it as a result of a calm and sober assessment of the political situation that had arisen after many years of tyranny, exploitation, and oppression of my people by whites." He defended his actions by emphasizing his efforts to avoid harm to people while destroying buildings. Nonetheless, Mandela's operations put lives at risk.

Pyrite has found a variety of industrial uses. Currently, pyrite is used in solar panels and batteries to collect and conduct energy. Previously, pyrite has been used to convey information in primitive radios of the early 20th century. Pyrite was also used as a source of ignition in firearms in the 16th and 17th centuries.[4] Like pyrite, antiheroes harness energy and convey messages with explosive, often destructive, power.

Malcolm X's militant message divided a nation. Some viewed him as a hero. But by casting others as the enemy, Malcolm X alienated more people than he incorporated, including those he vilified outside and inside the African American community in the United States. Like the pre-prison Mandela, Malcolm X was neither a hero nor a villain. Malcolm X was an anti-hero, fighting a noble cause with ignoble means.

Malcolm X demonstrated that, ultimately, anti-heroism promotes tribalism. Malcolm X unified a tribe by vilifying another tribe. Malcolm X tried to push people into two separate realms: black villages and white villages, with black owners and white owners, black customers, and white customers, led by black leaders and white leaders. By welcoming only certain people into the tribe, Malcolm X's black nationalist tribe remained relatively small as Dr. King's movement grew exponentially—in number, influence, and diversity of its members. Dr. King worked to bring everyone together to live as one tribe in one village. Dr. King was a hero.

---

4   The name "pyrite" derives from a Greek word for fire because, when struck, pyrite emits sparks.

Bad Cop, Good Cop

There are antiheroes in the real world just as there are antiheroes in comic books and feature films. Unlike fictional characters, we usually only remember—and celebrate—the heroes. Like the gritty characters that adorned the pages of pulps in the 1930s, anti-heroes are more likely to fade into obscurity. In early 1960's America and early 1990's South Africa, millions of angry young people looked for someone to champion their cause. To some, Malcolm X and Chris Hani looked like attractive options. But their attraction was like that of fool's gold.

Dr. King and Nelson Mandela were more effective than Malcolm X and Chris Hani. Both Dr. King and (post-prison) Mandela resisted the temptation to express anger in public or respond to violence with more violence. At best, the anti-heroism of Malcolm X and Chris Hani was effective only to the extent that it assisted their more heroic counterparts in the quest for freedom, justice, and equality. This possibility is best expressed in a remark Malcolm X made to Mrs. Coretta Scott King: "I want Dr. King to know that I didn't come to Selma to make his job difficult. I really did come thinking I could make it easier. If the white people realize what the alternative is, perhaps they will be more willing to hear Dr. King."

Iron pyrite sometimes contains "invisible gold." Trace amounts of actual gold within fool's gold remind us that, within anti-heroes, there is often an element of heroism concealed. Dr. King's public life was marked by heroism from beginning to end. Mandela, on the other hand, transitioned from anti-hero to hero. But even under the edifice of "The Black pimpernel," it was possible to see Mandela's potential. During the time Nelson Mandela spent as a political prisoner, his character changed. He mellowed. He matured. He honed his arguments, understood his adversary, and recognized that violence was not a viable path to peace. Long before his release from prison, Mandela had transformed into a hero.

When government officials agreed to secret talks, Mandela answered the call to help transform South Africa into a rainbow nation, to protect the vulnerable, unite the village, and uphold sacred values as he led the effort to defeat the villain of apartheid. Initially, Afrikaners were skeptical. But Mandela put immature, anti-hero ways behind him. Mandela did not seek revenge against those who had arrested him, incarcerated him, threatened him, or harassed him while he was in prison. In a spirit of forgiveness and reconciliation, Mandela sought redemption, rather than revenge—for all South Africans—regardless of whether they were formerly oppressed or former oppressors. In so doing, Mandela overcame a powerful temptation.

Unlike anti-heroes, heroes look the same from every vantage point. As a presidential candidate, Mandela demonstrated the nature of true heroism. Nelson Mandela became increasingly popular among people from every demographic during his time in office. After serving only a single term, he became even more popular as the *de facto* spiritual leader of the rainbow nation. Mandela entered prison as an anti-hero. But Mandela emerged from prison as an elder statesman—the hero that South Africa so desperately needed.

Chapter 14

The Great Escape

Forgiveness is more manly than punishment
-Gandhi

The United States sent two million American soldiers to Europe during WWII. Approximately 407,316 servicemen did not return, leaving behind grieving wives and fatherless children. One of those widows, Agnes, used alcohol to cope with her husband's death—and the reality that she was now a single mother to a 3-year-old son, Andy Robinson.

Andy found refuge in local theatres. Movies were a way to keep his father's memory alive, especially while watching brave soldiers at the Battle of the Bulge, where his father fought years earlier. As Andy later recalled, "no matter what my mother said to convince me otherwise, I believed that if these men could make it, so could my father." Andy found closure after seeing *The Fighting Sullivans*—a true story of five brothers who fought together on the same Navy ship, which was sunk by the Japanese at Guadalcanal.

As he exited the theatre on that winter evening in Hartford, Connecticut, Andy made five snowballs, which he threw at the side of a passing bus to represent each of the Sullivan brothers as "people on the bus shook their heads in disapproval—another pain-in-the-ass juvenile delinquent."

For Andy, the local theatre was a sanctuary. As he explained, "The only place I felt released from a constant, constricting tension was at the movies. It was the only place I felt safe. The screen gave me this lighted, rectangular opening to the world where there was no threat of personal danger. I could sit in the darkness and enjoy the crimes committed and the punishment justly administered. And yet, my identification with these giants also ensured that I wouldn't be left out and neglected."

Andy was so terrified while watching *The Thing* that he threw up a carton full of popcorn. But he convinced his mother to finish the movie from the back row. Andy knew that no matter how scary a movie was, it would end up ok in the end. However, he was less confident in his own prospects. Andy was always worried some vague danger might arise.

That danger came on his way home from yet another movie, when Andy was 9 years old. After watching Gene Kelly and Debbie Reynolds dance across colorful sets in *Singin' in the Rain*, Andy skipped out of the theater, imagining that he was dancing through puddles to the film's title song. His joyous performance drew the attention of two boys, who corralled him into an alley and pushed him against a brick wall. What happened next, foreshadowed his adolescence—and his career. As Andy recalled,

> *The violence happened with such a sudden and sadistic fury, I wasn't able to catch my breath. Between the pain of their physical abuse and the frustration of being completely dominated by their size and meanness, I experienced a suffocating fear I had never felt before. The panic was rising, I couldn't catch my breath, and I believed that they were going to kill me and stuff me into one of the cans. So I went crazy. It was where I was going anyway, but I accelerated the process by grabbing at the emerging physical symptoms of a berserker behavior I had seen my mother exhibit when she was drunk and got into a fight…eyes rolling and bugging, limbs shooting out in all directions, now bouncing myself*

off the cans, the walls and the ground and feeling none of the previous pain when I had been on the receiving end.

Andy felt a new sense of power after fighting off the bullies. But he still had a difficult time making friends or fitting in. Andy was desperate for attention and approval; he would perform for anyone who would watch. "From the beginning," he recalled, "I intuitively understood the value of an audience. Without people watching, I was just another kid kicking a can down the street. With an audience, everything was expanded, elevated. It was like…I had stepped out of the shadows into the light." Andy alluded to this transcendent feeling in the title of his memoir, *Stepping Into the Light*.

The "shadow" that he stepped out of was the string of cheap, dirty hotels that he and his mother lived in—and the dark, dangerous streets he wandered after his mother passed out each night. Andy broke into stores, stole merchandise, and vandalized buildings. Assaulting a police officer proved to be the last straw. In juvenile detention, Andy found himself at the mercy of a judge. A kindly social worker convinced the judge that there was still hope for the young man. Instead of prison, the judge sent Andy to an Episcopal boarding school for boys from broken homes, which was, quite fittingly, named St. Andrew's. There, Andy met an assistant headmaster who ran the drama program. The old Andy had gotten into trouble; the new Andy got into theatre. Andy's good fortune continued when he received a Fulbright scholarship to hone his craft at the London Academy of Music and Dramatic Arts. The merciful intervention of a social worker and drama teacher changed the trajectory of Andy's life.

Reprieve

Throughout the Civil War, President Lincoln received a constant stream of appeals from family members of soldiers who had violated military rules and regulations. On one occasion, an old man visited the Whitehouse to plead with President Lincoln to pardon his son, who had been found guilty of dereliction of duty. The despondent father was disappointed by Lincoln's response:

"I am sorry. I can do nothing for you. Listen to this telegram I received from General Butler yesterday: 'President Lincoln, I pray you not to interfere with the court martial of the army. You will destroy all discipline among our soldiers.'"

Seeing the anguish in the old man's face, Lincoln scribbled a note and handed it to his visitor: "Job Smith is not to be shot until further orders come from me."

Not yet understanding the implications of the statement, the father protested, "Why, I thought you wrote out a pardon. You may order him to be shot next week." Lincoln responded, "I see you are not very well acquainted with me. If your son never dies until orders come from me to shoot him, he will live to be a great deal older than Methuselah[1]."

On another occasion, Lincoln received an appeal from a Union army private that arrived as a single sheet of paper, lacking the usual letters of support from powerful friends. "What? Has this man no friends?" asked Lincoln. "No sir," his assistant responded, "not one." Before signing the pardon, Lincoln sighed, "Then I will be his friend."

Lincoln would sometimes spend an entire workday reviewing court-martials. His secretary, John Hay, remarked at "the eagerness with which the President caught at any fact which would justify him in saving the life of a condemned soldier." After several hours, Hay was "in a state of entire collapse" but Lincoln "found relief and renewed vigor as he exercised the power to pardon." Lincoln truly relished the administration of mercy, saying, "I go to bed happy as I think how joyous the signing of my name will make him and his family and his friends." In most cases, Lincoln was willing to uphold a conviction only "where meanness or cruelty were

---

1   In the book of Genesis, Methuselah was the son of Enoch and the grandfather of Noah. He was said to have lived for 969 years.

shown."

"If I have one vice," Lincoln observed, "it is not being able to say no." As he signed another pardon, Lincoln quipped, "I thank God I was not born a woman, because I never could refuse an impassioned plea." Lincoln's inability "to say no" prompted criticism from those (including cabinet members) who felt that Lincoln's generous use of his power to pardon undermined military discipline. Lincoln was aware of the criticism, acknowledging that he was often "charged with making too many mistakes on the side of mercy."

Lincoln's secretary of war, Edwin Stanton, argued that punishments for desertion or dereliction of duty must be severe, to which Lincoln would sometimes respond with the rhetorical question: "Must I shoot a simple-minded soldier boy who deserts, while I must not touch a hair of a wiley agitator who induces him to desert?"

Lincoln expressed his feelings toward deserters more generally with an additional question: "I put it to you and I leave it for you to decide for yourself. If Almighty God gives a man a cowardly pair of legs, how can he help their running away with him?" Lincoln recognized the very human urge to escape danger and he was especially forgiving when it came to younger troops who suffered from "runners itch." Lincoln feared that "It would frighten the poor devils too terribly to shoot them." Before a sixteen-year-old soldier was brought before the firing squad, Lincoln telegraphed General George Meade a message: "I am unwilling for any boy under eighteen to be shot."

Lincoln's tendency to forgive Union soldiers also extended to soldiers who wore the uniform of the Confederacy. Before the end of the war, Lincoln advocated for clemency and the release of captured soldiers who were willing to take an oath of loyalty to the Union. While some argued that former Confederate soldiers should be asked to declare their innocence, Lincoln responded, "on principle I dislike an oath which requires a man to swear he has not done wrong. It rejects the Christian principle of forgiveness on terms of repentance. I think it is enough if the man does no wrong hereafter."

Repentance

In the 1986 film, *The Mission*, Robert De Niro plays a mercenary and slave trader named Mendoza, who discovers that the woman he loves is, in fact, in love with his brother Felipe. Mendoza forces the overmatched Felipe into a sword duel whereby the expert swordsman Mendoza quickly dispatches his brother in a fit of jealous rage. Overcome by grief and remorse, Mendoza sits in jail in a catatonic state until a local priest, Father Gabriel, offers Mendoza a penance. Mendoza refuses, saying, "for me there is no redemption…there is no penance hard enough for me." Despite continued resistance from a hardened man who has lost faith in himself, Father Gabriel does not give up on Mendoza: "but do you dare try it!?"

After accepting his penance, Mendoza drags a net behind him, which is filled with the tools of his former trade—swords, guns, and armor—toward the mission, where he intends to devote his life to prayer, contemplation, and humble service to the indigenous people who live "above the falls." Weighted down by symbols of his past sins, Mendoza climbs hill after hill through unrelenting rains. After slipping down a muddy hill once again, one of the brothers, John Felding, cuts the rope, freeing Mendoza from his burden. But Mendoza pushes Felding aside, slides down the hill, grabs the bag, re-ties the rope, and struggles up the muddy hill once again.

As the exhausted Mendoza sleeps between two boulders below the falls, Felding pleads with his superior, Father Gabriel: "Father, he's done this penance long enough, and well, the other brothers think the same." Father Gabriel looks up from his writing and responds, "But *he* doesn't think so, John. Until he does, neither do I." The penance will not be satisfied until Mendoza is satisfied.

The term penance comes from the same root word as repentance.

Mendoza's penance is a voluntary act of repentance—an outward sign of an inward change. In some Christian denominations, a penance is an official religious sacrament. In other congregations, a penance is simply a form of self-discipline, motivated by sincere contrition, which is aimed at overcoming sin and restoring spiritual health to one's soul.

The term penance also comes from the same root word as penitentiary. A penitentiary is a place of involuntary—and sometimes artificial—penance, meant to house the most serious offenders, regardless of whether the prisoner feels any remorse for their crimes.

Incarceration is a form of punishment, which is sometimes referred to as "doing time" or "paying one's debt to society." The amount of time—and the size of the debt—depends on the offense. In administering justice, decisions are guided by the notion that "the punishment should fit the crime." The bigger the crime, the longer the time.

In the film, *Shawshank Redemption*, prisoners who have served sufficient time are asked by a parole board, "do you feel that you've been rehabilitated?"

The word *rehabilitation* refers to helping someone return to his or her original state—a point before which some unfortunate event occurred, such as a crime that was committed, an accident that was suffered, or an addiction that was developed. Rehabilitation is—or ought to be—the goal of incarceration. The objective is to restore someone or something to a state that existed before the injury, before the addiction, or before the crime. Not to merely house the malady but to heal the malady.

A penitentiary is not just a place of punishment but a form of prevention. Incarceration immediately prevents the criminal from committing further crimes. But a penitentiary that truly rehabilitates prisoners will prevent a criminal from committing additional crimes well beyond the length of the sentence. Ultimately, the success of criminal justice is not measured by what the convict does in prison, but what they do when they are released.

A penitentiary is effective only to the degree to which it promotes a change within a person, resulting in less criminal behavior. A penance is effective only to the degree that it initiates a transformation, which leads to a less sinful heart. The point of punishment, imprisonment, and penance is change. Religious sacraments and prison sentences are successful to the extent that they, in Lincoln's words, "ensure he does no wrong hereafter."

Restoration

Lincoln's inclination to extend forgiveness and grace became a hallmark of his presidency as he dealt with the delicate questions that came before him as Commander In Chief.

From a Union perspective, Confederate leaders were responsible for "the mighty scourge of war," which led to the deaths of around 620,000 Americans. Some lawmakers sought revenge against those who supported the Confederate cause. This is why Lincoln considered it fortuitous that the Civil War ended shortly after Congress had adjourned, believing that "there were men in Congress who, if their motives were good, were nevertheless impractical, and who possessed feelings of hate and vindictiveness in which he did not sympathize and could not participate." With Congress in recess, Lincoln and his cabinet were better able to ensure the process of restoration would not be sabotaged by vengeful colleagues.

Toward the end of the Civil War, General Sherman asked Lincoln what should become of the rebel soldiers after they were defeated. Lincoln explained to Sherman that "all he wanted of us was to defeat the opposing armies, and to get the men composing the Confederate armies back to their homes, at work on their farms and in their shops." Lincoln then instructed General Sherman and his fellow military leaders to allow defeated soldiers to "have their horses to plow with, and, if you like, their guns to shoot crows with." He explained further, "I want no one punished; treat them liberally all round. We want those people to return to their allegiance to the Union and submit to the laws."

Based on his expressed beliefs that "mercy bears richer fruit than strict justice" and that "The severest justice may not always be the best policy," Lincoln offered Confederate soldiers—and the Confederate states—a path to redemption. In promoting reconstruction, Lincoln was guided by the notion that "Enough lives have been sacrificed. We must extinguish our resentments if we expect harmony and union."

By approaching people with kindness and generosity, in a spirit of true friendship, Lincoln was able to turn enemies into friends while avoiding the emergence of new enemies. By offering forgiveness to those who chose to secede from the Union (rather than concede that he was their democratically elected leader), Lincoln left his former opponents with no reason for resentment and no cause to seek revenge. With malice toward none and generosity toward all, Lincoln turned enemies into friends.

After General Lee surrendered to Grant at the Appomattox Court House, the 16th president "spoke very kindly of General Lee and others of the Confederacy," exhibiting "the kindness and humanity of his disposition, and the tender and forgiving spirit that so eminently distinguished him." Lincoln bolstered his reputation in the North and gained the respect of many in the South. With kindness, tenderness, and forgiveness, Lincoln helped heal the wounds of a long-divided nation.

Release

In 1944, a group of allied soldiers organized a mass escape from a POW camp in Nazi Germany. A fictionalized version of their story was depicted in the 1963 film, *The Great Escape*. In an attempt to force Nazi leaders to devote resources to their search, capture, and return, the allied soldiers pooled their individual talents to concoct an elaborate escape plan. The plan involved digging three underground tunnels that they nicknamed "Tom," "Dick," and "Harry." The soldiers fashioned civilian clothing, forged documents, and organized transportation by train, plane, and motorcycle to the safety of nearby countries, including Switzerland.

The theme of duty is explored throughout *The Great Escape*. Rather than wait out the war in the relative safety and comfort offered by the warden, the soldiers risked their lives to distract enemy forces and, possibly, return to battle. *The Great Escape* reminds us that heroes put themselves at risk for a greater cause. The film also demonstrates that heroism looks different in different situations. Sometimes heroism involves escaping from villains. But sometimes heroism involves letting villains escape.

Despite the opinions of some that Jefferson Davis and other Confederate leaders "must be hung," Lincoln expressed his intentions clearly: "None need expect he would take any part in hanging or killing those men, even the worst of them."

Toward the end of the Civil War, Lincoln explained his intentions to General Sherman with a parable about an itinerant preacher who had pledged to refrain from drinking alcohol:

> *When visiting a friend, he was invited to take a drink, but declined, on the score of his pledge; when his friend suggested lemonade, [the man] accepted. In preparing the lemonade, the friend pointed to the brandy bottle, and said the lemonade would be more palatable if he were to pour in a little brandy; then his guest said, if he could do so 'unbeknown' to him, he would not object.*

General Sherman understood Lincoln's desire to allow Davis and the other Confederate leaders to escape "unbeknown to him."

Lincoln remained true to his intention to "frighten them out of the country, open the gates, let down the bars, scare them off." When Jacob Thompson, the former Confederate envoy to Canada, was caught boarding a ship bound for London, the "conspicuous secessionist" was detained at Stanton's order. Having been asked whether he wished to retain custody, Lincoln replied "Well, no, I rather think not. When you have an elephant by the hind leg, and he's trying to run away, it's best to let him run."

Confederate leaders like Davis and Thompson were no longer a threat to the Union. Therefore, Lincoln saw no further need to capture them as a form of prevention. Davis, Thompson, and fellow Confederates would be even less able to harm the union in exile. Lincoln also thought it unwise to punish them on punitive grounds. Self-imposed banishment from their homeland was punishment enough. Lincoln's wish to restore the Union on friendly terms was greater than any personal desire for revenge against those who had torn the nation apart. By offering mercy, forgiveness, and grace, even to "the worst of them," Lincoln chose national objectives over personal resentments. Lincoln let go of Confederate leaders in the hope that citizens of formerly Confederate states would let go of *their* resentments.

Redemption

When someone has been wronged, the natural inclination is to seek revenge. Some pursue vigilante justice while others see the criminal justice systems as a more acceptable vehicle of revenge. Pressing charges can inflict suffering upon those who cause suffering, via the power of the state.

Mother Teresa had different ideas. She often asked for compassionate exceptions for some of the most heinous criminals, dictators, and perpetrators of all kinds—especially when they were sentenced to death or were nearing their natural death while in prison. Mother Teresa believed that tender love was always the best course of action—both for victim and villain alike.

Mother Teresa's response to those who had suffered *and* those who had caused others to suffer was the same—tender love. Her response was also the same while caring for those who had, unintentionally and unknowingly, inflicted harm on themselves. As many condemned those who were dying from a mysterious new disease called AIDS, Mother Teresa comforted them and created new homes where these individuals could die enveloped in tender love rather than bitter judgment.

In any and every situation, tender love can work wonders. But, in each situation, tender love works in different ways.

Tender love *comforts* victims. Tender love heals wounds and calms fears. But tender love *confronts* villains. Anger and disgust pushes people in the direction of bitterness and resentment but tender love draws people in toward remorse and repentance. Anger and contempt are *arming*—they compel people to raise their voices, raise their fists, or raise weapons against their enemy. Tender love is *disarming*. Tender love encourages people to lay down their weapons, both figurative and literal. Tender love is the most powerful and the most reliable way to break a cycle of anger.

Gandhi taught that tender love brings people to shame. When people do bad things, they *should* feel bad. Negative emotions like guilt, shame, and remorse serve an important purpose—they motivate us to change our behavior. If the consequences of an action cause us to feel bad, we are more likely to try a different approach in the future. But there are different ways to feel "bad." Anger is an approach emotion, which tempts people to retaliate against someone. Shame, on the other hand, causes people to withdraw and look within. People who have harmed others *should be* ashamed of themselves.

Because people don't like to think of themselves as harmful people, shame creates what social psychologists call "cognitive dissonance[2]." The discomfort of cognitive dissonance prompts people to change their behavior. Tender love brings people to a place where they can confront their own actions (and beliefs) because they are not preoccupied by a need to defend themselves against attacks from others.

Mother Teresa was strong enough to resist the temptation to judge or condemn villains or those who unintentionally victimized themselves. Her pro-life stance was unwavering. She was against capital punishment for the same reason she was against abortion—she valued every human life. No

---

2   Cognitive dissonance has been defined as inconsistency between one's thoughts, beliefs, attitudes, and their actual behavior.

exceptions. She maintained a belief that nobody was beyond redemption. Even if, in the past, they had destroyed a life, Mother Teresa never tried to destroy *their* life or their livelihood. Instead, through tender love, she always encouraged them on their path to redemption.

Typecasting

One mark of a great actor is that the audience forgets that they are watching someone pretend to be someone else. Andy Robinson's portrayal of the psychotic killer Scorpio in *Dirty Harry* was so convincing that he—the actor, not the character—received death threats. Andy Robinson survived the death threats but his career didn't. In the minds of audiences, producers, and casting directors, Andy Robinson *was* Scorpio. Andy was pigeon-holed as a maniac. The only roles offered to him were other psychopaths. He accepted a few of these parts but began to decline offers, later admitting, "there is only so much your psyche can take."

Andy Robinson continued to perform on stage but he was not offered another major role for twenty-two years.[3] Andy Robinson was both a master of his craft and a victim of his expertise. His performance as the Zodiac Killer cemented his reputation as a villain. He fell victim to what many actors fear most—to be typecast into a certain role. The phenomenon is especially troubling when the actor is typecast in a role that depletes, rather than nourishes, the actor's psyche.

As a troubled young man, Andy Robinson received his break in life when a social worker and a drama teacher recognized his potential. He was allowed to leave his criminal life behind. He was allowed to stop being a villain. But as a screen actor, Andy Robinson was not permitted to escape his past.

Andy Robinson's life is emblematic of our times. When we refuse to forgive those who have sinned—even if they have repented—we typecast

---
[3] When he was asked to play Elim Garak in *Star Trek: Deep Space Nine*.

them into a role that is not helpful to society. We ensure that the world has one more villain than was otherwise necessary. When we refuse to give people an off-ramp, we ensure there is one more reckless driver on the highway. If the judge and social worker had insisted on keeping a delinquent in his place, the world would have lost a great character actor and mentor to the next generation.

Heroes seek redemption, not revenge.

Heroes seek to console, not to cancel.

There is nothing heroic about forcing a villain to remain a villain.

A few years ago, a slew of egregious behaviors, perpetrated by public figures, came to light. Some of the most notorious perpetrators were successful in their fields but used their power to do despicable things to women in less powerful positions. Their actions were sick, depraved, and inappropriate.

How would Mother Teresa respond if she were alive today? She would certainly comfort the many victims with tender love—which the public would celebrate. But if she could show tender love to violent dictators like Saddam Hussein, Jean-Claude Duvalier, and Enver Hoxha, it seems likely that she would also offer the same tender love to even the worst offenders. She would be criticized, of course. Vehemently. She might even be "cancelled" by individuals who consider themselves worthy to stand in judgment of someone like Mother Teresa. But, as always, Mother Teresa would be less concerned by her reputation than the redemption of every individual she encountered.

Recently, some have attacked the legacies of historical figures, including some of the heroes highlighted in this book. The mob has torn down statues, re-named buildings, and written under-informed and poorly reasoned critiques.

Fictional heroes are deliberately created with imperfections—such as a sensitivity to kryptonite—to remain relatable. But real-life heroes are simply born that way. Nobody is perfect. Even heroes are imperfect.

Lincoln, Gandhi, Dr. King, Mother Teresa, and Nelson Mandela had considerable flaws. The Big Five were aware of some of their imperfections, which they worked to remedy.

Ironically, Lincoln, Gandhi, Dr. King, Mother Teresa, and Mandela were admired, in part, *because* they were so consistently gracious and forgiving of others. Perhaps it is best to evaluate people with a similar measure of grace that they used to judge—or refrain from judging—those who opposed them.

To be sure, there should be consequences for inappropriate behavior. People should take responsibility for their actions. In seeking restoration, the wrongdoer should proceed with a penitent spirit rather than a carefully worded apology written by a publicist. Perpetrators should be expected to "repent and sin no more." But we must allow villains a path to redemption. Otherwise, villains will remain villains. The world needs less villains, not more villains. Helping a villain repent and work toward redemption is the best way to eliminate a villain—and perhaps create a hero—without creating new villains.

Amazing Grace

Mother Teresa devoted her life to free service to the poorest of the poor. But she considered poverty to be a spiritual condition rather than an economic state. She noticed that some of the wealthiest people suffer most profoundly from what she called "spiritual poverty." Mother Teresa recognized the profound spiritual poverty of bad actors and confronted them with tender love. In Mother Teresa's eyes, nobody was beyond redemption. A healthy society allows sick people to get well—even if they appear terminally ill.

Those who brand others as irredeemable are also in need of redemption. Those who insist on typecasting others as villains are not heroes. There is nothing heroic about euthanizing and eulogizing another person. Heroes don't kill, they apprehend. If a villain is killed, the possibility of redemption dies with them. When the village mob begins throwing stones, heroes offer mercy, forgiveness, and grace. Heroes seek redemption, not revenge.

The hymn "Amazing Grace" summons power from a captivating melody and simple lyrics. The words are especially profound when considering the life story of their author. John Newton was not just a slave owner but also a slave trader. He bought and sold human beings. But after a spiritual conversion at sea, Newton recognized the error of his ways.

John Newton could not undo the terrible harm that he had caused fellow human beings. He could not change his past. But he could "change course" by seeking forgiveness for his sins and atonement for his crimes. With a humble heart and a penitent spirit, John Newton opened himself up to change—a transformation that he described in his most famous lines:

> *Amazing grace, how sweet the sound*
> *that saved a wretch like me.*
> *I once was lost, but now I'm found,*
> *was blind, but now I see.*

As a younger man, John Newton made the world a worse place. But John Newton devoted his later years to changing the world for the better. He became a pastor, a prominent abolitionist, and worked alongside William Wilberforce to see the elimination of slavery in his native England, which occurred only months before his death.

Redemption—or atonement—is a central theme in literature and film because life is a process of learning from the past and preparing for the next chapter. The hero must conquer his inner demons before he can step up to the final challenge. The hero's real battle is within. Sometimes the hero needs others to help him, rather than harm him, along his path to heroism.

The world needs more heroes and less villains. For a villain to become a hero, the villain must change his ways—and the villagers must allow the villain a path to redemption. Only then will the village have one more hero, one less villain, and fewer victims.

Dr. King stressed the importance of forgiveness to his congregants who had been, in many cases, the victims of the despicable actions of others. "We must develop and maintain the capacity to forgive," he explained, "He who is devoid of the power to forgive is devoid of the power to love."

Heroes are forgiving and gracious, even to those who might seem undeserving of forgiveness and grace.

Heroes provide tender love. Heroes offer amazing grace. Heroes allow people to change. Heroes help villains make their great escape.

Chapter 15

The World's A Stage

There are no small parts, there are only small actors.
-Konstantin Stanislavski

In William Shakespeare's *As You Like it*, the contemplative nobleman Jacques delivers one of the Bard's most familiar monologues:

All the world's a stage,
And all the men and women merely players;
They have their exits and their entrances,
And one man in his time plays many parts,
His acts being seven ages.

Between the first and final acts, we indeed play many parts. Whether we are born into a role, assigned to a role, hired for a role, elected to a role, volunteer for a role, or we create an entirely new role for ourselves, it is not the role we play, but *how we play the role*, that defines our character.

The word "character" comes from the Old French word *caractere*, derived from a Greek word, *kharakter*, which refers to a stamping tool. Over time, the word took on additional meanings and began to denote a "distinctive mark" or a "token, feature, or trait."

The way fictional characters treat other fictional characters reveals their distinctive mark—and exposes their character. Throughout this book we have identified the distinctive marks of heroes: they answer the call, disregard their own wellbeing, protect the vulnerable, defend the village, defeat the villain, and stand up for sacred values. We have also revealed the distinctive marks of anti-heroes: rather than seeking redemption for villains, anti-heroes use violence in pursuit of revenge. Villains also have a distinctive mark: they intentionally harm others to fulfill their selfish desires for money, power, or psychological rewards.

Actors are usually placed in roles by casting directors who work at the behest of directors and producers. Some actors, like Andy Robinson, are typecast as villains. Others, like Tom Hanks, have an "everyman" quality that helps them land roles playing likeable, relatable, sympathetic characters. But, in the real world, people cast *themselves* into roles.

You cast yourself into roles by the way you treat other people. There is no such thing as a petty, cruel, vindictive hero. And there is no such thing as a warm, caring, compassionate, benevolent villain. Like fictional characters, we evaluate other people—especially people in positions of prominence—based on the way they relate to others. The way we treat other people becomes our distinctive mark.

It would be delusional to consider ourselves heroic if our actions bear the distinctive marks of villainy or anti-heroism. Regardless of how we may view ourselves, or what adjectives we might self-ascribe, our actions define us. We don't get to act like a villain and be regarded as a hero. It just doesn't work that way.

Method Acting

During the first half of the 20th century, most stage and screen actors in the United States performed in the Shakespearian tradition of character acting, which emphasized the precise delivery of carefully written (often by Shakespeare himself) lines. Excellence in the classical tradition was measured by the projection of one's voice, the articulation of their words, and the stylized movements of their limbs. Delivering an authentic performance meant delivering lines as Shakespeare might have intended.

Then, a highly regarded Russian actor and director named Konstantin Stanislavski began sharing the secrets of his success. Stanislavski craved a different sort of authenticity. Compared to the classical, Shakespearian approach full of booming voices and exaggerated movements, Stanislavski taught a less-is-more approach, full of subtlety and believability. Rather than merely projecting their words, Stanislavski wanted actors to project their emotions—to replace guarded masculinity with emotional vulnerability.

Based on his premise that excellent performances originate from the "art of experiencing" rather than the "art of representation," Stanislavski developed a "System" to help actors embody their character rather than merely play the character. While preparing for a role, Stanislavski taught actors to search for the character's motivations and to consider what the character was trying to achieve in each scene. If the character was betrayed by a friend, the appropriate response would be something like anger. Stanislavski encouraged actors to not just act angry but *be* angry—to *feel* the anger that their character was feeling.

Stanislavski's ideas were adopted by three teachers at The Actor's Studio in New York City—Lee Strasberg, Stella Adler, and Sandford Meisner—who borrowed the central tenants of Stanislavski's System to create what came to be known as "The Method." Strasberg, Adler, and Meisner trained a parade of future stars, including Marilyn Monroe, Paul Newman, Dustin Hoffman, Jack Nicholson, Al Pacino, and Robert De Niro.

For many viewers, their first exposure to method acting was through the on-screen performances of Marlon Brando, who was a student of Adler. As Stanley Kowalski in *A Streetcar Named Desire* (1951), Brando's performance was gut-wrenching and included one of the most iconic lines in film history: "Stella! Hey, Stella!" Some of Brando's most enduring performances were improvised, including the taxicab scene in *On the Waterfront* (1951). Brando, who played promising young boxer-turned-reluctant-cheat Terry Malloy, lamented to his brother: "You don't understand! I coulda' had class. I coulda' been a contender. I coulda' been somebody instead of a bum, which is what I am." Brando added to his already impressive body of work with another performance for the ages as Vito Corleone in *The Godfather* (1972).

If evaluated against the standards of classic character acting, Brando would be considered an abject failure. His posture was wrong. His enunciation was terrible. He often mumbled his lines. Audiences weren't always able to decipher his words. But Brando was fluent in emotion. Brando was able to conjure feelings and reveal inner conflicts in a way that had seldom been seen before on stage or screen. He connected with audiences on an emotional level because he made audiences feel what his character was feeling. Brando earned a reputation for eccentricity off screen, but while in character, he impressed both critics and colleagues. In 1999 Brando was named Actor of the Century by *Time* Magazine.

1,000 Journeys

While filming the first *Star Wars* movie, Mark Hamill shared a concern with one of his co-stars, Harrison Ford. Given that Hamill's character, Luke Skywalker, had just escaped from a wet, dirty trash compacter, why were his hair and costume perfectly clean in the next scene? Harrison Ford, who was nine years older than Hamill, turned to his less experienced colleague and replied, "it's not that kinda' movie kid."

Harrison Ford understood that *Star Wars: A New Hope* was not created in the image of *The Godfather* films and their job was not to emulate the nuanced performances delivered by method actors like Marlon Brando, Al Pacino, and Robert De Niro. The mass appeal of *Star Wars* was based on symbolism rather than realism. George Lucas' objective was not to maintain believability but to delve into the extraordinary. *Star Wars* movies are filled with implausible physics and unrealistic plot elements but the stories are rich in symbolism.

In the tradition of all great epics, the main protagonist in each *Star Wars* movie progressed through the stages included in Joseph Campbell's Hero's Journey. The first film, *Star Wars: A New Hope* (1977), followed the transformation of young Luke Skywalker from an anonymous villager to the heroic pilot who was responsible for destroying the Empire's Death Star and saving the galaxy. The sequel, *The Empire Strikes Back* (1980), follows Luke Skywalker as he retreats to the planet Dagobah to receive advanced Jedi training from Yoda *en route* to facing his villainous father Darth Vader. In the third installment, *Return of the Jedi* (1983), Luke Skywalker rescues Han Solo from Jabba the Hut before defeating the evil Emperor Palpatine.

Like each of the first Star Wars stories, the three sequels—*The Force Awakens* (2015), *The Last Jedi* (2017), and *The Rise of Skywalker* (2019)—follow the same hero's journey structure of the original stories. But instead of focusing on Luke Skywalker, these stories focus on Rae's journey and transformation.

The hero's journey plot structure resonates with viewers because the experiences of protagonists mirror our experiences. Throughout our lives, we go through trials of many kinds, and along the way, we change. If we respond to adversity by getting better rather than getting bitter, tough times help us learn, grow, mature, and transform into an improved version of ourselves. Every story that includes trials, temptations, transformation, and triumph whispers this timeless truth.

Taken as a whole, the entire *Star Wars* saga can be viewed as an intergenerational family drama with a beginning, middle, and an end, set against the backdrop of a perpetual struggle between good and evil. But if the viewer focuses just on the linear story, rather than the circular structure, they miss an important lesson.

A movie franchise is a collection of stories, divided into hero's journeys, which are held together by the continuity of characters and setting. Each movie franchise—from *James Bond* to *Indiana Jones*, *Harry Potter* to *The Hunger Games*—follows the formula.[1] And each installment in the grand saga follows the hero's journey structure. Each new episode in a movie franchise reminds us that the previous battle may be over but the war is never really won. Victory is fleeting.

At certain points in our lives, our tasks may be completed and we may experience a season of rest. But our work is never really done. The hero's journey is not a metaphor for a lifetime. Life is more like a movie franchise than a single film. Life is *a series* of hero's journeys. Just as fictional characters transform between the first and third acts of a movie, our character is shaped over time by our experiences—especially our most difficult experiences. The way we respond to adversity determines how we change (and what type of character we become). When we overcome a trial, undergo a transformation, and, once again, emerge victorious, we are not finished. But we are prepared for even more daunting trials, even more profound transformations, and even greater triumphs.

Description = Prescription

This book provided a *description* of heroes who were guided by a set of principles. On the surface, the Big Five—Lincoln, Gandhi, Dr. King, Mother Teresa, and Mandela—looked nothing alike. Lincoln and Mandela were tall in stature; Mother Teresa and Gandhi were much shorter. But they were all giants. When conventional labels and titles are insufficient to honor the impact of such exceptional leaders, we call them "heroes."

The nature of heroism is not mysterious or complicated. When heroes encounter suffering or injustice, they answer the call to help. Heroes protect

---

[1] This is especially true of superhero films. From the initial release of *Iron Man* in 2008 to *Avengers: Endgame* in 2019, the twenty-two movies set in the "Marvel Cinematic Universe" tell a more-or-less contiguous story.

the vulnerable, disarm opponents, defeat villains, and unite the village—all while adhering to timeless values. Heroes don't avoid conflicts. They engage in conflicts with discipline and restraint—in a spirit of forgiveness and reconciliation.

The heroes of history look a lot like their comic book counterparts. All heroes—whether real or imaginary—bare the same distinct mark and display the same features and traits. Real-life heroes abide by the same laws that govern the heroes of comic books and novels: Heroes don't kill, they apprehend. Heroes defeat injustice, not individuals. Heroes stand for principles, not against people. Heroes seek redemption, not revenge.

One of the best ways to improve in any area of your life is to identify and adopt the characteristics and behaviors of people who have found success in that area. A description of exceptional leaders is a prescription for exceptional leadership. A description *of* their heroism is a prescription *for* our heroism.

Doing Things

During his tenure at the Actors Studio in New York City, Lee Strasberg emphasized Stanislavski's idea of memory recall. Strasberg's "Method" required actors to summon the appropriate emotions for each scene by recalling emotions and bodily sensations that they had previously experienced in similar real-life situations. Then, those affective memories and sense memories are substituted for the emotions that the character might experience in the scene. Through emotional recall and substitution, actors were able to convey genuine emotions because they were genuinely experiencing the emotions being conveyed.

One of Strasberg's students, Elia Kazan, left the Actors Studio to focus on directing. When casting roles, Kazan preferred method actors. And while directing films, Kazan encouraged method acting techniques he had learned under Strasberg. As Kazan explained, "I want the breath of life from them rather than the mechanical fulfillment of the movement which I asked for." Kazan directed Marlon Brando in *A Streetcar Named Desire* and *On The Waterfront*. For his next project—a film adaptation of John Steinbeck's *East of Eden*—Kazan cast another Actor's Studio alum and Strasberg student—an unknown young actor named James Dean.

After meeting James Dean in New York City, Kazan saw him as "an extreme grotesque of a boy, a twisted boy." Kazan later explained that "As I got to know his father, as I got to know about his family, I learned that he had been, in fact, twisted by the denial of love." Under Kazan's direction, Dean harnessed these experiences while portraying Cal Trask, the less favored of two brothers, a troubled young man who was desperate for the approval of his legalistic father.[2]

After only three feature films, James Dean managed to transcend his craft. He was enshrined alongside Humphrey Bogart, Marilyn Monroe, and Elvis Presley, in Gottfried Helnwein's painting, *Boulevard of Broken Dreams*,[3] a Mount Rushmore of nostalgic, golden age Americana.

As a method actor, James Dean's performances were raw, realistic, and often improvised. In each of his roles, Dean employed Stanislavski's technique of experiencing rather than merely representing the character's emotions. When asked about his approach, James Dean explained:

You've got to learn how to smoke the cigarette,
not act smoking the cigarette.
You need to drink the drink, not act drinking the drink.
You've got to do things and not show them.

---

2 *East of Eden* was the only film released before 24-year-old James Dean died in a car accident East of Paso Robles, CA. James Dean's final two films were released posthumously: *Giant* (1955) and *Rebel Without A Cause* (1955), in which James Dean played Jim Stark, a disillusioned teenager in search of his father's love. Dean became the standard-bearer for suburban, middle-class teen angst and film's title became synonymous with the late actor's defiant image.

3 Gottfried's work was based on Edward Hopper's (1942) Nighthawks painting.

Full Commitment

In teaching "The Method," Stella Adler emphasized the importance of thorough research to understand each character. She also emphasized the role of imagination in considering how the character would act and feel in the "given circumstances" of a scene.

In acceptance speeches and interviews, actors sometimes applaud the performances of fellow actors by praising their "commitment." Full commitment is a prerequisite for excellence both during the preparation phase and the performance phase. In the preparation phase, actors must commit to understanding a role so that, later, they can commit to embodying the role. Some method actors have taken Adler's insistence on meticulous preparation to almost comical extremes, which have become the stuff of Hollywood legend.

Jack Nicholson and his co-stars attended group therapy sessions at the psychiatric ward where *One Flew Over the Cuckoo's Nest* was filmed. Robert De Niro, who played Travis Bickle in *Taxi Driver*, obtained a taxi driver's license so that he could transport passengers around New York City between scenes. Daniel Day-Lewis lived on the set of *The Crucible* in a 17th century-style colonial house that he built himself, using only 17th century-style tools. Years later, when he was cast in the title role of *Lincoln*, Daniel Day-Lewis refused to break character, even off set. He addressed other members of the caste by their character names and insisted on communicating only with the language that would have been common during the 1860's.

Convincing performances are a result of thorough preparation and full emersion in the role. During the performance phase, the actor "stays in character" to maintain a sense of realism or "verisimilitude." Any reluctance, any doubt, any self-consciousness, which causes the actor to display emotions that *they* are feeling—as opposed to emotions their *character* is feeling—can be fatal to a performance.

An American acting coach, Uta Hagen, built on the ideas of Stanislavski,

Strasberg, and Adler by describing acting as a game of make believe. But acting is not just about making the audience believe. As Hagen stated in her best-selling book, *Respect for Acting*, "I use substitution in order to 'make believe' in its literal sense—to make *me* believe, in order to send me into the moment-to-moment spontaneous action of my newly selected self on stage." To convince other people, an actor or a hero must first convince herself. Only then does the illusion become reality.

Your Best Bet

In life, as in literature, there are many parts to play. You might be hired *by* a CEO or you might *be* the CEO. Regardless of the position you are placed in, hired for, or elected to, only you can decide which part you play. You caste yourself into a role with the choices you make, the actions you take, and the way you treat other people. Your relationships—with subordinates, peers, and superiors—as well as your parents, your siblings, your children, and your neighbors—reveal your distinctive mark and establish your character.

If a person helps, protects, or defends people—especially if they do so at a personal cost—they are a hero. If a person seeks revenge against those who have done wrong, they are an anti-hero. If a person harms others on purpose—to receive some financial or psychological reward—they are a villain. And there are additional, less prominent, roles that people play. If a person waits passively for something to change, instead of working to change something, they are a villager. If a person is paralyzed by self-pity, rather than energized by the desire to protect others from a similar fate, they are a victim. With the choices a person makes and the actions that a person takes, they caste themselves into a role. That's just how things work.

In every context—whether at home, at the office, around the neighborhood, or on a basketball court—playing the role of the hero is always your best bet. Evil villains and insensitive bosses can achieve some measure of success—at least in the short-term. But acting like a villain or an antihero is a risky wager if you hope to achieve long-term success and lasting satisfaction.

In movies, the mentor is often old and wise but the villain is young and foolish. Why? Because the success of villains and antiheroes is usually short-lived. Tyrants tend to have short lifespans. And there is a good reason for this.

Help and harm are reciprocal. People feel compelled to help those who help them and harm those who harm them. Little in life can be accomplished alone. The hero is surrounded by people who are eager to reciprocate. But the villain is surrounded by people who lie in wait, hoping for an opportunity to retaliate. Heroes achieve more because they attract people, earn loyalty, and walk with a crowd of admirers in tow. But villains repel people, trigger animosity, and leave a mob of enemies in their wake. Enemies who will do anything they can to destroy them!

Heroes are attractive because their toughness makes people feel protected and their tenderness makes people feel comforted. Villains, on the other hand, are repulsive. Their cruelty and callousness make people feel angry and afraid. People cheer when the hero wins but long for the villain's defeat. When all is said and done, people celebrate the hero's life but revel in the villain's demise.

Playing Your Part

Heroism is helpful during times of calm and essential during tumultuous times. When times get tough, heroes step up to the challenge. When the villagers run from danger, the hero runs toward the sound of gunfire.

Lincoln, Gandhi, Dr. King, Mother Teresa, and Nelson Mandela began their transformation from villager to hero when they saw opportunities, took responsibility, and opened new possibilities for those who were suffering. They didn't ignore or avoid challenges. They took risks and encountered danger. They faced some of the most daunting problems of their times.

Compelling stories involve high stakes. That is why so many stories are set on battlefields and in operating rooms. These are life-or-death situations. High stakes bring out the best in heroes. The stakes could not have been higher when Lincoln, Gandhi, Dr. King, and Mandela fought for freedom, equality, and justice on behalf of those who were oppressed.

Compared to the villains faced by The Big Five, your adversaries may not be as enigmatic or as evil. The villagers that you serve may not be as vulnerable or as oppressed. Your endeavors might not be broadcast for millions to see. Your battles may not be fought on such a global stage. Instead of battle fields, court rooms, or slums, your stage might be a home, a workplace, a school, or a gymnasium. The stakes might not be as high when making decisions in a living room, office, classroom, or a basketball court, but the principles of heroism are the same.

In some stories, there is one hero who saves the day. But the real world is an ensemble cast, with interrelated stories about a team of heroes. There is always a need for more ordinary people who do extraordinary things on behalf of others.

Big people almost always start small. The Big Five began their lives in obscurity. But they were invited to perform on larger and larger stages by people who admired their actions and wanted to see more. The many small, seemingly insignificant performances outside the public view led to greater visibility, larger crowds, and bigger parts. As John Wooden observed, "little things make big things happen."

Mother Teresa believed in the enormous power of small actions. Her advice to those who approached her was always simple, memorable, and actionable. When people asked how they could make a difference, Mother Teresa would respond, "love one another."

Mother Teresa's life was a compilation of "small things done with great love." While performing ordinary acts of service, she modeled to her sisters how to *be* joyful—not just *act* as if she was joyful. Mother Teresa asked her sisters to start within and to "give always a happy smile."

Mother Teresa played her role and her sisters played their roles. Together, they changed the world. Mother Teresa—like all great heroes—embodied the tough and tender sides of love. She demonstrated that love is not a leadership tactic. Love is a way of being. Love is the essence of heroism.

Heroism is like method acting. You've got to hero, not act as if you are a hero. You've got to embody the part, not just act the part.

The world needs less villains and less antiheroes. The world needs less villagers waiting on the sidelines for others to take action. The world needs more heroes. The world needs *you* to be a hero. The people in your life need you to play your part. And whether you perform on a global stage or in a community theatre, remember the words of Konstantin Stanislavski:

There are no small parts, there are only small actors.

Afterword

Nathaniel

My cousin Nathaniel wanted two things. As a child, he wanted to be a superhero. As a young adult, he wanted someone to write a book about him.

Nathaniel was a pediatric heart transplant recipient. He made the most of his new heart as a dominant little league pitcher who gained a reputation for post-strikeout theatrics. He was a lights-out trap shooter, joined a bowling league, and followed his father's path in becoming an accomplished woodworker. Nathaniel never lacked enthusiasm and he was always willing to take on new challenges.

But due to the immunosuppressant medications needed to prevent Nathaniel's body from rejecting his transplanted heart, he was vulnerable to certain forms of cancer. Unfortunately, he went through several rounds of cancer and chemotherapy. Nathaniel earned the title, "cancer survivor," multiple times.

Eventually, after nearly two decades of appointments, biopsies, blood tests, infusions, and side effects, Nathaniel made the decision to forego further treatments. He was ready to go home. So he requested his friends and family gather for an "almost home" party. He wanted to see the people he loved and share with them what he loved most.

One of the things Nathaniel loved was coffee. He planned to set up his espresso machine so that he could personally make and serve mochas, lattes, and macchiatos to his guests. But, since everyone would be there to see him, Nathaniel's parents talked him out of it.

On a beautiful late summer's day in a suburb of Seattle, Nathaniel welcomed his loved ones as they arrived in the backyard. Despite the lack of artisanal coffee, the party was very much on-brand for Nathaniel. Full of love and laughter. Refreshments and friendships. Great grandparents and newborns. And Nathaniel was the keynote speaker.

Everyone at the party knew Nathaniel had been dealt a tough hand. He had as much reason as anybody to feel sorry for himself. But he didn't want pity. He didn't want sorrow. He wanted to share the reason for his joy. And he did so with conviction.

Nathaniel passed away a few weeks after his party. At the memorial service, his mother, Becky, read Nathaniel's obituary. His father, David, delivered Nathaniel's eulogy. And some of Nathaniel's closest family members shared memories on stage. After three hours of tears and laughter, it became obvious that there would not be time for the open-mic session that had been planned. There were simply too many stories to tell from such an eventful life.

In her remembrances, Becky mentioned Nathaniel's childhood wish to be a superhero. And at his party, Nathaniel had reminded me of his other wish—that someone would write a book about him. He envisioned an inspirational biography, filled with obstacles and triumphs, and centered around the theme of God's faithfulness. To my knowledge, the book he envisioned has yet to be written. But, as I listened to family members share stories of Nathaniel's impact on their lives and the lives of others, I realized there is at least one book that is about Nathaniel—this one.

Nathaniel's story is that of a little boy who grew up to become a hero. He knew *How Heroes Hero* because he lived the principles of heroism.

Nathaniel's brief time as an adult was spent doing the things heroes do: Answering the Call, Uniting the Village, and Protecting the Vulnerable. He acted on behalf of others. He stood for something (and Someone) bigger than himself. And he faced adversity with confidence, conviction, and a sense of peace that Dr. King described as "radiant assurance."

Nathaniel became increasingly heroic as he approached the end of his time with us. When friends or family members asked how they could help, Nathaniel's answer was usually the same—he asked people to pray for his mom and his three older sisters. His passing, he explained, was going to be especially tough on them.

After years of almost relentless suffering—Nathaniel was focused on protecting those he loved. Love is the heart of heroism. Nathaniel was a hero. And protecting other people is what heroes do.

Having courageously endured more than most of us could imagine, while focusing on alleviating the suffering of those around him, Nathaniel's wish was fulfilled. He became a super-hero. And like all great heroes, Nathaniel is fondly remembered and sorely missed.

Bibliography

Axelrod, A. (1999). *Patton on leadership: Strategic lessons for corporate warfare.* Prentice Hall.

Basler, R. P. (1953). *The Collected Works of Abraham Lincoln.* Rutgers University Press.

Bayne, J. T. (1931). *Tad Lincoln's Father.* Little, Brown, and Company.

Bender, Jill C. (2016). *The 1857 Indian Uprising and the British Empire.* Cambridge University Press.

Berry, W. H. (1893). *Abraham Lincoln. Address at Simpson College.*

Boller, P. F., Jr. (1981). *Presidential anecdotes.* Oxford University Press.

Bowerman, W. J., & Harris, W. E. (1967). *Jogging: A physical fitness program for all ages.* Ace Books.

Braude, J. M. (1964). *Braude's treasury of wit and humor.* Prentice-Hall.

Bullock, A. M. (1913). *Headlights of American History*, No. 2: Lincoln.

Busey, S. C. (1895). *Personal reminiscences and recollections of forty-six years' membership in the Medical Society of the District of Columbia.* Dornan.

Campbell, J. (2008). *The Hero With 1,000 Faces.* Pantheon Press.

Carpenter, F. B. (1866). *Six months at the White House.* Hurd & Houghton.

Case, C. B. (1916). *Wit and humor of Abraham Lincoln.* Shrewesbury Publishing Co.

Chafin, E. W. (1908). *Lincoln: The man of sorry.* Lincoln Temperance Press.

Colfax, S. (1865). *Life and Principles of Abraham Lincoln.* J. B. Rodgers.

Conwell, R. H. (1922). *Why Lincoln Laughed.* Harper Bros.

Covey, S. R. (1989). *The 7 Habits of Highly Effective People.* Free Press.

Cramer, J. H. (1948). *Lincoln under enemy fire.* Louisiana State University Press.

Dalal, C. B. (1971). *Gandhi: 1915-1948: A detailed chronology.* Bharatiya Vidya Bhavan.

Dana, C. A. (1996). *Recollection of the Civil War.* Bison Books.

Davis, S. (2014). *Wooden: A coach's life.* St. Martin's Griffin.

Denenberg, D., & Roscoe, L. (2001). *50 American Heroes Every Kid Should Meet!* Millbrook Press.

Dweck, C. S. (2006). *Mindset: The New Psychology of Success.* Random House.

Easwaran, E. (2011). *Gandhi the man: How one man changed himself to change the world.* Nilgiri Press.

Edison, T. A. (1931). *The diary and sundry observations of Thomas Alva Edison.* Edited for 1968 edition by Dagobert David Runes. Greenwood Pub Group.

Festinger, L. (1957). *A theory of cognitive dissonance.* Stanford University Press.

Frome, S. (2001). *Actor's Studio: A History.* McFarland Publishing.

Gandhi, A. (2017). *The Gift of anger. And other observations from my Grandfather Mahatma Gandhi.* Jeter.

Gandhi, M. K. (1921). *The Pilgrims' march: Their messages.* Ganesh & Co.

Gandhi, M. K. (1927). *An Autobiography or the Story of My Experiments with Truth*, p. 233. Navajivan.

Gandhi, M. K. (1942). *Nonviolence in peace and war.* Navajivan Publishing.

Gandhi, M. K. (1943). *The wisdom of Gandhi in his own words.* A Dakers.

Garrow, D. J. (1986). *Bearing the cross: Martin Luther King, Jr., and the Southern Christian Leadership Conference.* William Morrow and Company, Inc.

Goodwin, D. K. (2005). *Team of rivals: The political genius of Abraham Lincoln.* Simon & Schuster.

Grant, J. D. (1893). *Personal Memoirs of Julia Dent Grant* (John Y. Simon, Ed.). G. P. Putnam's Sons.

Guha, R. (2018). *Gandhi: The years that changed the world, 1914-1948.* Alfred A. Knopf.

Hagen, U. (2008). *Respect for Acting.* John Wiley & Sons, Inc.

Hani, C. (1991). *My life, an autobiography written in 1991.* SA Communist Party.

Hatfield, Edwin F. (1884). *John Newton, The Poets of the Church: A Series of Biographical Sketches of Hymn-Writers.* Anson D.F. Randolph & Company.

Hay, J. (1999). *Inside Lincoln's White House: The Complete Civil War Diary of John Hay.* (Burlinggame, M., & Ettlinger, J. R. T. (Eds). Southern Illinois University Press.

Herndon, W. H., Weik, J. W. (1930). *Herndon's Life of Lincoln: The historical and personal recollections of Abraham Lincoln.* Albert & Charles Boni.

Hertz, E. (1941). *Lincoln talks: A biography in anecdote.* Halcyon House.

Hill, A., & Wooden, J. (2001). *Be quick-but don't hurry!: Finding success in the teachings of a lifetime.* Simon & Schuster.

Hugo, V. (1862). *Les Misérables.* Dodd, Mead & Company.

Humes, J. C. (1996). *The Wit and Wisdom of Abraham Lincoln.* Gramercy:

Johnson, N. L. (2010). *Woodenisms: The wisdom and sayings of coach John Wooden.* Cool Titles.

Keane, M. (2012). *Patton: Blood, Guts, and Prayer.* Regnery Publishing, Inc.

Kimmel, S. (1957). *Mr. Lincoln's Washington.* Coward-McCann, Inc.

King, M. L., Jr. (1958). *Stride Toward Freedom: The Montgomery Story.*

King, M. L., Jr. (1963). *Strength of Love.* Harper and Row.

King, M. L., Jr. (1967). *Where Do We Go From Here?: Chaos or Community.* Harper & Row.

King, M. L. (1998). *Autobiography of Martin Luther King Jr.* (Clayborn Carson, ed.). Warner Books.

Knight, B. & Hammel, B. (2002). *Knight: My Story.* Thomas Dunne.

Maasburg, L. (2011). *Mother Teresa of Calcutta: A personal portrait.* Ignatius.

Mandela, N. (1995). *Long walk to freedom.* Little Brown.

Mandela, N. (2011). *Nelson Mandela by himself: The authorized book of quotations.* Macmillan.

Moore, S. (1984). *The Stanislavski System: The professional training of an actor* (2nd ed.). Penguin.

Mother Teresa (1983). *Words to Love By.* Ave maria Press.

Mother Teresa. (1995). *No Greater Love: The most accessible and inspirational collection of her teachings ever published.* MJF Books.

Mother Teresa. (1997). *No greater love: The most accessible and Inspirational Collection of her teachings ever published.* MJF Books.

Mother Teresa. (2007). *Come be my light: The private writings of the "Saint of Calcutta."* (edited by B. Kolodiejchuck). Doubleday.

Muggeridge, M. (1971). *Something beautiful for God: Mother Teresa of Calcutta.* Harper & Row.

Myers, W. D. (1992). *Malcolm X: By any means necessary.* Pathfinder Press.

Newton, J. (1806). *Olney hymns, in three books: I: On select texts of scripture.* J. Johnson Printing.

Oates, S. B. (1982). *Let the trumpet sound: A life of Martin Luther King, Jr.* HarperCollins.

Oldroyd, O. H. (1882), *The Lincoln memorial: Album-Immortelles.* G. W. Carleton & Co.

Palache, C. H., et al. (1944). *Dana's system of mineralogy, 7th Ed.* Wiley & Sons.

Pascal B. (1852). *Pensées,* pp. 659. Firmin-Didot.

Phillips, D. T. (1999). *Martin Luther King, Jr. on Leadership.* Warner Books.

Piaget, J., & Inhelder, B. (1969). *The psychology of the child* (translated by H. Weaver). Basic Books.

Pickren, D. A., et al (Eds.), *Portraits of pioneers in developmental psychology* (pp. 277–296). New York, NY, US: Psychology Press.

Porter, D. D. (1886). *Incidents and Anecdotes of the Civil War.* Appleton and Company.

Ricca, B. (2013). *Super boys. The amazing adventures of Jerry Siegel and Joe Shuster.* St. martin's Press.

Robinson, A. (2015). *Stepping into the light: Sources of an actor's craft.* Figueroa Press.

Scott, D. (2005). *A revolution of love: The meaning of Mother Teresa.* Loyola Press.

Sherman, W. T. (1889). *Memoirs of General W. T. Sherman.* Appleton and Company.

Smith, S. G. (1902). *The Hero Series: Abraham Lincoln.* Jennings & Pye.

Snyder, B. (2005). *Save the cat!: The last book on screenwriting you'll ever need.* Michael Wiese Productions.

Solzhenitsyn, A. I. (1974) *The Gulag Archipelago.* Collins.

Spink, K. (1997). *Mother Teresa: A complete authorized biography.* Harper.

Stanislavski, K. (1924). *My life in art.* Little Brown.

Stengel, R. (2009). *Mandela's Way: Fifteen Lessons on Life, Love, and Courage.* Crown.

Stevens, G., Jr. (2006). *Conversations with the great moviemakers of Hollywood's golden age at the American Film Institute.* Random House: New York.

Swett, A. T. (1971) Lincoln's story of his own life, in *Reminiscences of Abraham Lincoln,* (A. T. Haskell, ed.). House Publishers Ltd.

Tandy, F. D. (1908). *An anthology of the epigrams and sayings of Abraham Lincoln.* Francis D. Tandy Company.

Tarbell, I. M. (1890), *The Life of Abraham Lincoln.* Doubleday & McClure co.

Thomas, B. P., & Hyman, H. M. (1962). *Stanton: The life and times of Lincoln's secretary of war.* Alfred A. Knopf.

Thompson, D. D. (1894). *Abraham Lincoln, the first American.* Cranston & Curts.

Tzu, S. (2010). *The art of war.* Capstone Publishing.

Van Biema, D. (2010). *Mother Teresa: The life and works of a modern saint.* Time Books.

Varela, et al. (1991). *The Embodied Mind: Cognitive Science and Human Experience.* MIT Press.

Villard, H. (1904). *Memoirs of Henry Villard, Vol. I.*, p. 147. Houghton, Mifflin and Company.

Villard H. (1941) *Lincoln on the Eve of '61.* A. A. Knopf.

Watson, B. (2000). *The Father of Judo: A Biography of Jigoro Kano:* Kodansha International.

Whitney, S. A. (1897). *Abraham Lincoln's Lost Speech.* The De Vinne Press.

Wooden, J., & Jamison, S. (2005). *Wooden on Leadership.* McGraw-Hill.

Wooden, J., & Yaeger, D. (2009). *A game plan for life: The power of mentoring.* Bloomsbury.

Notes

Ch. 1 | Answering The Call

"There are those who see the need and respond. I consider those people my heroes." Spoken by Fred Rogers in 1994, cited in his obituary printed in the *Pittsburgh Post-Gazette*, February 28, 2003.

While on a rickety train en route to Darjeeling: Spink (1997), p. 22.

"Call within a call." Mother Teresa (2007), p. 40.

"I thirst." Mother Teresa (2007), p. 41.

"Quench the thirst...for love of souls." Mother Teresa (2007), p. 395.

"Wholehearted free service to the poorest of the poor." Muggeridge (1971), p. 97.

"Sitting in a first-class seat on a train...to Pretoria." Gandhi (1927), 111-112.

"Should I fight for my rights or...next available train to Pretoria." Gandhi (1927), pp. 112.

"No man is good enough to govern another without the other's consent." Speech at Peoria, October 16, 1854

"If slavery is not wrong, nothing is wrong." Letter to Albert G. Hodges, April 4, 1864.

"A chance to escape the long night of segregation..." King (1958), p. 21.

"The victim of a threefold malady...in the uneducated." King (1958), p. 37.

"Martin, Martin, come quickly!...Darling, it's empty!" King (1958), p. 52.

"I neither started the protest nor suggested it. I simply responded to the call of the people for a spokesman." Speech, March 31, 1958.

"The reward for work well done is..." Denenberg & Roscoe (2001), p. 99.

Like Mandela and Gandhi, Dr. King was incarcerated. King (1998).

"I am in Birmingham because injustice is here." King (1958), p. 159.

"I am here because...any one of them concerns all individuals." Letter, April 16, 1963.

"For the past several days I have been...I must go back to the valley." King (1963).

"This is not the life I expected to lead," he explained, *"but gradually you take some responsibility, then a little more."* King's personal notes, 1956.

Ch. 2 | Protecting The Vulnerable

"Life's most persistent and urgent question is, 'What are you doing for others?'" Speech delivered May 17, 1967 at Sproul Plaza in Montgomery, Alabama.

Riding horseback…Lincoln heard the squeal of a pig. Humes (1996), pp. 77-78.

An aggrieved man entered a law office in Springfield, IL. Humes (1996), p. 56.

"One day…Mother Teresa was swarmed by a group of children." Spink (1997), p. 35.

"I picked her up and took her to the hospital." Spink (1997), p. 36.

"Today I learned a good lesson." Muggeridge (1971), p. 72.

"In order to understand and help those who are suffering." Spink (1997), p. 44.

"We have come to give tender love and care." Spink (1997), p. 239.

Psychologists use the term "directed altruism." De Wall, F. B. M. (2008). Putting the altruism back into altruism: The evolution of empathy. *Annual Review of Psychology, 59,* 279-300.

"There is more hunger in the world for love and appreciation than for bread." Maasburg (2011), p. 39.

"I never look at the masses… Just one, one, one." Mother Teresa (1983), p. 79.

"I feel called to help individuals…person-to-person encounters." Mother Teresa (1995), p. 69.

"Cared about…not from some grand theoretical perspective." Gandhi (2017), p. 6.

A Kantian philosopher…used the terms "idiographic" and "nomothetic." History and Natural Science (1998). *Theory and Psychology,* 6–22.

"If only one man dies of hunger, that is a tragedy." Washington Post (January 20, 1947).

Superman's debut. Siegel, J., & Shuster, J. (April 18, 1938). *Action Comics #1.* DC Comics.

"Some people are suffering…I am going to fight for them." Sermon at Ebenezer Baptist church, June 5, 1966.

"He who is the greatest among you shall be your servant." Speech, February 4, 1968.

Gandhi's first notable acts of public service… Gandhi (1927), pp. 215-216.

"All other pleasures and possessions pale…spirit of joy." Gandhi (1927), p. 175.

"Power comes from sincere service." Gandhi (2017), p. 261.

"For show or for fear of public opinion…crushes his spirit." Gandhi (1927), p. 175.

"Selfishness and egotism." Gandhi (1927), p. 396.

"Service can have no meaning… unless one takes pleasure in it." Gandhi (1927), p. 175.

"Why did we come here?...do that with a smile!" Maasburg (2011), p. 133.

"No one thinks of the pen while reading a letter…." Scott (2005), p. 37.

"Yes, for a million dollars I wouldn't do it either." Maasburg (2011), p. 36.

"I freely acknowledge myself the servant of the people…I am responsible to them." Letter to James Conkling, August 26, 1863.

Ch. 3 | Projecting Calm

"Fearlessness presupposes calmness and peace of mind." Gandhi, M. K. (March 11, 1946). *Harijan*, p. 388.

"Coach Wooden just raised an eyebrow. He must be very upset about something." Wooden & Jamieson (2005), pp. 111-112.

"Emotion is your enemy." Wooden & Jamieson (2005), p. 107.

"Be quick but don't hurry." Hill & Wooden (2001), p, 69.

"If you don't have time to do it right, when will you have time to do it over?" Johnson (2010), p. 30.

"Stood in front...what those Sisters are doing in there." Maasburg (2011), p. 158.

"Man, I was terrified up there." Stengel (2009), p. 25.

"Calm is what people look for in tense situations...." Stengel (2009), pp. 39-40

"Now let's not become panicky...Go home with this glowing faith and radiant assurance." King (1958), p. 137.

"We must not return violence under any condition...We must somehow believe that unearned suffering is redemptive." King (1958), pp. 178-179.

"I'm not going to run, Hosea." Oates (1982), p. 299.

"I was scared they were going to jump us... if he can do it, somehow nothing will happen to me." Oates (1982), p. 299.

"We need leadership that is calm...no place for misguided emotionalism." Speech, May 17, 1957.

"I want to make a point that I think everyone here should consider...And I want you to think about it." Oates (1982), p. 213.

"I can't promise you that it won't get you killed." Speech, February 26, 1965.

"I have a job to do... if I should lose my life, in some way it would aid the cause." Speech, January, 1965.

"The people know I come among them without fear." Thomas & Hyman (1962), p. 395.

"Rather be dead than to live in continued dread." Joshua Speed, recorded September 16, 1885.

"If I am killed, I can die but once; but to live in constant dread of it, is to die over and over again." Sanger, W. T. (February, 1907). The assassination of Lincoln. *The Philomathean Monthly*, volume XI, p. 12.

"The President evinced a remarkable coolness and disregard for danger." Cramer (1948), p. 30.

"One morning, Edwin Stanton, Lincoln's secretary of war, stormed into the President's office... Now burn it and write another letter." Humes (1996), p. 202.

"*Pocket the insult.*" Gandhi (1927), p. 114.

"*I am glad to see you can be moved to anger…It is an energy that compels us to define what is just and unjust.*" Gandhi (2017), pp. 17-18.

"*When we channel electricity intelligently…use anger wisely for the good of humanity.*" Gandhi (2017), p. 20.

"*People make bad choices when they're mad or scared or stressed.*" Buck, C., & Lee, J. (Directors). (2013). *Frozen* [Film]. Walt Disney Pictures.

There is a psychology to vicious circles. Omli, J. (2008). The MVP Model: From phenomenology to performance. *The Sport Psychologist, 22,* 229-243.

"*Ironic processing.*" Janelle, C. M. (1999). Ironic mental processes in sport: Implications for sport psychologists. *The Sport Psychologist, 13,* 201-220.

You cannot fail in any laudable object…unless you allow your mind to be improperly directed." Letter to William H. Herndon, July 10, 1848

"*When I hear a man preach, I like to see him act as if he were fighting bees.*"
Leonard Volk, as quoted in Hertz (1941), p. 77.

"*We must not be led by excitement…to do that which our sober judgments would not approve in our cooler moments.*" Speech, May 29, 1956 printed in Whitney (1897), pp. 11-12.

"*In grave emergencies, moderation is generally safer than radicalism.*" Speech, May 29, 1956 printed in Whitney (1897), pp. 11-12.

"*Nothing valuable can be lost by taking time."* Lincoln's first inaugural address, March 4, 1961

"*I promise to 'keep cool' under all circumstances:"* Letter to General John J. Hardin, January 19, 1845.

Humans engage in…"social referencing." Bandura, A. (1992). Social Cognitive theory of social referencing. In S. Feinman (ed.), *Social Referencing and the Social Construction of Reality in Infancy,* pp. 175-208. Springer Science + Business Media.

Ch. 4 | Remaining Vigilant

"*No decision is difficult to make if you will get all the facts.*" Axelrod (1999), p. 88.

"*Old blood and guts.*" Keane (2012).

"*We must step down from our pedestals and live with them.*" Easwaran (2011), p. 80.

"*I do not think much of a man who is not wiser today than we was yesterday.*" Bullock (1913), p. 156.

"*They don't want much, they get but little, and I must see them.*" Hay (1890). Life in the White house in the time of Lincoln, pp. 33. *Century.*

"*Public opinion baths… invigorating to my perceptions of responsibility and duty.*" Carpenter

(1869), pp. 281-282.

"*Serve to renew in me a clearer and more vivid image of that great popular assemblage out of which I sprung.*" Carpenter (1869), p. 281.

"*We are in the midst of a great movement...we are destined to win.*" Remarks, October, 1962.

"*You can't really get close to the poor without living and being here with them.*" Speech, January 26, 1966.

"*To other countries I may go as a tourist, but to India I come as a pilgrim.*" Statement, February 2, 1959.

"*A deep study of the social, economic, and political conditions...was to be of invaluable service to me in the future.*" Gandhi (1927), p. 128.

"*I can give no opinion without seeing the conditions with my own eyes.*" Gandhi (1927), p. 405.

"*A tour through India travelling third class...their comforts are sheep's comforts.*" Gandhi (1927), p. 238.

"*The indifference of the railway authorities...regardless of the convenience or comfort of fellow passengers.*" Gandhi (1927), p. 240.

"*Latrines for us!...Latrines are for the big people.*" Gandhi (1927), p. 170.

"*The sari I am wearing is the only one I have...merely with a rag to cover their shame.*" Gandhi (1927), p. 423.

"*Inside and outside, upside and downside...he was remorseless in his analysis of facts and principles.*" Herndon & Weik (1930), p. 478.

"*During the first six months after my release...taste different foots, speak with all manner of people.*" Mandela (1995), p. 413.

"*a world radically different...it was sometimes difficult to keep up with them.*" Mandela (1995), p. 413.

"*Mother Teresa acknowledged with girlish pleasure.*" Spink (1997), p. 83.

"*Gift for giving her whole attention to the person she encountered.*" Spink (1997), p. vi.

"*Her warmth and...Mother Teresa did not regard visitors as a bothersome disturbance.*" Maasburg (2011), p. 96.

"*He took off his shoes and went into the chapel...utterly immersed again in prayer.*" Maasburg (2011), pp. 2-3.

"*For that moment... many people who met her felt that they were her best friend.*" Maasburg (2011), p. 96.

"*If you wanted to talk to him, he was going to take time to talk... that was his nature.*" Garrow (1986), p. 603.

"*It would literally take him...an hour to walk one and a half blocks.*" Garrow (1986), p. 603.

"*A thousand miles to sit and wait...I will not have the time to come one mile to see him.*"

Interview, June 11, 1967.

"*I have always endeavored to listen…in the discussion.*" Mandela (1995), 25-26.

"*Express as radical a view as possible and somebody to express as conservative a view as possible.*" Garrow (1986), p. 464.

"*I remember that some time previously…his painstaking description of the Baton Rouge experience was invaluable.* King (1958), p. 75.

"*Empty drums make the loudest noises.*" Gandhi (2017), p. 183.

"*Beyond occasionally exposing me to laughter…It has helped me in my discernment of truth.*" Gandhi (1927), p. 63.

Ch. 5 | Finding Solitude

"*The best thinking has been done in solitude.*" Edison (1931), p. 56.

"*It is the joy of giving, the joy of bringing love into people's lives that keeps us all going.*" Spink, K. (1997), p. 216.

On flights, she kept a tablet of paper on her seatback table: Maasburg, L. (2011), p. 45.

"*Silence gives us a new outlook on life…silence of the eyes, ears, tongue, mind, and heart.*" Spink, K. (1997), pp. 74-75.

After his return from South Africa, Gandhi spent 43% of his days traveling outside the Ashram in Ahmedabad. Dalal, C. B. (1971), p. ix.

In total, Gandhi spent 18% of his time in prison, which amounts to nearly 6 years of his life. Dalal, C. B. (1971), p. ix.

"*You did not disturb my solitude. My solitude is taken in the midst of many.*" Easwaran (2011), p. 156.

Big chair by the window. Bayne (1931), p. 32.

Sleep is important to our physical and emotional health: Ramar, K., et al. (2021). Sleep is essential to health: an American Academy of Sleep Medicine position statement. *Journal of Clinical Sleep Medicine, 17*(10), 2115-2119.

Dr. King was in-and-out of the hospital with exhaustion and infections. King (1958).

"*The doctors tell me I can't get by on two or three hours of sleep a night.*" Remarks, 1966.

"*Sleeping a third of your life adds a third to your life span.*" Gandhi (2017), pp. 68-69.

His 1927 autobiography: Gandhi (1927).

"*I believed then…one should always find some time for exercise…adds to it.*" Gandhi (1927), p. 233.

Two decades before the term "jogging" was popularized by…Bill Bowerman." Bowerman & Harris (1967).

"*I have always believed…the inflexible disciplines of my life.*" Mandela (1995), pp. 319-320

While practicing as a young lawyer, Mandela also trained as a boxer. Mandela (1995).

"*Stationary running in my cell…and various other calisthenics.*" Mandela (1995). pp. 319-320.

"*Sharpen your saw.*". Covey (1989).

1 in 50 Americans lost their lives as a direct or indirect result of combat: National Park Service (2023). *Civil War Facts: 1861-1865.*

"*Where he was assured of good conversation and much-needed relaxation.*" Goodwin (2005), p. 506.

"*With the fearful strain that is on me night and day, if I did not laugh, I should die.*" Conwell (1922).

"*I must have some relief from this terrible anxiety, or it will kill me.*" Colfax (1865), p. 12.

"*To plant a seed, watch it grow, to tend it and then harvest it, offered, a simple but enduring satisfaction.*" Mandela (1995), *p. 318.*

Mother Teresa referred to her network of volunteer "coworkers" as the "most disorganized organization in the world." Spink (1997), p. vi.

"*Father, do you know what the abbreviation MC after our name really stands for?…Mental Case, Multiple Change.*" Maasburg (2011), pp. 47-48.

"*Most of us think of important people as being serious…swing his legs off the ground with childlike joy.*" Gandhi (2017), p. 190.

"*Embodied cognition.*" Varela (1991).

"*I am a specialist…probably the world's best specialist in cleaning toilets.*" Maasburg (2011), p. 175.

"*How do you learn humility? Only through humiliations!*" Maasburg (2011), p. 179.

"*To know oneself and not to be untrue.*" Spink (1997), p. 230.

"*I have a PhD from the London School of Economics…change the economy of the country.*" Gandhi (2017), pp. 180-181.

"*Mother Teresa…You and me!*" Maasburg (2011), p. 194.

"*Self-knowledge puts us on our knees…needed sharpening just a little more.*" Spink (1997), p. 230.

"*Fill yourself first and then only will you be able to give to others.*" Spink (1997), p. 181.

Ch. 6 | Preparing for Battle

"*Failing to prepare is preparing to fail.*" Johnson (2010), p. 144.

"*The will to win is not as important as the will to prepare to win.*" Knight & Hammel (2002), p. 21.

"*Think weeks.*" Clifford, C. (July 28, 2019). Bill Gates took solo 'think weeks' in a cabin in the woods---why it's a great strategy." CNBC.com.

"*I insist on a lot of time being spent, almost every day, to just sit and think.*" Schwantes, M. L. (2021). In a few words, Warren Buffett reminds us of a forgotten habit that led to his success. Inc, Nov. 8.

"*Most of my reading since 1893 has been done in jail.*" Gandhi (1972), p. 166.

"*I know nothing so pleasant…at once new and valuable.*" Humes (1996), p. 39.

"*Want of education.*" Swett (1971), p. 458.

"*He read hard works.*" Interview, December 20, 1855.

"*The Bible, Blackstone, and the Bard.*" Humes (1996), p. 79.

"*A loss to a man not to have grown up among books.*" Case (1916), p. 95.

"*A capacity, and a taste for reading.*" Address at the Wisconsin State Fair, September 30, 1859.

"*Books serve to show a man that those original thoughts of his aren't very new after all.*" Case (1916), p. 95.

"It's what you learn after you know it all that counts." Johnson (2010), p. 8.

"*Drink deeply of good books.*" Johnson (2010), p. 162.

"*When we go into action…we must be as armed with knowledge as they are.*" King (1967), p. 155.

"*Education gives us not only knowledge…but wisdom, which is control.*" King (1958), p. 206.

"*I began the only way I knew…fundamental questions.*" Mandela (1995), p. 102.

"*As freedom fighters and political prisoners…at night our cell block seemed more like a study hall than a prison.*" Mandela (1995), p. 229.

"*See the enemy's point of view…and profit from the wisdom.*" Stengel (2009), p. 79.

"*If you know the enemy and know yourself.*" Tzu (2010).

"*When you speak Afrikaans…you go straight to their hearts.*" Mandela (2011), p. 144.

Lincoln announced that he would "not receive callers." *National Republican*, March 2, 1865.

"*I want to think it over.*" Common response to important questions.

"*Rarely do we find men who willingly engage in hard, solid thinking.*" A Tough Mind and a Tender Heart Sermon, August 30, 1959, Montgomery, AL, Dexter Baptist.

"*Advertisers have long since learned that most people are soft minded.*" A Tough Mind and a Tender Heart Sermon, August 30, 1959, Montgomery, AL, Dexter Baptist.

"*Cold, calculating, unimpassioned reason.*" Smith (1902), p. 31.

Calling Lincoln his "favorite American." Wooden & Yaeger (2009).

Wooden's notecards. Hill & Wooden (2001), p. 156.

Mother Teresa was affectionately called the "Benevolent Dictator." Maasburg (2011), p. 90.

"*She had all the elements assembled…Her decision then stood firm as a rock.*" Maasburg (2011), pp. 89-90.

"*Don't hurry; think, analyze, then act.*" Stengel (2009), p. 53.

"*I think it cannot be shown that when I have once taken a position, I have ever retreated from it.*" Liberator, January 29, 1864."

"*Hard, solid thinking.*" A Tough Mind and a Tender Heart Sermon, August 30, 1959, Montgomery, AL, Dexter Baptist.

Ch. 7 | Disarming Opponents

"*Do I not destroy my enemies when I make them friends?*" King (1963), p. 39.

"*Suddenly...she invited them to eat with us.*" Maasburg (2011), pp. 97-98.

"*We were led into a windowless room...the poorest of the poor in the slums of Managua!*" Maasburg (2011), pp. 59-60.

Mother Teresa received the permission she sought: Spink (1997), p. 290.

"*What do you want...if I can do anything to help you, please let me know.*" Spink (1997), pp. 98-99.

"*Perhaps there might be some people...bring hope to the discouraged.*" Spink (1997), p. 199.

"*No, I am coming from Calcutta.*" Spink (1997), p. 201.

"*We have no poor people here...whom I am offering.*" Maasburg (2011), pp 118-119.

"*That charisma—that of opening doors which others cannot.*" Spink (1997), p. 272.

"*Don't go near Gandhi. He'll get you.....and stayed to serve*" Easwaran (2011), p. 85.

"*You are always talking about revolution...the rest of your family too.*" Easwaran (2011), p. 86.

"*See here, Lincoln...sure to hit me inside this mark or it won't be fair.*" Braude (1964), p. 74.

"*Was remarkably gentle with young lawyers...personal affection.*" Unidentified lawyer, quoted in Tarbell (1890).

"*As a poor man I don't have a carriage...vote for my opponent who is a fine gentleman.*" Humes (1996), p. 167.

"*Always attracted the riveted attention...kept his company in a roar of laughter.*" Oldroyd (1882), p. 241.

"Was always ready with a story or anecdote...Everybody prepared for the explosion of laughter to follow." Busey (1985), p. 25.

"A very offensive man... provoking unpleasant discussion." Busey (1895), p. 26.

"*Did not wish to introduce or discuss subjects...made him very popular with the household.* Busey (1895), p. 27.

"*Is the very embodiment of good temper and affability...strongly and favorably impressed with his general disposition.*" Villard (1941), pp. 39-40.

"*To explain a meaning or enforce a point... heal wounded feelings and mitigate

disappointments." Villard (1904), p. 175.
"*Deliberately strode across the room…planned and practiced.*" Mandela (1995), p. 33.
"*The meeting was not even half an hour…he could not do that.*" Mandela (1995), p. 387.
"*Something decent and honorable…since they were children.*" Stengel (2009), p. 122.
"*He was a very decent chap…he was very polite.*" Stengel (2009), pp. 117-118.
"*The line separating good and evil…small corner of evil.*" Solzhenitsyn (1974), p. 168.
"*Just as pretending to be brave can…reveal their better selves.*" Stengel (2009), p. 117.
"*People will feel I see too much good…with whom you work.*" Stengel (2009), p. 129.
"*There's as much crookedness as you want to find… trust too much than distrust and be miserable all the time.*" Davis (2014).
"*The coach who…tells his players they are rotten is sure to make them so.*" Davis (2014).
"*I know very well…and I have decided to see the good.*" Maasburg (2011), p. 92.
"*Always insisted that she knew nothing about politics…she was not there to mix in politics but to support life.*" Spink (1997), p. 183.
"She, as a matter of principle, never said a negative word about anyone…local politicians had assisted in her work." Maasburg (2011), p. 90-91.
"*I do not feel like judging or condemning…never judge.*" Van Biema (2010), p. 67.
"*Rather excuse than accuse…If you judge someone, then you have no time to love him.*" Maasburg (2011), p. 91.
"*The authors of all the vice and misery and crime in the land…even to his own best interest.*" Lincoln's *Address to the Springfield Washington Temperance Society,* February 22, 1842.
Lincoln was careful not to "impugn the motives of anyone opposed." Response to a crowd serenading Lincoln after his re-election, as cited in Kimmel (1957), p. 154.
"*The better part of one's life consists of friendships… The loss of enemies does not compensate for the loss of friends.*" Telegram to Secretary Seward, June 30, 1862.
"*I want it said of me that I always plucked a thistle and planted a flower when I thought a flower would grow.*" Berry (1893), p. 24.
"*Damned long armed ape.*" William Herndon to Jessie Weik, January 6, 1887, reel 10, Herndon-Weik Collection, DLC.
"*I choose always to make my statute of limitations a short one.*" Carpenter (1966), p. 257.
A man has not time…remember the past against him." Conversation with Gideon Wells.
"*Why Madam, do I not destroy my enemies when I make them friends?*" King (1963), p. 39.

Ch. 8 | Defeating Villains

Opening paragraphs: Donner, R. (Director). (1978). *Superman: The movie* [Film]. Dovemead, Ltd.

NOTES 251

History of slavery in America. History.com editors (November 12, 2009). *Slavery in America*. A&E Television network.

"*Whenever I hear anyone arguing for slavery, I feel a strong impulse to see it tried on him personally.*" Address to Indiana Regiment, March 17, 1865, cited in Tandy (1908), p. 52.

"*If slavery is not wrong, nothing is wrong.*" Lincoln letter to Albert G. Hodges, April 4, 1864.

"*The slave is a man who cannot be considered 'mere merchandise.'*" Lincoln speech in Peoria, IL, October 16, 1854.

"*House Divided Speech.*" Delivered June 16, 1858 at the Illinois State Capitol, Springfield, IL.

Demographic statistics for Montgomery, AL in 1954: King (1958), pp. 28-29.

"*A threefold malady…could ever be achieved in Montgomery.*" King (1958), pp. 37-38.

"*One way is acquiescence…it is the way of the coward.*" King (1958), p. 212.

"*Physical violence and corroding hatred…merely creates new and more complicated ones.*" King (1958), p. 212.

"*Violence as a way of achieving racial justice…creates bitterness in the survivors and brutality in the destroyers.*" King (1958), pp. 212-213.

"*The nonviolent resister agrees…in order to right a wrong.*" King (1958), pp. 213-214.

Rosa Parks refused to give up her seat. Arrest occurred on December 1, 1955.

Dr. King's "Give Us the Ballot" speech." Delivered at the Prayer Pilgrimage for Freedom in Washington, D.C., May 17, 1957.

"*Our most urgent question…we want it back.*" For the "Give us the Ballot" speech, May 17, 1957.

"*Injustice anywhere is a threat to justice everywhere.*" From Dr. King's *Letter from a Birmingham Jail*, written April 16, 1963.

Kanō Jigorō, founder of jūdō: Watson (2000).

"*Bloody Sunday" and the Edmunds Pettis Bridge.* King (1998).

A popular uprising known to Indians as the First Indian War of Independence and to the British as the Indian Rebellion of 1857. Bender (2016).

He was swarmed by a cheering crowd as he and his family disembarked the S. S. Arabia: Bombay Chronicle, January 11, 1915.

"*For a bowl of water…return with gladness good for evil done.*" Gandhi (1972), p. 35.

"*Went straight to my heart.*" Gandhi (1972), p. 69.

"*You have heard that it was said to the people long ago, 'You shall not murder…in danger of the fire of hell.*" Matthew 5: 21-22, *New International Version*. Biblica, Inc.

"You have heard that it was said, 'Eye for eye, and tooth for tooth'…hand over your coat as well." Matthew 5: 38-40, *New International Version*. Biblica, Inc.

"You have heard that it was said, 'Love your neighbors…that you may be children of your father in heaven." Matthew 5: 43-45, *New International Version*. Biblica, Inc.

"*Ahimsa is a comprehensive principle…but he can never become entirely free from outward himsa.*" Gandhi (1927), p. 349.

"*That renunciation was the highest form of religion appealed to me greatly.*" Gandhi (1927), p. 70.

"*Found that the term 'passive resistance' was too narrowly construed.*" Gandhi (1927), p. 318.

"*Should not be to punish the opponent…rendering him humanitarian service whenever possible.*" Easwaran (2011), p. 194.

"*I've come to tell you that…with your help.*" Easwaran (2011), p. 64.

"*Never resort to violence…by any other honest labour.*" Gandhi (1927), pp. 427-428.

"*However much I may sympathize…the evil it does is permanent.*" Easwaran (2011), p. 60.

"*This is a struggle of not one man, but millions of us.*" Gandhi (2017), p. 119.

"*Come to arrest Mr. M. K. Gandhi… This is all I need.*" Easwaran (2011), p. 93.

"Nonviolence is the weapon of the brave…unadulterated fearlessness." Gandhi, M. K. (March 25, 1939). *Harijan*, p. 64.

"*Satyagraha is gentle…It is never the intention of a satyagrahi to embarrass the wrongdoer.*" Gandhi, M. K. (March 25, 1939). *Harijan*, p. 64.

"*Man and his deed are two distinct things…why the poison of hatred spreads throughout the world.*" Gandhi (1927), p. 276.

"*The appeal is never to his fear…convert, not to coerce, the wrongdoer.*" Gandhi (March 3, 1939), *Harijan*, p. 64.

"*Let's join forces… I want to educate them and change their hearts.*" Gandhi (2017), p. 32.

"*The sympathy of everyone—including the police—not to hurt or embarrass them.*" Gandhi (2017), p. 32.

"*Does not seek to destroy the opponent…but not the antagonists themselves.*" Gandhi, M. K. (1930). Some Rules for Satyagraha. *Navajivan*, p. 23.

"*Segregation is totally un-Christian…those who believe in segregation.*" Letter to Sally Canada, September 19, 1956.

"*A conflict between justice and injustice…so low as to hate them.*" Speech, February, 1956.

"*Should seek to persuade the perpetrators of segregation through love, patience, and understanding.*" Letter to Sally Canada, September 19, 1956.

"*I knew that people expected…the system that turned us against one another.*" Mandela (1995), pp. 407-408.

"*We had been taking turns…I defeated my opponents without dishonoring them.*" Mandela

(1995), p. 11.

"South Africa belongs to all who live in it, black and white…I do not want to drive you into the sea." Mandela (1995), p. 373.

"Wanted to impress upon the reporters…our struggle for a democratic, nonracial South Africa." Mandela (1995), p. 408.

"To Every Briton… I know of no single case in which it has failed." Open letter from Gandhi on July 3, 1940.

Gandhi was never elected to political office and had no official role in the British or Indian governments. Guha (2018).

"There is no force in the world that is so direct or so swift in working." Gandhi, M. K. (April 6, 1925) *Young India*, p. 189.

Within 24 hours of his speech…they would not win the war. Guha (2018).

"Mr. Gandhi, you may know all about…that does not mean that it cannot take place in the future." Easwaran (2011), p. 69.

Ch. 9 | Uniting the Village

"If you want to make peace with your enemy, you have to work with your enemy. Then he becomes your partner." Mandela (1995).

"More than any of his other speeches…reverence, and belief in God—his justice and overruling power—increased in him." Goodwin (2005), p. 699.

"Both read the same Bible and pray to the same God, and each invokes His aid against the other." Lincoln's Second Inaugural Address, March 4, 1865.

"Fondly do we hope, fervently do we pray…a just and lasting peace among ourselves and with all nations." Lincoln's Second Inaugural Address, March 4, 1865.

"I am very greatly rejoiced…but I insisted yesterday that we fairly captured it." National Intelligencer, April 10, 1865.

"I presented the question to the Attorney General…I now request the band to favor me with its performance." National Intelligencer, April 10, 1865.

"It is good to show the rebels that with us they will be free to hear it again." Chambrun, A. D. (1893), Personal Recollections of Mr. Lincoln. *Scribner's*, p. 34.

"The crowd went off in high good-humor." National Intelligencer, April 11, 1865.

"Today we are entering a new era…one nation is at hand." Mandela Inauguration Speech, May 9, 1994.

"The time for the healing of the wounds has come… God bless Africa!" Mandela Speech in Pretoria, South Africa, May 10, 1994.

"In awe as a spectacular array of South African jets, helicopters, and troop carriers roared in

perfect formation over the Union Buildings." Mandela (1995), p. 455.

"*The day was symbolized for me by the playing of our two national anthems…they would soon know the words by heart.*" Mandela (1995), p. 456.

"*Not just as the leader of the ANC…their struggle was indivisible.*" Mandela (1995), p. 316.

"*Always choose an Indian or a Colored prisoner… for a leader to do.*" Stengel (2009), p. 94.

"*Afrikaners were Africans…a symbol of South African culture.*" Stengel (2009), pp. 138-139.

"*No man or woman…one-vote on a common voters' roll.*" Mandela (1995), p. 410.

"*One of preaching reconciliation…together into the future.*" Mandela (1995), pp. 453-454.

"*Free at last! Free at last.*" Mandela Inauguration Speech, May 9, 1994.

"*Living tomorrow with the very people against whom [they are] struggling today.*" King (1967), p. 72.

"*Let us remember that as we struggle, we must have love, compassion and understanding goodwill for those against whom we struggle.*" Speech, May 17, 1956.

"*I would be terribly disappointed if any of you go back to the buses bragging…a victory for justice and democracy.*" Speech, November 14, 1956.

"*Respond to the decision with… new adjustments that the court order poses for them.*" King (1958), p. 171.

"*Integration based on mutual respect…on the basis of a real harmony of interests and understanding.*" King (1958), p. 171.

"*Go back to the buses in all humility with gratitude to Almighty God for making this decision possible.*" Speech, November 14, 1956.

"*Just as determined to see us free as we are to be free ourselves.*" Interview, June 26, 1966.

"*I always have in the past and will in the future… society toward which we work.*" Interview, 1959.

"*Would take each volunteer by the hand…or just sit by him, pray beside him, or shave him.*" Maasburg (2011), p. 35.

"*Had put the volunteers physically in touch…she would smile broadly and contentedly.*" Maasburg (2011), p. 36.

"*An elegantly dressed man came into the House…I just wanted to bring them to you personally.*" Maasburg (2011), p. 5.

"*The most important twenty minutes of my life—cleaning toilets.*" Maasburg (2011), p. 106-107.

"*Doesn't matter race, doesn't matter religion… We are all children of God, created to love and to be loved.*" Maasburg (2011), p. 155.

"*It is not your money but your time we need…we want all of you to donate YOURSELVES to the poor people.*" Rotary international speech

"*She did not want to set people against each other…She wanted the rich to save the poor and*

the poor to save the rich." Spink (1997), p. 247.
"I am praying so much for her happiness...Prayer can help them through their troubles." Spink (1997), p. 263.
"And how is your grandson, Prince William?" Spink (1997), p. 180.
"The great and the humble were treated alike...even in mayors, ministers and presidents." Maasburg (2011), p. 152.
"Did nothing to alter...regardless of nationality, standing or creed." Spink (1997), p. 180.
"When Mother Teresa picked a human being...could all count just the same on her love and care." Maasburg (2011), p. 155.
"I hate from the bottom of my heart the hideous system of untouchability for which millions of Hindus have made themselves responsible." Gandhi, M. K. (June 8, 1925). *Young India*, p. 272.
"All of us are one... If God were here, everyone would have access." Easwaran (2011), p. 79.
"Big folks" church...a social club with a thin veneer of religiosity." King (1958), p. 25.
Dr. King joined several organizations, including the NAACP. King (1958), p. 35.
"Deep down within all of us," [we have] an instinct...a desire to be first." Speech, February 4, 1968.
"The ability of Negroes to enter alliances...not of weakness." King (1967), p. 60.
"Whenever Pharaoh wanted to keep the slaves in slavery, he kept them fighting among themselves." Speech, August 31, 1966.
"There is amazing power in unity...every effort to disunite only serves to strengthen the unity." King (1958), p. 150.
"The victim of the deferred dreams, of blasted hopes." Speech, December, 1967.
"Was met with all the natural human emotions of jealousy, apprehension, and distrust—even in his own hometown." Phillips (1999), p. 138.
"Orchestrate a group of individuals that probably pretty much approached egomania." Garrow (1986), p. 464.
"Remarkable facility for...summarizing what everybody had said and synthesizing." Garrow (1986), p. 464.
"The biggest job in getting any movement...is to keep together the people who form it." King (1958), p. 84.

Ch. 10 | Disregarding Speed Limits

"An unjust law is no law at all." Letter from a Birmingham Jail, April 16, 1963.
"There is a higher court than...the court of conscience. It supersedes all other courts." Gandhi (1921), p. 108.

"*This has got potential for a major incident. Still working on access.*" St. John, P., et al. (November 18, 2018). California fire: What started as a tiny brush fire became the state's deadliest wildfire. Here's how. *LA Times*.

"*There is, even now, something of ill-omen, amongst us…the worse than savage mobs, for the executive ministers of justice*. Lincoln's Lyceum Address, January 27, 1838.

"*Let every American, every lover of liberty…let it be preached from the pulpit, proclaimed in legislative halls, and enforced in courts of justice.*" Lincoln's Lyceum Address, January 27, 1838.

Plot and characters from *Les Misérables*: Hugo (1862).

In the 1920's…Jean Piaget developed an interest in the intellectual development of children: Burman, J. T. (2012). "Jean Piaget: Images of a life and his factory". *History of Psychology*. 15 (3): 283–288.

Piaget's stages: Piaget & Inhelder (1969).

Jean Valjean, who was transformed by forgiveness and grace offered by Bishop Myriel: Hugo (1862). *Les Misérables*.

"*While I never violated a recruiting rule…A young person should be with family on an important day.*" Wooden & Jamieson (2005), pp. 84-85.

"*Bailed players out of jail for minor traffic violations…It was no different than what I would do for my own children.*" Wooden & Jamieson (2005), p. 85.

"*When I so pressingly urge a strict observance of all the laws… let them, if not too intolerable, be borne with.*" Lincoln's Lyceum Address, January 27, 1838.

"*You express a great deal of anxiety…one has a moral responsibility to disobey unjust laws.*" *Letter from a Birmingham Jail*, April 16, 1963.

"*Now, what is the difference…disobey segregation ordinances, for they are morally wrong.* *Letter from a Birmingham Jail*, April 16, 1963.

"*I hope you are able to see the distinction…the highest respect for law.*" *Letter from a Birmingham Jail*, April 16, 1963.

"*We should never forget that…I would openly advocate disobeying that country's antireligious laws.*" *Letter from a Birmingham Jail*, April 16, 1963.

"*Bring tender loving care…the idea of being a law-breaker for God was on which obviously amused her.*" Spink (1997), p. 238.

"*Then the Sisters should visit as many families as possible; they cannot lock them all up.*" Maasburg (2011), pp. 103-104.

"*People had rushed down to get arrested…for the cause of freedom.*" King (1958), p. 146.

"*Injunction or no injunction, we're going to march…an injunction can't stop us.*" Speech, April 10, 1963.

"*I don't know that will happen…But' I'm going to jail.*" Speech, April 1, 1963.

"*Some years ago…patterned a great deal after Gandhi.*" Press conference, July 5, 1963.

"*A Satyagrahi obeys the laws of society intelligently and…then does the right accrue to him of the civil disobedience of certain laws in well-defined circumstances.*" Gandhi (1927), p. 472.

"*Civility is the most difficult part of Satyagraha…a desire to do the opponent good.*" Gandhi (1927), p. 438.

"*They should thoroughly understand its deeper implications.*" Gandhi (1927), p. 472.

"*Its roots not in hatred, but in love.*" Easwaran (2011), p. 76.

"*Must be sincere, respectful, restrained… no ill will or hatred behind it.*" Easwaran (2011), p. 96.

"*I have learnt…a power which can move the world.*" Easwaran (2011), p. 96.

"*Satyagraha is essentially a weapon of the truthful…observe it in thought, word, and deed.*" Gandhi (1927), pp. 468-469.

"*Old John Brown has been executed for treason…in neither case, is the interposition of mob law, either necessary, justifiable, or excusable.*" Speech in Leavenworth, Kansas, December, 1859.

Ch. 11 | Defending Values

"*The Greatest of all virtues is love.*" King (1967), p. 144.

"*Faster than a speeding bullet!…Able to leap tall buildings at a single bound!*" Ricca (2013).

"*Look! Up in the sky!…truth, justice and the American way.*" Ricca (2013).

"*Five score years ago…finds himself in exile in his own land.*" The "I Have a Dream" speech, delivered August 28, 1963.

"*So we've come here today…the time to make justice a reality for all of God's children.*" The "I Have a Dream" speech, delivered August 28, 1963.

"*I say to you today, my friends…but by the content of their character.*" The "I Have a Dream" speech, delivered August 28, 1963.

"*With this faith we will be able to work together…we are free at last!*" The "I Have a Dream" speech, delivered August 28, 1963.

"*It has been affirmed that…our ultimate allegiance to God and His will, rather than to man and his folkways.*" King (1958), p. 117.

"*When Peace Becomes Obnoxious*" sermon: Delivered March 18, 1956 at Dexter Baptist.

"*Peace is not merely the absence of this tension… if peace means this, I don't want peace.*" Sermon, March 18, 1956 at Dexter Baptist.

"*If peace means accepting second-class citizenship, I don't want it… we must revolt against this peace.*" Sermon, March 18, 1956 at Dexter Baptist.

"*Permanent, positive peace…But this is not true peace.*" King (1958), p. 117.

"*The lack of human dignity experienced by Africans…whether the African is employed by him or not.*" Closing statement, delivered April 20, 1964 in Rivonia, South Africa.

"*Poverty and the breakdown of family life…not only politically, but everywhere.*" Closing statement, delivered April 20, 1964 in Rivonia, South Africa.

"*Africans want a just share in the whole of South Africa…It is a struggle for the right to live.*" Closing statement, delivered April 20, 1964 in Rivonia, South Africa.

"*Crowds came to meet her wherever she went…to prevent her from being crushed.*" Spink (1997), p. 198.

"*I only have to cough and the world knows about it.*" Spink (1997), p. 276.

"*Her presence alone…gave her a capacity to influence.*" Spink (1997), pp. 178-179.

"*Dear President George Bush and President Saddam Hussein…the suffering, pain and loss of life which your weapons will cause.*" Letter written January 2, 1991.

"*Maybe in our own family…do we put our own interests first?*" Prayer Breakfast Speech delivered in Washington, DC, February 3, 1994.

"*Why is it like that… These are the things that break peace.*" Prayer Breakfast Speech delivered in Washington, DC, February 3, 1994.

"*But I feel that the greatest destroyer of peace today…abortion which brings people to such blindness.*" Prayer Breakfast Speech delivered in Washington, DC, February 3, 1994.

"*I will tell you something beautiful… we have a tremendous demand from couples who cannot have a child.*" Prayer Breakfast Speech delivered in Washington, DC, February 3, 1994.

"*Please don't kill the child… joy to their adopting parents and have grown up so full of love and joy.*" Prayer Breakfast Speech delivered in Washington, DC, February 3, 1994.

"*Belonged to a little circle of privileged persons…that Mother Teresa had just shown her so tangibly.*" Maasburg (2011), pp. 171-172.

"*How is it that he is able to speak so well for such a long time…so we need notes and files to keep track.*" Easwaran (2011), p. 134.

"*At the time of writing… I have discovered no inconsistency between the two.*" Gandhi (1927), p. 135.

"*I think it cannot be shown that once taken a position, I have ever retreated from it.*" Response to Fredrick Douglass.

"*Important principles may and must be inflexible.*" Final speech, April 11, 1865.

"*No party can command respect which sustains this year, what it opposed last.*" Letter to Judge Samuel Galloway, July 28, 1859.

"*Mother Teresa had a gift of…slogans that were easy to remember.*" Maasburg (2011), p. 38.

"*Life is opportunity, avail it… Life is too precious, do not destroy it.*" Poem hanging in a home for the dying, New York City, 1985.

"*You did it to me.*" From Matthew 25:40, NIV.
"*The fruit of silence is prayer…the fruit of service is peace.*" Mother Teresa (2007), p. 315.
"*This is good business.*" Spink (1997), p. 267.
"*All you have to do…victory complete and permanent is sure at last.*" Speech given March 1, 1859.
"*During my lifetime…it is an ideal for which I am prepared to die.*" Closing statement, delivered April 20, 1964 in Rivonia, South Africa.
"*Even went the length of threatening me with assassination if I went to the Punjab.*" Gandhi (1927), p. 476.
"*Never liked to live for the sake of living.*" Gandhi (1927), p. 454.
"*Fit to live.*" Sermon at Ebenezer, November 5, 1967.
"*Stand up for some great principle, some great issue, some great cause.*" Sermon at Ebenezer, November 5, 1967.
"*You refuse to do it… stand up for truth.*" Sermon at Ebenezer, November 5, 1967.
"*The end of life is not to be happy, nor to achieve pleasure and avoid pain, but to do the will of God, come what may.*" King (1963), p. 143.

Ch. 12 | Noah's Character Arc

"*One of the most difficult things is not to change society — but to change yourself.*" From an Interview with John Battersby, Johannesburg, South Africa, *Christian Science Monitor*, February 10, 2000.
The Biblical story of the Flood: From Genesis 6-9.
"*Only of evil all the time.*" Genesis 6:5, NIV.
"*A hero ventures forth from the world of common day…with the power to bestow boons on his fellow man.*" Campbell (2008), p. 30.
"*Multifinality" and "equifinality.*" Cicchetti, D., & Rogosch, F. A. (1996). Equifinality and multifinality in developmental psychopathology. *Development and Psychopathology, 8*, 597-600.
Thalidomide. Campbell, Denis. (July 29, 2009). "Wonder Drug" left babies with deformed limbs. *Guardian*.
Zika Virus: Sikka, V., et al. (February 11, 2016). The emergence of Zika Virus as a global health security threat. *Journal of Global Infectious Diseases, 8*, 3-15.
"*Very shy and avoided all company…thieves from another and serpents from a third.*" Gandhi (1927), p. 20.
"*Preposterously early…assuming the authority of a husband.*" Gandhi (1927), p. 8.
"*Felt tempted to speak…sad at heart for [his] incapacity.*" Gandhi (1927), p. 62.

"I stood up, but my heart sank into my boots...I decided not to take up any more cases until I had courage enough to conduct them." Gandhi (1927), 94-95.
"Mother Teresa called her associates...Gandhi Centre of Love." Spink (1997), p. 127.
"A popular child...something of a driving force in all the activities she undertook." Spink (1997), p. 9-10.
"A gathering place for the poor...some of them are our relations but all of them are our people." Spink (1997), p. 7
"Growth mindset" and the "fixed mindset." Dweck, C. S. (2006).
"If you think you can or if you think you can't, you are probably right." Reader's Digest (1947), volume 51, p. 64.
A desperate villager, Jean Valjean: *Les Misérables*: Hugo (1862).
"Stories are about change...the promise of a fresh start." Snyder (2005), p. 136.
"Atonement with the father." Campbell (2008), p. 105.
"Strict and disciplined with herself, but at the same time kindly, considerate and extremely patient with others." Maasburg (2011), p. 1.
"Whether I shall ever be better...I must die or be better." Chafin (1908), p. 15.

Ch. 13 | Fool's Gold

"Violence and hate only breed violence and hate." King. (1998), ch. 25.
"Must one kill to ensure there are no evildoers? That makes two evildoers instead of one." Pascal (1852).
"As long as you got a sit-down philosophy...some fighting to back that up." From "The Ballot or the Bullet" Speech, April 12, 1964.
"Part of what's wrong with you, you do too much singing...Swinging helped him." From "The Ballot or the Bullet" Speech, April 12, 1964.
"This is why I say it's the ballot or the bullet...everything that's due him, everything." From "The Ballot or the Bullet" Speech, April 12, 1964.
Chris Hani...*Umkhonto we Sizwe:* Hani (1991).
Lawrence Kohlberg and his theory of moral development: Snarey, J. R. (2012). Lawrence Kohlberg: Moral biography, moral psychology, and moral pedagogy. In Pickren (2012), pp. 277–296.
"Truth, justice, and the American way." Ricca (2013).
"If you prick us, do we not bleed?...And if you wrong us, shall we not take revenge?" William Shakespeare, *The Merchant of Venice*, Act III, Scene I.
"Affect forecasting." Carlesmith, K. M., et al. (2008). The paradoxical consequences of revenge. *Journal of Personality & Social Psychology*, 95, 1316-1324.

Manilal Gandhi believed in nonviolence…Mandela saw nonviolence as merely tactical. Mandela (1995), p. 78.

"By any means necessary." Myers (1992).

Iron Pyrite aka "Fool's gold." Palache (1944).

Malcolm X tried to push people into two separate realms: See "The Ballot or the Bullet" Speech, April 12, 1964.

"I want Dr. King to know that…perhaps they will be more willing to hear Dr. King." Personal conversation, February, 1965.

Ch. 14 | The Great Escape

"Forgiveness is more manly than punishment." Gandhi (1942), p. 16.

Approximately 407,316 servicemen did not return: Congressional Research Report – American War and Military Operations Casualties. Updated July 29, 2020.

"No matter what my mother said to convince me otherwise… I wouldn't be left out and neglected." Robinson (2015), pp. 12-13.

"The violence happened with such a sudden and sadistic fury… when I had been on the receiving end." Robinson (2015), pp. 14-15.

"From the beginning…out of the shadows into the light." Robinson (2015), p. 17.

"I am sorry. I can do nothing for you… he will live to be a great deal older than Methuselah." Thompson (1894), pp. 86-87.

"What? Has this man no friends…then I will be his friend." Humes (1996), p. 64.

"The eagerness with which the President caught at any fact…as he exercised the power to pardon." Journal entry from July 18, 1863, in Hay (1999), p. 64.

"I go to bed happy…him and his family and his friends." Carpenter (1866), p. 142.

"Where meanness or cruelty were shown." Entry from July 18, 1863, in Hay (1999), p. 64.

"If I have one vice," Lincoln observed, *"it is not being able to say no."* Viele, E. L. (October, 1878). A trip with Lincoln, Chase, and Stanton. *Scribners Monthly*, 16, p. 818.

"I thank God I was not born a woman, because I never could refuse an impassioned plea." Humes (1996), p. 168.

"Charged with making too many mistakes on the side of mercy." Tarbell (1890), p. 225.

"Must I shoot a simple-minded soldier boy…a wiley agitator who induces him to desert?" Lincoln to Erastus Corning and Others, June 12, 1863, in Basler (1953), pp. 264, 266-267.

"I put it to you…how can he help their running away with him?" Boller (1981), p. 139.

"It would frighten the poor devils too terribly to shoot them." Entry from July 18, 1863, in Hay (1999), p. 64.

"*I am unwilling for any boy under eighteen to be shot.*" Basler (1953), volume VI, p. 506.

"*On principle I dislike an oath...I think it is enough if the man does no wrong hereafter.*" Letter to Secretary of War Edwin Stanton, February 5, 1864.

"*For me there is no redemption... but do you dare try it?*" Joffé, R. (Director). (1986). *The Mission* [Film]. Goldcrest Films.

"*Father, he's done this penance long enough... Until he does, neither do I.*" Joffé, R. (Director). (1986). *The Mission* [Film]. Goldcrest Films.

"*Do you feel that you've been rehabilitated?*" Darabont, F. (Director). (1994). *The Shawshank Redemption* [Film]. Castle Rock Entertainment.

"*The mighty scourge of war.*" Lincoln's Second Inaugural Address, March 4, 1865.

"*There were men in Congress who... would not be undercut by a punitive agenda.*" Gideon Welles (April, 1872), "Lincoln and Johnson." *Galaxy 13*, p. 526.

"All he wanted of us was...work on their farms and in their shops." Sherman (1889), p. 682.

"*Have their horses to plow with...and submit to the laws.*" Porter (1886), p. 314.

"*Mercy bears richer fruit than strict justice.*" Bullock (1913), p. 156.

"*The severest justice may not always be the best policy.*" Veto message, written July 17, 1862 but not executed, in response to the Second Confiscation Act passed by Congress.

"*Enough lives have been sacrificed...expect harmony and union.*" Lincoln to his cabinet, April 14, 1965.

"*Spoke very kindly of General Lee...that so eminently distinguished him.*" Edwin Stanton to John A. Dix, April 15, 1865, *The War of the Rebellion: A Compilation of the Official Records of the Union and Confederate Armies*, Ser. 1, Vol. XLVI, Part III, p. 70.

"*Tom,*" "*Dick,*" and "*Harry.*" Sturges, J. (Director). (1963). *The Great Escape* [Film]. The Mirisch Company.

"*Must be hung.*" Grant (1893), p. 149.

"*None need expect he would take any part in hanging or killing those men, even the worst of them.*" Gideon Welles (April, 1872). "Lincoln and Johnson." *Galaxy 13*, p. 526.

"*When visiting a friend...if he could do so 'unbeknown' to him, he would not object.*" Sherman (1889), pp. 682-683.

"*Frighten them out of the country, open the gates, let down the bars, scare them off.*" Gideon Welles (April, 1872), "Lincoln and Johnson." *Galaxy 13*, p. 526.

"Conspicuous secessionist...it's best to let him run." Dana (1996), pp. 273-274.

"*She often asked for compassionate exceptions...nearing their natural death while in prison.*" Mother Teresa (1995).

"*Cognitive dissonance.*" Brehm, J. W. (1956). Postdecision changes in the desirability of alternatives. *The Journal of Abnormal and Social Psychology*, 52(3), 384-389; Festinger

(1957).
Andy Robinson's portrayal of the psychotic killer Scorpio: Siegel, D. (Director). (1971). *Dirty Harry* [Film]. The Malpaso Company.
He was not offered another major role for twenty-two years. Robinson (2015).
"*Spiritual poverty.*" Prayer Breakfast Speech delivered in Washington, DC, February 3, 1994.
John Newton: Hatfield (1884); McCann, I. (July 18, 2016). The Life of a Song: 'Amazing Grace." *Financial Times.*
"*Amazing grace.*" Newton (1806), p. 53.
"*We must develop and maintain...the power of love.*" King (1963), p. 42.

Ch. 15 | The World's A Stage

"*There are no small parts, there are only small actors.*" Stanislavski (1924).
"*All the world's a stage...seven ages.*" Shakespeare, W. (1599). As You Like It, Act II, Scene VII.
"*Then, a highly regarded Russian actor and director.*" Stanislavski (1924).
"*Stanislavski developed a 'System.'*" Moore (1984).
"*The Method.*" Frome (2001).
"*Stella! Hey, Stella!*" Kazan, E. (Director). (1951). *A Streetcar Named Desire* [Film]. Warner Bros. Pictures.
"*You don't understand! I coulda' had class...instead of a bum, which is what I am.*" Kazan, E. (Director). (1954). *On the Waterfront* [Film]. Horizon Pictures.
Coppola, F. F. (Director). (1972). *The Godfather* [Film]. Paramount Pictures.
Brando was named Actor of the Century by Time Magazine. Schickel, R. (June 8, 1998). "The Actor: Marlon Brando." *Time.*
The first Star Wars: Lucas, G. (Director). (1977). *Star Wars* [Film]. Lucasfilm Ltd.
"*I want the breath of life...fulfillment of the movement which I asked for.*" Stevens (2006), p. 395.
Kazan, E. (Director). (1955). *East of Eden* [Film]. Warner Bros. Pictures.
"*An extreme grotesque of a boy... twisted by the denial of love.*" Stevens (2006), pp. 389-408.
"*I use substitution in order to 'make believe' in its literal sense...my newly selected self on stage.*" Hagen (2008), p. 36.
"*Little things make big things happen.*" Wooden & Jamieson, (2005), p. 146.
"*Give always a happy smile.*" Muggeridge (1971), p. 69.
"*Love one another.*" Nobel Prize Lecture, December 11, 1979. Oslo, Norway.

About the Author

Jens Omli is an author, speaker, and consultant who has helped mobilize and equip hundreds of heroes in North America, Africa, and Asia. His experience on stage started at an early age, as the youngest member of an opening act for notable figures such as President Reagan, Johnny Cash, and Mickey Mouse. Dr. Omli's contributions have been mentioned in *The Wall Street Journal*, *The Guardian*, *ESPN.com*, the *LA Times*, and *NPR*. He studied Psychology and Philosophy at Westmont College, earned a PhD in Sport & Exercise Psychology at the University of Minnesota, and completed an NIH-funded postdoctoral position at the Institute of Child Development. Dr. Omli has taught undergraduate and graduate classes in Leadership, Psychology, Sociology, Human Development, and Coaching. He enjoys travel, playing with his daughters, and trying everything twice.

Jens Omli is available for select speaking events and consulting opportunities. Contact via requests@jensomli.com

jensomli.com

www.ingramcontent.com/pod-product-compliance
Lightning Source LLC
Chambersburg PA
CBHW020631220526
45464CB00001B/110